Lonely planet

B ARCELONA

TO P SIGHTS, AUTHENTIC EXPERIENCES

D0226887

Contents

Gràcia & Park Güell
Gaudí's fairy-tale woodland park and the intriguing district of Gràcia, full of *barrio* life, await exploration. *(Map p254)*

La Sagrada Família ⊙

La Ribera
The trendiest part of the old town, with first-rate tapas, medieval architecture and a stunning Modernista concert hall. *(Map p250)*

ⓜ Quadrat d'Or

⊙ La Pedrera

Passeig de Gràcia ⓜ

Casa Batlló

Palau de la Música Catalana ⊙

El Fòrum *(4km)*

⊗ La Ribera
Museu Picasso
ⓜ ⊗ El Born
ⓞ Basílica de Santa Maria del Mar

Museu Frederic Marès ⓜ
(Museu d'Art de Barcelona) ⓜ
La Catedral ⊙ ⓜ
Mercat de la Boqueria ⊙
Museu d'Història de Barcelona

La Rambla ⊙
Palau Güell ⓞ

Museu Marítim ⓜ

Barceloneta & the Waterfront
Pretty beaches, a waterfront promenade and bountiful seafood make for a memorable day on the Mediterranean.

Fundació Joan Miró ⓜ

Colònia Güell ⊙ *(15km)*

⊙ Gardens of Montjuïc

Port Vell

Mediterranean Sea

La Rambla & Barri Gòtic
Stroll Barcelona's famous boulevard, then lose yourself in the Gothic quarter. *(Map p250)*

Welcome to Barcelona

From sunrise over the Mediterranean to the last dance-floor whirl of an action-packed night, Barcelona holds your attention 24 hours a day. Its combination of natural attractions, hedonism and serious cultural cachet makes it one of the world's great cities.

Barcelona's architectural treasures span millennia. Temple columns, ancient city walls and subterranean stone corridors provide a window into the Roman era. Then skip a thousand years to the Middle Ages by taking a stroll through the Gothic quarter, all shadowy lanes, tranquil plazas and soaring churches. Later bloomed the sculptural masterpieces of Modernisme, a heady mix of ingenuity and whimsy created by Gaudí and contemporaries. La Sagrada Família, still under construction, is already one of the planet's most sublime buildings.

Barcelona has long inspired artists too, including Salvador Dalí, Pablo Picasso and Joan Miró, whose works are on bold display in the city's myriad museums.

Art of another sort adorns the groaning bar tops and stylish plates of Barcelona's tapas bars and avant-garde restaurants. Catalan cooking has a long tradition of using flavourful, market-fresh ingredients, garnished with a soupçon of French savoir faire. The molecular wizardry of modern Catalan gastronomy gives it a real twist.

Add to this spending lazy days on the beach, paddling or cruising the deep blue sea, strolling into classy boutiques and quaffing sessions in sociable *cava* bars and you have just a fraction of the intoxicating cornucopia that is Barcelona.

> *Its combination of natural attractions, hedonism and serious cultural cachet makes it one of the world's great cities.*

View over Port Vell from Teleférico del Puerto (p63)
EVGENIYA TELENNAYA/SHUTTERSTOCK ©

★ BARCELONA ★

Tibidabo
Mountain
(1km)

Park
Güell

**Camp Nou, Pedralbes
& La Zona Alta**
A medieval monastery,
an intriguing museum
and lofty Tibidabo – all
capped by football
thrills at Camp Nou.

Museu-Monestir
de Pedralbes

**La Sagrada Família &
L'Eixample**
Modernisme rules in
the city's 19th-century
'extension', replete
with masterpieces
by Gaudí and others.
(Map p254)

MACB
Contemporani

Camp Nou

Estació
Sants

El Raval
A once-seedy area
that's now home
to cutting-edge
museums and
bohemian bars and
eateries. *(Map p249)*

Museu Nacional d'Art
de Catalunya (MNAC)

**Montjuïc, Poble Se
& Sant Antoni**
Home to manicured
parks, excellent
museums and
cinematic city views
(Maps p249 & p256

SCOTTT13/SHUTTERSTOCK ©, ANGELA N PERRYMAN/SHUTTERSTOCK ©,
EVGENIYA TELENNAYA/SHUTTERSTOCK ©, MATT MUNRO/LONELY PLANET ©,
ARSENIE KRASNEVSKY/SHUTTERSTOCK ©, ARTUR BOGACKI/SHUTTERSTOCK ©,
ESME FOX/LONELY PLANET LP LOCALS

This Year in Barcelona

2019

IAKOV FILIMONOV/SHUTTERSTOC

Barcelona

Barcelona is a place where there's always something happening. Traditional fiestas maintain a riotous blend of popular religion, devil-may-care revelry and time-honoured customs. Meanwhile, concerts, festivals and modern celebrations keep things ticking right through the year.

From left: Festes de la Mercè (p14); Primavera Sound (p10); Festa Major de Gràcia (p13)

2019

CHRISTIAN BERTRAND/SHUTTERSTOCK ©

★ **Top Festivals & Events**

Festes de Santa Eulàlia, February (p7)

Primavera Sound, May (p10)

Festival del Grec, July (p12)

Festa Major de Gràcia, August (p13)

Festes de la Mercè, September (p14)

MARCIN D/500PX ©

Plan Your Trip
This Year in Barcelona

January

Barcelonins *head to the Pyrenees for action on the ski slopes, while others simply enjoy a bit of post-holiday downtime (school holidays go to around 8 January).*

✿ Reis (Reyes)   5 Jan
On 5 January, the day before Epifanía (Epiphany), children delight in the Cavalcada dels Reis Mags (Parade of the Three Kings; pictured above), a colourful parade of floats and music, spreading bonhomie and boiled sweets in equal measure.

☆ Barcelona World Race   12 Jan
This nonstop round-the-world sailing race (www.barcelonaworldrace.com) starts and ends in Barcelona and only happens every two years or so. Two-person crews kick off the next edition here...next stop: Sydney, Australia.

✿ Festes dels Tres Tombs   17 Jan
In addition to live music and *gegants* (papier-mâché giants worn over the shoulders of processionists), the festival dedicated to Sant Antoni features a parade of horse-drawn carts in the neighbourhood of Sant Antoni (near the Mercat de Sant Antoni) every 17 January.

☆ Mozart Requiem   28 Jan
The Palau de la Música Catalana (p106) sees the Balthasar Neumann choir and ensemble, conducted by Thomas Hengelbrock, take on Mozart's unfinished masterpiece. Kerll's *Non sine quare* mass precedes it. It's one of a series of winter and spring concerts.

◉ Sabartés por Picasso por Sabartés   Jan-24 Feb
This exhibition at the Museu Picasso (p80) documents the painter's relationship with Jaume Sabartés, a writer and intellectual who was an important Barcelona conduit for the artist-in-exile and instrumental in establishing the museum.

IAKOV FILIMONOV/SHUTTERSTOCK ©

February

02

Often the coldest (and seemingly the longest) month in Barcelona, February sees few visitors. Nonetheless, some of the first big festivals kick off, with abundant Catalan merriment amid the wintry gloom.

☆ Nights at the Opera   Jan-Jun

The Gran Teatre del Liceu (p199; pictured above) opera season runs right through winter and spring. While there are better-known works performed (Liudmyla Monastyrska sings *Tosca* in June), February sees the world premiere of a new Catalan opera, *L'Enigma di Lea*, that should be intriguing.

🎎 Festes de Santa Eulàlia   12 Feb

Around 12 February this big winter fest (http://lameva.barcelona.cat/santaeulalia) celebrates Barcelona's first patron saint with a week of cultural events, including parades of *gegants*, open-air art installations, theatre, *correfocs* (fire runs) and *castells* (human castles).

☉ Art at the Gates of 1968   Jan-Mar

At the Museu Nacional d'Art De Catalunya (MNAC; p56), this exhibition examines the nascent Pop Art movement in Catalonia in the Francoist '60s. The movement laid the groundwork for the cultural flowering after the end of the dictatorship.

☉ Jaume Plensa   Jan-Apr

A major exhibition at MACBA (p94) concentrates on this prominent Catalan sculptor and installation artist, covering bases from his early work of the 1980s to challenging, up-to-the-minute material.

Plan Your Trip
This Year in Barcelona

March

After chillier days of winter, March brings longer, sunnier days, though still cool nights (light-jacket weather). There are relatively few tourists and fair hotel prices.

🎭 Carnestoltes (Carnaval) 28 Feb-6 Mar

Seven weeks before Easter, the carnival (http://lameva.barcelona.cat/carnaval; pictured above) involves several days of fancy-dress balls, merrymaking and fireworks, ending on the Tuesday before Ash Wednesday. More than 30 parades happen around town on the weekend. Down in Sitges a wilder version takes place.

🎭 Festa de Sant Medir 3 Mar

This characterful religious procession in Gràcia includes throwing sweets to the masses, who await with buckets and bags to catch the treats.

☆ Barcelona Obertura Spring Festival 4-17 Mar

A top-notch line-up of classical musicians and singers makes this festival an exciting prospect. Choral performances, opera, chamber music and orchestral works are scheduled across two venues, with some high-profile Russian artists featuring.

🏃 Barcelona Marathon 10 Mar

Runners converge on Barcelona every March to participate in the city's spring marathon; it usually starts and finishes at Plaça d'Espanya, passing Camp Nou, La Pedrera, La Sagrada Família, Torre Agbar, El Fòrum, Parc de la Ciutadella, Plaça de Catalunya and La Rambla.

☆ Disney on Ice 14-17 March

A guaranteed hit with the children, this spectacular Disney show takes place at the Palau Sant Jordi (p203) over four consecutive days. You might have to rely on re-sales for tickets.

🍺 Barcelona Beer Festival mid–late Mar

Craft beer has hit the scene in full force in Barcelona. Come see the latest taste-makers in action at this three-day beer and food fest (www.barcelonabeerfestival.com), with over 300 craft beers on hand. So many beers, so little time!

04

April

Spring arrives with a flourish, complete with wildflowers blooming in the countryside, Easter revelry and school holidays, although April showers can dampen spirits. Book well ahead if coming around Easter.

⚜ Setmana Santa 14-21 Apr

On Palm Sunday people line up to have their palm branches blessed outside the cathedral, while on Good Friday you can follow the floats and hooded penitents in processions from the Església de Sant Agustí (Plaça de Sant Agustí 2), located in El Raval.

☆ Barcelona Open 20-28 Apr

The city's premier tennis tournament, an important fixture of the international clay-court season, sees some top names slug it out.

⚜ Día de Sant Jordi 23 Apr

Catalonia honours its patron saint, Sant Jordi (St George), on 23 April. Traditionally men and women exchange roses (pictured above) and books – and La Rambla and Plaça de Sant Jaume fill with book and flower stalls.

⚜ Feria de Abril de Catalunya 26 Apr-5 May

Andalucía comes to the Parc del Fòrum with this weeklong southern festival featuring flamenco, a funfair and plenty of food and drink stalls.

✘ Alimentaria late Apr

Though it's a serious trade fair (www.alimentaria-bcn.com) rather than a gastro festival, this is well worth visiting for foodies. A highlight is the show cooking area, where top chefs demonstrate their skills.

🏃 Passejada Amb Barret 29 Apr

Inspired by New York's Easter Parade, this 'Stroll with a Hat' welcomes spring with a casual walk along Rambla de Catalunya. Make sure you wear your hat!

Plan Your Trip
This Year in Barcelona

SHUTTERSTOCK/NATURSPORTS ©

May

With sunny, pleasant days and clear skies, May can be one of the best times to visit Barcelona. The city slowly gears up for summer with the opening of the chiringuitos (beach bars).

☆ D'A – Festival Internacional de Cinema d'Autor
de Barcelona   late Apr–early May
This well-curated film festival (www.dafilmfestival.com) presents a selection of contemporary art-house cinematic works over a few days.

☆ Salón del Cómic   early May
Spain's biggest comics event (www.ficomic.com) takes place over three days. It's generally in early May but has been held as early as late March, so keep an eye out.

☆ Spanish Grand Prix   mid-May
One of the fixtures of the motor-racing calendar, the Spanish Grand Prix (pictured above) is held at the Circuit de Barcelona-Catalunya, northeast of the city.

☆ Primavera Sound   late May or early Jun
For one week the open-air Parc del Fòrum stages an all-star line-up (www.primaverasound.com) of international bands and DJs. There are also associated concerts around town, including free open-air events at the Parc de la Ciutadella and the Passeig Lluís Companys.

SHUTTERSTOCK/CHRISTIAN BERTRAND ©

☆ Ciutat Flamenco   mid-May
One of the best occasions to see great flamenco in Barcelona, this concentrated festival (www.ciutatflamenco.com) is held over four days in May at the Teatre Mercat De Les Flors and other venues.

June

Tourist numbers are soaring as Barcelona plunges into summer. Live music festivals and open-air events give the month a festive air.

✿ Cors Muts   10 Jun

After a weekend of out-of-town revelry over Pentecost (or 'Second Easter' weekend), these gaudily-dressed bands of musicians return to the *barrios* of Raval and Barceloneta in a big parade on the Monday afternoon.

☆ Sónar   mid-Jun

Usually held in mid-June, Sónar (www.sonar.es) is Barcelona's massive celebration of electronic music and technology, with concerts, DJs, exhibitions, sound labs, record fairs and urban art.

☆ Festival Pedralbes   mid-Jun–early Jul

This summertime fest (www.festival pedralbes.com) takes place in lovely gardens and stages big-name performers – many of them old-timers (Beach Boys, Sting, Blondie) – from mid-June to early July.

✿ L'Ou com Balla   20 Jun

On Corpus Christi, L'Ou com Balla (the Dancing Egg) bobs on top of flower-festooned fountains around the city. There's also an early-evening procession from La Catedral and traditional Catalan folk dancing.

✿ La Revetlla de Sant Joan   23 Jun

On 23 June locals hit the streets or hold parties at home to celebrate the Revetlla de Sant Joan (St John's Night), which involves drinking, dancing, bonfires and fireworks. In Spanish, it's called 'Verbenas de Sant Joan'.

✿ Pride Barcelona   late Jun or early Jul

The Barcelona Gay Pride festival (www.pridebarcelona.org; pictured above) is a week of celebrations held late June or early July with a crammed program of culture and concerts, along with the traditional Gay Pride march on Sunday.

Plan Your Trip
This Year in Barcelona

CHRISTIAN BERTRAND/SHUTTERSTOCK ©

July

07

Prices are high and it's peak tourist season, but it's a lively time to be in the city, with sun-filled beach days, open-air dining and outdoor concerts.

☆ **World Roller Games**   5-15 Jul
Covering a range of disciplines from roller derby to artistic skating via hockey and skateboarding, this is the second edition of this world championship (www.wrg2019.com).

☆ **Rock Fest Barcelona**   early Jul
This three-day summer festival (www.rockfestbarcelona.com) pulls some very big names indeed from the hard rock and metal end of the spectrum.

☆ **Cruïlla**   mid-Jul
This well-attended music festival (www.cruillabarcelona.com; pictured above) runs over three days and features an eclectic line-up covering everything from rock to flamenco.

☆ **Sala Montjuïc**   Jul–early Aug
Picnic under the stars while watching a movie at this open-air cinema (www.salamontjuic.org), which also features concerts.

☆ **Festival del Grec**   Jul
The major cultural event of the summer is a month-long fest (http://grec.bcn.cat) with dozens of theatre, dance and music performances held around town, including at the Teatre Grec amphitheatre (pictured below) on Montjuïc, from which the festival takes its name.

FELIX LIPOV/SHUTTERSTOCK ©

☆ **Brunch in the Park**   Jul-Sep
Every Sunday from late June to September, you can enjoy a day of electronic music (http://barcelona.brunch-in.com) at an outdoor space on Montjuïc. It attracts a mix of young families and party people.

SHUTTERSTOCK/IAKOV FILIMONOV ©

08

August

The heat index soars; barcelonins leave the city in droves for summer holidays as huge numbers of tourists arrive. It's a great time to hit the beach.

☆ **Música als Parcs**　　Jun–Aug
Music in the Parks is a series of open-air concerts held in different parks and green spaces around the city. More than 40 different concerts feature classical, blues and jazz groups.

🎆 **Festes de Sant Roc**　　mid-Aug
For four days in mid-August, Plaça Nova in the Barri Gòtic becomes the scene of parades, the *correfoc,* a market, traditional music and magic shows for kids.

🎆 **Festa Major de Gràcia**　　around 15 Aug
Locals compete for the most elaborately decorated street in this popular weeklong Gràcia festival (www.festamajordegracia. org; pictured above) held around 15 August. The fest also features free outdoor concerts, street fairs and other events.

🎆 **Circuit Festival**　　mid-Aug
Running for about two weeks, this is a major gay fiesta (www.circuitfestival.net) with numerous party nights, including an epic final all-day, all-night bash in a waterpark. There's a parallel lesbian event, GirlieCircuit (www.girliecircuit.net).

🎆 **Festa Major de Sants**　　late Aug
The district of Sants hosts a five-day fest (www.festamajordesants.net) with concerts, outdoor dance parties, *correfocs* and elaborately decorated streets.

Plan Your Trip
This Year in Barcelona

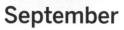

09

September

After a month off, barcelonins *return to work, although several major festivals provide ample amusement. Temperatures stay warm through September, making for fine beach days.*

🎉 Diada Nacional de Catalunya
11 Sep

Catalonia's national day (pictured above) curiously commemorates Barcelona's surrender on 11 September 1714 to the Bourbon monarchy of Spain, at the conclusion of the War of the Spanish Succession.

🍷 Mostra de Vins i Caves de Catalunya
late Sep

At this wine and *cava* event, you can taste your way through some of the top wines of Catalunya. It's usually held on Passeig Lluís Companys near the Arc de Triomf over four days, coinciding with the Festes de la Mercè at the end of September.

🎉 Festa Major de la Barceloneta
around 29 Sep

This big September celebration in Barcelona honours the local patron saint, Sant

🎉 Festes de la Mercè
around 24 Sep

Barcelona's co-patron saint is celebrated with fervour in this massive five-day fest (www.bcn.cat/merce). The city stages sporting events, free concerts, dance performances, human towers of *castellers*, parades of *gegants* and a fiery *correfoc* (fire run).

Miquel, on 29 September. It lasts about a week and involves plenty of dancing and drinking, especially on the beach.

10

October

While northern Europe shivers, Barcelona enjoys mild October temperatures and sunny days. With the disappearance of the summer crowds, and lower accommodation prices, this is an excellent month to visit.

🔒 Liber   2-4 Oct
This major international book fair (www. libereurope.eu) brings together authors, publishers and keen readers for a few days at the beginning of October.

✗ Mercat de Mercats   mid-Oct
The 'market of markets' is a celebration of Catalan cooking (pictured above) and those wonderfully locally sourced ingredients that have made Barcelona such a foodie destination. Over one weekend in October, this food fair features great foods, wines and workshops. Held in front of La Catedral.

☆ Symphony for the Ears   Oct
L'Auditori (p196) is a modern building with amazing acoustics, and seeing a show here is a must for music lovers. Visit www. auditori.cat to see the program and buy tickets.

Human Castles
One of the highlights of a traditional Catalan festival is the building of human *castells* (castles). Teams from across the region compete to build towers up to 10 'storeys' tall.

☆ Festival de Jazz de Barcelona   throughout Oct
With an excellent program of high-quality concerts throughout the month, this long-standing festival (www.jazz. barcelona) is a musical highlight.

Plan Your Trip
This Year in Barcelona

November

Cooler days and nights arrive in Barcelona, along with occasional days of rain and overcast skies. For beating the crowds (and higher summer prices), though, it's an excellent month to visit.

🍂 Día de Todos los Santos 1 Nov
All Saint's Day is traditionally when locals visit the tombs of family members, then get together for the Castanyada, when roasted chestnuts and other winter foods are eaten.

☆ LOOP Barcelona mid-Nov
LOOP features video art and avant-garde films shown in museums, theatres and non-traditional spaces (like food markets) around the city. It usually runs for a few days and its timing can vary substantially, so check the dates.

☆ L'Alternativa mid-Nov
Showcasing feature-length and short films, plus premieres by new directors, the Barcelona Independent Film Festival (www.alternativa.cccb.org) includes free and ticketed events.

☆ Camp Nou Nov
See a football match at Camp Nou (p72), hallowed ground for football fans across the globe. There are likely league, cup or Champions League games to choose from this month. Or take a self-guided tour of the stadium and learn about the sport's most famous players at FC Barcelona's museum.

☆ Festival Mil·lenni late Nov–May 2020
Running from November to May every year, this festival (www.festival-millenni.com) consists of a series of high-profile concerts in various venues around town.

GURB1008P/SHUTTERSTOCK ©

CHRISTIAN BERTRAND/SHUTTERSTOCK ©

2019

December

As winter returns barcelonins *gear up for Christmas, and the city is festooned with colourful decorations. Relatively few visitors arrive, at least until Christmas, when the city fills with holidaying out-of-towners.*

🏠 Fira de Santa Llúcia   late Nov-Christmas

Held from late November to Christmas, this holiday market (www.firadesantallucia.cat) has hundreds of stalls selling all manner of Christmas decorations and gifts – including the infamous Catalan nativity scene character, the *caganer* (the crapper).

🎄 Christmas   24 Dec-6 Jan

Christmas in Spain is a two-week affair, with the major family meals on the night of Christmas Eve, New Year's Eve and 6 January.

🎄 Nochevieja (New Year's Eve)   31 Dec

On 31 December, the fountains of Montjuïc (Font Màgica) take centre stage for the biggest celebration in town. Crowds line

Christmas Crappers

At Christmas some rather unusual Catalan characters appear. The *caganer* (crapper) is a chap with dropped pants who balances over his unsightly offering (a symbol of fertility for the coming year). There's also the *caga tío* (poop log), which on Christmas Day is supposed to *cagar* (crap) out gifts.

up along Avinguda Reina Maria Cristina to watch a theatrical procession and audio-visual performance (plus *castells*), followed by fireworks at midnight.

Plan Your Trip
Hotspots For...

CULTURE VULTURES

GASTRONAUTS

◉ **Mercat de la Boqueria** (p48; pictured below) This legendary produce market is a cornucopia of sights and smells.

◉ **La Ribera** Stroll this intriguing district and browse its gourmet shops.

✖ **Cinc Sentits** (p147) Delight in the superb tasting menu at this top-notch modern restaurant.

✖ **Disfrutar** (p147) Have the meal of your trip at this highly inventive molecular gastronomy restaurant.

⚲ **Espai Boisà** (p209) Learn to whip up some classic tapas and Catalan dishes in this excellent cooking school.

◉ **MACBA** (p94; pictured above) The city's top destination for contemporary art, with amazing views to boot.

◉ **Fundació Joan Miró** (p60) A comprehensive collection of this local's works, in a brilliant building.

✖ **Els Quatre Gats** (p142) Admire the Modernista decor in this historic restaurant.

✖ **Tickets** (p149) If food can be art, then this is the most spectacular performance in town.

☆ **Gran Teatre del Liceu** (p199) Enjoy state-of-the-art acoustics in this atmospheric venue on La Rambla.

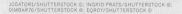

VIEW SEEKERS

◉ **Teleférico del Puerto** (p63) Old-fashioned cable car with awesome perspectives.

◉ **Basílica del Sagrat Cor de Jesús** (p99) Worth the trip for the mesmerising view.

✕ **Barraca** (p135) Superb seafood to match the sublime sea outlook.

✕ **Martínez** (p149) Paella and tapas high up on Montjuïc.

🍷 **Mirablau** (p178) At the foot of Tibidabo, with magnificent vistas out over the city.

ROMANTICS

◉ **Park Güell** (p68) Stroll the gardens and admire the views among Gaudí's Modernista fantasies.

◉ **Barri Gòtic** (pictured above) Amble around the historic centre and explore its hidden corners.

✕ **La Vinateria del Call** (p140) This exquisite little old-town eatery is perfect for cosy dining.

✕ **Caelum** (p142) Beautiful medieval cafe with a candlelit downstairs.

🕺 **Swing Maniacs** (p210) Learn swing dancing at a drop-in course, then hit the dance floor.

HISTORY BUFFS

◉ **Museu d'Història de Barcelona** (p113; pictured above) Probe the city's Roman past.

◉ **Temple d'August** (p67) Examine the best of Barcelona's ancient temples.

◉ **Via Sepulcral Romana** (p47) This assemblage of tombs originally stood outside the city limits.

🛁 **Aqua Urban Spa** (p208) Relax in bathhouse style.

✕ **La Granja** (p142) Check out the section of old city wall in this cafe.

Plan Your Trip
Top Days in Barcelona

TAKASHI IMAGES/SHUTTERSTOCK ©

Barcelona's Must-Sees

On your first day in Barcelona, visit the city's major highlights: stroll La Rambla, explore the atmospheric lanes of the Barri Gòtic and linger over the stunning artistry of La Sagrada Família. History, great architecture and a celebrated food market are all part of this sensory-rich experience.

❶ La Rambla (p42)

Start with La Rambla. Don't miss the human statues, the Miró mosaic, and key buildings facing La Rambla, including the 18th-century Palau de la Virreina.

➲ La Rambla to Mercat de la Boqueria

🚶 Find the market's entrance on La Rambla's west side.

❷ Mercat de la Boqueria (p48)

Packed with culinary riches, this staggering food market is the favoured stomping ground for chefs and conjurors, weekend cooks and hungry-looking tourists. Don't leave without having a few snacks – perhaps from one of the delectable tapas bars in the back.

➲ Mercat de la Boqueria to Barri Gòtic

🚶 Head back down La Rambla, then turn left into Plaça Reial after passing Carrer de Ferran.

Day
01

ANSHARPHOTO/SHUTTERSTOCK ©

❸ Barri Gòtic

Delve into Barcelona's old city. Cross picturesque Plaça Reial (p47) before wandering narrow lanes that date back to at least the Middle Ages. Make your way to the magnificent La Catedral (p64), then visit the Temple d'August (p67).

➲ Barri Gòtic to Cafè de l'Acadèmia

🏃 Cross Plaça de Sant Jaume, walk along Carrer de la Ciutat and take the first left.

❹ Lunch at Cafè de l'Acadèmia (p140)

Arrive early to get a seat at this small atmospheric restaurant serving excellent Catalan cuisine. The multicourse lunch special is fantastic value.

➲ Cafè de l'Acadèmia to La Sagrada Família

Ⓜ Take Line 4 north from Jaume I; transfer at Passeig de Gràcia for Line 2 to Sagrada Família.

❺ La Sagrada Família (p36)

Roll the drums, turn on the stage lights and get ready for Spain's most visited sight. This one-of-a-kind religious monument is as unique as the Pyramids and as beautiful as the Taj Mahal.

➲ La Sagrada Família to Tapas 24

Ⓜ Take Line 2 back to Passeig de Gràcia. Walk southeast down the street of the same name, then take the second left.

❻ Evening Bites at Tapas 24 (p145)

This great basement spot does a smart line in innovative takes on traditional tapas. It's a top place for a light bite or a full meal.

From left: La Rambla; Plaça Nova, Barri Gòtic

Plan Your Trip
Top Days in Barcelona

KERT/SHUTTERSTOCK ©

Mar i Muntanya (Sea & Mountain)

This itinerary takes you along the promenade that skirts the Mediterranean, then into the old fishing quarter of Barceloneta before whisking you up to the heights of Montjuïc for fine views, fragrant gardens and superb art galleries – including two of the city's top museums.

Day

02

❶ Barceloneta Beach

Start the morning with a waterfront stroll; this scenic but once derelict area experienced a dramatic makeover around the 1992 Olympics. Look north and you'll see Frank Gehry's shimmering fish sculpture, while to the south rises the spinnaker-shaped tower of the W Hotel.

➲ Barceloneta Beach to Can Ros

🏃 Look for Carrer del Almirall Aixada just north of the rectangular beach sculpture. Can Ros is about 350m back from the beach on this road.

❷ Lunch at Can Ros (p136)

Take your pick of the seaside restaurants if you want the view, but otherwise head back a few streets to this family-run gem, which has been dishing up excellent seafood for generations.

➲ Can Ros to Teleférico del Puerto

🏃 Walk to the southern end of Barceloneta and you'll see the cable car to your right.

EVGENYA TELENNAYA/SHUTTERSTOCK ©

❸ Teleférico del Puerto (p63)

After lunch take a scenic ride on this aerial cable car for fantastic views over the port and the dazzling city beyond. At the top, you'll arrive in Montjuïc, a minimountain that's packed with gardens – both sculptural and floral – as well as hosting a few first-rate museums.

⟶ Teleférico del Puerto to Fundació Joan Miró

🚡 Take the cable car up to Montjuïc, disembark and follow the main road 800m west.

❹ Fundació Joan Miró (p60)

See a full range of works by one of the giants of the art world. Paintings, sculptures and drawings by the prolific Catalan artist are displayed along with photos and other media. Outside is a peaceful sculpture garden with views over Poble Sec.

⟶ Fundació Joan Miró to Museu Nacional d'Art de Catalunya

🚶 Follow the path through the sculpture gardens east, take the steps up to the main road and continue east to the museum.

❺ Museu Nacional d'Art de Catalunya (p56)

Not to be missed is the incomparable collection of artwork inside this enormous museum. The highlight is the impressive Romanesque collection – rescued from 900-year-old churches in the Pyrenees. Out front, you can take in the view over Plaça d'Espanya to the distant peak of Tibidabo.

⟶ Museu Nacional d'Art de Catalunya to Tickets

🚶 Descend toward Plaça d'Espanya. Turn right before the fountain, left on Carrer de Lleida and right on Avinguda del Paral·lel.

❻ Dinner at Tickets (p149)

You'll need to book weeks in advance, but it's well worth the effort to score a table at Tickets, one of Barcelona's hottest attractions. The celebrated restaurant, run by the Adrià brothers, showcases an ever-changing menu of molecular gastronomy.

From left: Barceloneta Beach; Teleférico del Puerto

Plan Your Trip

Top Days in Barcelona

KSL/SHUTTERSTOCK ©

La Ribera

Like adjacent Barri Gòtic, La Ribera has narrow cobblestone streets and medieval architecture galore. Yet it's also home to high-end shopping, a brilliant Modernista concert hall and a treasure trove of artwork by Picasso. Great restaurants and a fanciful green space complete the Ribera ramble.

Day

03

❶ Museu Picasso (p80)

You can see Picasso's early masterpieces inside this inspiring museum, which contains some 3500 of his works. Perhaps just as impressive as the artwork are the galleries themselves – set in a series of merchant houses dating back to the 1300s.

➲ Museu Picasso to El Born

🚶 Stroll southeast along Carrer de Montcada.

❷ Window Shopping in El Born

The medieval streets of El Born hide an abundance of shopping intrigue, from magic shops to purveyors of fine wines, along with plenty of eye-catching fashion boutiques.

➲ El Born to Cal Pep

🚶 Walk across Plaça de les Olles.

❸ Lunch at Cal Pep (p143)

For lunch, head to this bustling eatery for some of the city's tastiest seafood tapas.

➲ Cal Pep to Basílica de Santa Maria del Mar

🚶 Stroll northwest along Carrer de la Vidriería and turn left on Carrer de Santa Maria.

❹ Basílica de Santa Maria del Mar (p116)

A few blocks away, this captivating church is built in the style of Catalan Gothic. The 14th-century masterpiece soars above the medina-like streets surrounding it.

➲ Basílica de Santa Maria del Mar to Parc de la Ciutadella

🏃 Walk northeast on Carrer de Santa Maria and continue around the former Mercat del Born site to the park.

❺ Parc de la Ciutadella (p84)

After the compact streets of La Ribera, catch your breath and stroll through the open green expanse of this manicured park. You'll find sculptures, a small zoo, the Parlament de Catalunya and the centre-piece, a dramatic if utterly artificial water-fall dating from the 19th century.

➲ Parc de la Ciutadella to Palau de la Música Catalana

🏃 Take Carrer de la Princesa back into El Born and turn right after 200m, making your way northwest.

❻ Palau de la Música Catalana (p106)

Designed by Domènech i Montaner in the early 1900s, this intimate concert hall is a Modernista work of art, with luminescent stained glass and elaborately sculpted details throughout. Come for a concert, but it's also worth returning for a guided tour.

➲ Palau de la Música Catalana to El Xampanyet

🏃 Make your way back (southeast) to Carrer de Montcada.

❼ El Xampanyet (p185)

Just up the road, El Xampanyet is a festive spot to end the night. Sample mouth-watering bites and let your cup brim with ever-flowing *cava* (Catalan sparkling wine). It's usually crowded but friendly; just polite-ly elbow your way in.

From left: Boutique shop in El Born; Stained-glass skylight of Palau de la Música Catalana

Plan Your Trip
Top Days in Barcelona

Art & Architecture

This tour takes you up to the enchanting (if accidental) park Gaudí designed overlooking the city, down the elegant architectural showpiece avenue of Passeig de Gràcia and into El Raval. There you'll find the city's top contemporary art museum anchoring Barcelona's most bohemian neighbourhood.

❶ Park Güell (p68)

Go early to Park Güell to beat the crowds and see the early morning rays over Barcelona and the Mediterranean beyond. Stroll the expanse of the park, ending your visit at Casa-Museu Gaudí (p70), where you can learn more about the life and work of the great Catalan architect.

➲ Park Güell to Gràcia

Ⓜ Take Line 3 from Vallcarca to Fontana.

❷ Gràcia

The village-like feel of Gràcia makes for some great exploring. Stroll from plaza to plaza along the narrow shop-lined lanes, stopping perhaps at open-air cafes along the way. Good streets for browsing include Carre de Verdi, Travessera de Gràcia and Carrer de Torrijos.

➲ Gràcia to Botafumeiro

🏃 Walk southwest along Travessera de Gràcia and turn right on Carrer Gran de Gràcia.

Day
04

ALIONABIRUKOVA/SHUTTERSTOCK ©

❸ Lunch at Botafumeiro (p139)

One of Barcelona's best seafood restaurants. If the tables are full, you can usually get a spot at the bar.

◯ Botafumeiro to Passeig de Gràcia

🏃 Amble southeast along Carrer Gran de Gràcia, which leads into Passeig de Gràcia after 400m.

❹ Passeig de Gràcia

Head to L'Eixample to see high-concept architecture. Passeig de Gràcia is a busy but elegant boulevard lined with exquisite Modernista buildings, including Gaudí's La Pedrera (p76) and Casa Batlló (p52).

◯ Passeig de Gràcia to MACBA

🏃 Continue on Passeig de Gràcia, cross Plaça de Catalunya to La Rambla and turn right on Carrer del Bonsuccés.

❺ MACBA (p94)

A few streets away from Plaça d'Espanya you'll reach the city's top contemporary art gallery, MACBA. It houses an excellent range of Catalan and European works from WWII to the present.

◯ MACBA to El Raval

🏃 Walk along Carrer dels Àngels and turn left on Carrer del Carme.

❻ El Raval

Spend the early evening strolling the lively multicultural street scene of El Raval. Stop for a breather in the pretty courtyard of the Antic Hospital de la Santa Creu (p51) and check out Gaudí's Palau Güell (p92).

◯ El Raval to Koy Shunka

Ⓜ Take Line 3 from Paral·lel to Catalunya.

❼ Dinner at Koy Shunka (p142)

Top off your night with a feast at Koy Shunka, where the haute cuisine is a magnificent marriage of Catalan creativity and Japanese tradition. The tasting menus are worth the hefty price tags.

From left: View of the city from Park Güell; Casa Batlló on Passeig de Gràcia

Plan Your Trip

Need to Know

Daily Costs

Budget: Less than €60

o Dorm bed: €17–28

o Set lunch: from €11

o Bicycle hire per hour: €5

Midrange: €60–200

o Standard double room: €80–140

o Two-course dinner with wine for two: €50

o Walking and guided tours: €15–25

Top end: More than €200

o Double room in boutique and luxury hotels: €200 and up

o Three-course meal at top restaurants per person: €80

o Concert tickets to Palau de la Música Catalana: around €40

Advance Planning

Three months before Book a hotel and reserve a table at a top restaurant.

One month before Check out reviews for theatre and live music, and book tickets.

One week before Browse the latest nightlife listings, art exhibitions and other events to attend while in town. Reserve spa visits and organised tours.

Useful Websites

Barcelona (www.bcn.cat) Town hall's official site with plenty of links.

Barcelona Turisme (www.barcelonaturisme.com) City's official tourism website.

Lonely Planet (www.lonelyplanet.com/barcelona) Destination information, hotel bookings, traveller forum and more.

BCN Més (www.bcnmes.com) Trilingual monthly mag of culture, food, art and more.

Spotted by Locals (www.spottedbylocals.com) Insider tips.

Opening Hours

Standard opening hours are as follows:

Restaurants 1pm to 4pm & 8.30pm to midnight

Shops 9am or 10am to 1.30pm or 2pm and 4pm or 4.30pm to 8pm or 8.30pm Monday to Saturday

Department stores 10am to 10pm Monday to Saturday

Bars 6pm to 2am (to 3am weekends)

Clubs Midnight to 6am Thursday to Saturday

Banks 8.30am to 2pm Monday to Friday; some also 4pm to 7pm Thursday or 9am to 1pm Saturday

Museums & art galleries Vary considerably; generally 10am to 8pm. Many close all day Monday and from 2pm Sunday.

Currency

Euro (€)

Languages

Spanish, Catalan

Visas

Generally not required for stays up to 90 days. Some nationalities need a Schengen visa.

Money

ATMs are widely available (La Rambla has many). Credit cards are accepted in most hotels, shops and restaurants.

Mobile Phones

Local SIM cards can be used in unlocked phones. Data packages are readily available.

Time

Spain is on CET, one hour ahead of GMT/UTC during winter and two hours ahead during daylight saving (the last Sunday in March to the last Sunday in October). Most other western European countries are on the same time as Spain year-round. The UK, Ireland and Portugal are one hour behind. Spaniards use the 24-hour clock for official business (timetables etc) but generally switch to the 12-hour version in daily conversation.

For more, see the **Survival Guide** (p235)

When to Go

The sweltering summer (July and August) is peak tourist season, when crowds swarm the city – and its beaches. For pleasant weather, but without the sea dips, come in late spring (May).

Barcelona

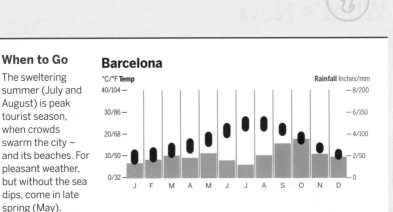

°C/°F **Temp**   **Rainfall** Inches/mm

Arriving in Barcelona

El Prat airport Frequent *aerobúses* make the 35-minute run into town (€5.90) from 6am to 1am. Taxis cost around €26.

Estació Sants Long-distance trains arrive at this large station near the centre of town, which is linked by metro to other parts of the city.

Estació del Nord Barcelona's long-haul bus station is located in L'Eixample, about 1.5km northeast of Plaça de Catalunya, and is a short walk from the Arc de Triomf metro station.

Girona-Costa Brava airport The 'Barcelona Bus' operated by Sagalés (one way/return €16/25, 1½ hours) is timed with Ryanair flights and goes direct to Barcelona's Estació del Nord.

Reus airport Buses operated by Hispano-Igualadina (one way/return €16/25, 1½ hours) are timed with Ryanair flights and go direct to Barcelona's Estació Sants.

Getting Around

Barcelona has abundant options for getting around town. The excellent metro can get you to most places, with buses and trams filling in the gaps. Taxis are the best option late at night.

Metro The most convenient option. Runs from 5am to midnight Sunday to Thursday, till 2am on Friday and 24 hours on Saturday. Targeta T-10 (10-ride passes; €9.95) are the best value; otherwise, it's €2.15 per ride.

Bus A hop-on, hop-off Bus Turístic (p210), from Plaça de Catalunya, is handy for those wanting to see the city's highlights in one or two days.

Taxi You can hail taxis on the street (try La Rambla, Via Laietana, Plaça de Catalunya and Passeig de Gràcia) or at taxi stands.

On foot To explore the old city, all you need is a good pair of walking shoes.

Plan Your Trip
What's New

Gaudí's Hidden Townhouse

In a quiet backstreet of Gràcia, the spectacular facade of Gaudí's Mudéjar-inspired Casa Vicens (p71) has long been an undervisited gem, but this changed at the end of 2017, when the building opened to the public for the first time.

Luxury with Pedigree

Soho House, London's famous member's club, has opened a **bolt-hole** (📞93 220 46 00 www.sohousebarcelona.com; Plaça del Duc de Medinaceli 4; r from €300) in Barcelona, where regular punters can rub elbows with celebs and creative types in the stunning bar area.

Three-Star Dining

Barcelona finally has a restaurant with three Michelin stars, in the shape of Lasarte (p147), on the Passeig de Gràcia. For the full, no-expense-spared extravaganza, order the tasting menu.

Meat-Free Revolution

Vegetarians and mindful eaters need not give Barcelona a pass when planning their next holiday. The city has seen an explosion of healthy, animal-free eateries in recent years – and even vegan clothing shops, such as Amapola Vegan Shop (p160).

Poblenou Renaissance

This formerly industrial hood is on the make, with new galleries, colourful shops and restaurants forming the intersection for the creative tech and design folk who are increasingly moving here.

Adrià's Culinary Kingdom

Famed chef Albert Adrià now runs six celebrated restaurants all within strolling distance of one another in Sant Antoni. His latest, Enigma (p149), opened in 2017 and is already considered one of the city's best.

Above: Casa Vicens (p71)

Plan Your Trip
For Free

With planning, Barcelona can be a surprisingly affordable place in which to travel. Many museums offer free days, and some of the best ways to experience the city don't cost a penny – hanging out on the beach, exploring fascinating neighbourhoods and parks, and drinking in the views from hilltop heights.

Festivals & Events

Barcelona has loads of free festivals and events, including Festes de la Mercè (p14) and Festes de Santa Eulàlia (p7). From June to August, the city hosts Música als Parcs (p13), a series of open-air concerts held in different parks and green spaces around the city. Stop in at the tourist office or go online (www.bcn.cat) for a schedule.

Walking Tours

Numerous companies offer pay-what-you-wish walking tours. These typically take in the Barri Gòtic or the Modernista sites of L'Eixample. Of course, the guides expect a contribution.

Sights

Entry to some sights is free on occasion, most commonly on the first Sunday of the month, while quite a few attractions are free from 3pm to 8pm on Sundays. Others, including the Centre d'Art Santa Mònica (p47), Palau del Lloctinent (p67), Temple d'August (p67) and Antic Hospital de la Santa Creu (p51), are always free, and the Basílica de Santa Maria del Mar (p116) is free in the morning and evening.

Picnics

It might not be for free, but you can eat very well on a budget if you stick to set menus at lunchtime. For even less, you can put together a picnic of fresh fruits, cheese, smoked meats and other goodies purchased at local markets such as Mercat de la Boqueria (p48), El Raval's Mercat de Sant Antoni (p169) or La Ribera's Mercat de Santa Caterina (p110).

Above: Mercat de Santa Caterina (p110)

Plan Your Trip
Family Travel

VITALI AND OLGA/SHUTTERSTOCK ©

Catalan Style

Going out to eat or sipping a beer on a late summer evening at a *terraza* (terrace) needn't mean leaving children with minders. Locals take their kids out all the time and don't worry about keeping them up late. To make the most of your visit, try to adjust your child's sleeping habits to 'Spanish time' early on, or else you'll miss out on much of Barcelona. Also, be prepared to look for things 'outside the box': there's the childlike creativity of Picasso and Miró (give your children paper and crayons and take them around the museums), the Harry-Potter-meets-Tolkien fantasy of Park Güell and La Pedrera, and the wild costumes, human castle-building and street food at festivals.

Babysitting

Most of the midrange and top-end hotels in Barcelona can organise babysitting services. Otherwise, contact **Tender Loving Canguros** (https://tlcanguros.wordpress.com)

or **5 Serveis** (☏93 412 56 76; www.5serveis. com; Carrer de Pelai 50; ⓂCatalunya).

Eating with Children

Barcelona – and Spain in general – is super friendly when it comes to eating with children. Spanish kids tend to eat the Mediterranean offerings enjoyed by their parents, but some restaurants have children's menus that serve up burgers, pizzas, tomato-sauce pasta and the like. Good local – and child-proof – food commonly found on tapas menus are *tortillas de patatas* (potato omelettes) or *croquetas de jamón* (ham croquettes).

Family-Friendly Meals

Fantastic for chocolate and all manner of sweet things, **La Nena** (p138) has a play area, and toys and books in a corner. A great all-weather option is **Bar del Convent** (p145), with a safe, traffic-free terrace

From left: A child plays on the stairs of Museu Nacional d'Art de Catalunya (p56); Jardí Botànic (p126)

IAKOV FILIMONOV/SHUTTERSTOCK ©

to play in, and a raft of games and toys indoors. Sit outside **Filferro** (☑93 221 98 36; Carrer de Sant Carles 29; tapas €5-8, mains €7-12; ☺10am-1am; 🔁📶; MBarceloneta), a tapas and snack bar, and enjoy the Mediterranean breeze, while junior busies about in the adjacent playground. At **Granja M Viader** (p137) no kid will be left unimpressed – and without a buzz! – by the thick hot chocolate. **Pepa Tomate** (☑93 210 46 98; www.pepa tomategrup.com; Plaça de la Revolució de Setembre de 1868 17; sharing plates €7-17; ☺8pm-midnight Mon, from 9am Tue-Fri, from 10am Sat, from 11am Sun; 👶; MFontana) is a winner with crayons provided and a tiny playground near the plaza-side tables. Along a street famed for its chocolate cafes, **Granja La Pallaresa** (☑93 302 20 36; www.lapallaresa. com; Carrer del Petritxol 11; ☺9am-1pm & 4-9pm Mon-Sat, 9am-1pm & 5-9pm Sun; 🔁; MLiceu) is a favourite for crispy churros dipped in steaming chocolate.

Best Parks & Gardens for Kids

Jardí Botànic (p126)
Parc de la Ciutadella (p84)
Parc de Diagonal Mar (p121)
Park Güell (p68)

Need to Know

Change facilities Generally widely available and clean.

Cots Usually available in hotels (ask for *una cuna*); reserve ahead.

Health High health-care standards.

Highchairs Many restaurants have at least one.

Infant supplies Nappies, dummies, creams and formula are sold at any of the city's many pharmacies. Nappies are cheaper in supermarkets.

Transport The metro is great for families with strollers – just be mindful of your bags, as pickpockets often target distracted parents.

TOP
EXPERIENCES

The very best to see & do

TOMASSEREDA/GETTY IMAGES ©

La Sagrada Família

If you have time for only one sightseeing outing, this is it. La Sagrada Família inspires awe with its sheer verticality, remarkable use of light and Gaudí's offbeat design elements.

Great For...

☑ **Don't Miss**

The apse, the extraordinary pillars and the stained glass.

In the manner of the medieval cathedrals La Sagrada Família emulates, it's still under construction after more than 100 years. When completed, the highest tower will be one and a half times as high as those that stand today.

A Holy Mission

The Temple Expiatori de la Sagrada Família (Expiatory Temple of the Holy Family) was Antoni Gaudí's all-consuming obsession. Given the commission by a conservative society that wished to build a temple as atonement for the city's sins of modernity, Gaudí saw its completion as his holy mission. As funds dried up, he contributed his own and in the last years of his life he was never shy of pleading with anyone he thought a likely donor.

Detail of the Passion Facade (p39)

ℹ️ Need to Know

(Map p254; 📞93 208 04 14; www.sagrada familia.org; Carrer de Mallorca 401; adult/child €15/free; 🕙9am-8pm Apr-Sep, to 7pm Mar & Oct, to 6pm Nov-Feb; Ⓜ Sagrada Família)

✕ Take a Break

Cantina Mexicana (📞93 667 66 68; www. cantinalamexicana.es; Carrer de València 427; mains €7-13; 🕙1pm-midnight; 🖋; Ⓜ Sagrada Família) dodges the crowds and does excellent tacos.

★ Top Tip

Buy tickets online to beat the frequently dispiriting queues.

Gaudí devised a temple 95m long and 60m wide, able to seat 13,000 people, with a central tower 170m high above the transept and another 17 towers of 100m or more. The 12 towers along the three facades represent the Apostles, while the remaining five represent the Virgin Mary and the four evangelists. With his characteristic dislike for straight lines (there were none in nature, he said), Gaudí gave his towers swelling outlines inspired by the weird peaks of the holy mountain Montserrat, outside Barcelona, and encrusted them with a tangle of sculpture that seems an outgrowth of the stone.

At Gaudí's death, only the crypt, the apse walls, one portal and one tower had been finished. Three more towers were added by 1930, completing the northeast (Nativity) facade. In 1936 anarchists burned and smashed the interior, including workshops, plans and models. Work began again in 1952, but controversy has always clouded progress. Opponents of the continuation of the project claim that the computer models based on what little of Gaudí's plans survived the anarchists' ire have led to the creation of a monster that has little to do with Gaudí's plans and style. It is a debate that appears to have little hope of resolution. Like or hate what is being done, the fascination it awakens is undeniable.

Having begun in 1882, the work is hoped (although by no means expected) to be finished in 2026, a century after the architect's death. Even before reaching that point, some of the oldest parts of the church, especially the apse, have required restoration work.

The Interior & the Apse

Inside, work on roofing over the church was completed in 2010. The roof is held up by a forest of extraordinary angled pillars. As the pillars soar toward the ceiling, they sprout a web of supporting branches, creating the effect of a forest canopy. The tree image is in no way fortuitous – Gaudí envisaged such an effect. Everything was thought through, including the shape and placement of windows to create the mottled effect you would see with sunlight pouring through the branches of a thick forest. The pillars are of four different types of stone. They vary in colour and load-bearing strength, from the soft Montjuïc stone pillars along the lateral aisles through to granite, dark grey basalt and finally burgundy-tinged Iranian porphyry for the key columns at the intersection of the nave and transept. The stained glass, divided in shades of red, blue, green and ochre, creates a hypnotic, magical atmosphere when the sun hits the windows. Tribunes built high above the aisles can host two choirs: the main tribune up to 1300 people and the children's tribune up to 300.

Nativity Facade

The Nativity Facade is the artistic pinnacle of the building, mostly created under Gaudí's personal supervision. You can climb high up inside some of the four towers (at extra cost) by a combination of lifts and narrow spiral staircases – a vertiginous experience. Do not climb the stairs if you have cardiac or respiratory problems. The towers are destined to hold tubular bells capable of playing complex music at great volume. Their upper parts are decorated with mosaics spelling out 'Sanctus, Sanctus, Sanctus,

View of the kaleidoscopic ceiling

Hosanna in Excelsis, Amen, Alleluia'. Asked why he lavished so much care on the tops of the spires, which no one would see from close up, Gaudí answered: 'The angels will see them'.

Three sections of the portal represent, from left to right, Hope, Charity and Faith. Among the forest of sculpture on the Charity portal you can see, low down, the manger surrounded by an ox, an ass, the shepherds, kings and angel musicians. Some 30 different species of plant from around Catalonia are reproduced here and the faces of the many figures are taken

from plaster casts done of local people and the occasional one made from corpses in the local morgue.

Directly above the blue stained-glass window is the archangel Gabriel's Annunciation to Mary. At the top is a green cypress tree, a refuge in a storm for the white doves of peace dotted over it. The mosaic work at the pinnacle of the towers is made from Murano glass, from Venice.

To the right of the facade is the curious Claustre del Roser, a Gothic-style mini cloister tacked on to the outside of the church (rather than the classic square enclosure of the great Gothic church monasteries). Once inside, look back to the intricately decorated entrance. On the lower right-hand side you'll notice the sculpture of a reptilian devil handing a terrorist a bomb. Barcelona was regularly rocked by political violence and bombings were frequent in the decades prior to the civil war. The sculpture is one of several on the 'temptations of men and women'.

Passion Facade

The southwest Passion Facade, on the theme of Christ's last days and death, was built between 1954 and 1978 based on surviving drawings by Gaudí, with four towers and a large, sculpture-bedecked portal. The sculptor, Josep Subirachs, worked on its decoration from 1986 to 2006. He did not attempt to imitate Gaudí; rather, he produced angular, controversial images of his own. The main series of sculptures, on three levels, are in an S-shaped sequence, starting with the Last Supper at the bottom left and ending with Christ's burial at the top right. Decorative work on the Passion Facade continues even today, as construction of the Glory Facade moves ahead.

NIKADA/GETTY IMAGES ©

To the right, in front of the Passion Facade, the Escoles de Gaudí is one of his simpler gems. Gaudí built this as a children's school, creating an original, undulating roof of brick that continues to charm architects to this day. Inside is a recreation of Gaudí's modest office as it was when he died and explanations of the geometric patterns and plans at the heart of his building techniques.

A Hidden Portrait

Careful observation of the Passion Facade will reveal a special tribute from sculptor Josep Subirachs to Gaudí. The central sculptural group (below Christ crucified) shows, from right to left, Christ bearing his cross, Veronica displaying the cloth with Christ's bloody image, a pair of soldiers and, watching it all, a man called the evangelist. Subirachs used a rare photo of Gaudí, taken a couple of years before his death, as the model for the evangelist's face.

Glory Facade

The Glory Facade is under construction and will, like the others, be crowned by four towers – the total of 12 representing the Twelve Apostles. Gaudí wanted it to be the most magnificent facade of the church. Inside will be the narthex, a kind of foyer made up of 16 'lanterns', a series of hyperboloid forms topped by cones. Further decoration will make the whole building a microcosmic symbol of the Christian church, with Christ represented by a massive 170m central tower above the transept and the five remaining planned towers symbolising the Virgin Mary and the four evangelists.

Museu Gaudí

Open the same times as the church, the Museu Gaudí, below ground level, includes interesting material on Gaudí's life and other works, as well as models and photos of La Sagrada Família. You can see a good example of his plumb-line models that showed him the stresses and strains he could get away with in construction. A side hall towards the eastern end of the museum leads to a viewing point above the simple crypt in which the genius is buried. The crypt, where Masses are now held, can also be visited from the Carrer de Mallorca side of the church.

What's Nearby?

Església de les Saleses   Church
(Map p254; ☑93 458 76 67; www.parroquia concepciobcn.org; Passeig de Sant Joan 90; ⏰10am-1pm & 5-7pm Mon-Sat, 10am-2pm Sun; Ⓜ Verdaguer) A singular neo-Gothic effort, this church was designed by Joan Martorell i Montells (1833–1906), Gaudí's architecture professor. Built between 1878 and 1885 with an adjacent convent (badly damaged in the civil war and now a school), it offers hints of what was to come with Modernisme, with the use of brick, mosaics and stained glass.

Passion Facade (p39)

Recinte Modernista
de Sant Pau · Architecture

(☎93 553 78 01; www.santpaubarcelona.org;
Carrer de Sant Antoni Maria Claret 167; adult/
child €13/free; ⊙9.30am-6.30pm Mon-Sat, to
2.30pm Sun Apr-Oct, 9.30am-4.30pm Mon-Sat,
to 2.30pm Sun Nov-Mar; Ⓜ Sant Pau/Dos de
Maig) Domènech i Montaner outdid himself
as architect and philanthropist with the
Modernista Hospital de la Santa Creu i de
Sant Pau, renamed the 'Recinte Modernista' in 2014. It was long considered one of
the city's most important hospitals but was
repurposed, its various spaces becoming
cultural centres, offices and something
of a monument. The complex includes 16
unique, lavishly decorated pavilions. It is a
a joint Unesco World Heritage Site together
with the Palau de la Música Catalana.

Museu del Disseny
de Barcelona · Museum

(☎93 256 68 00; www.museudeldisseny.cat;
Plaça de les Glòries Catalanes 37; permanent
exhibition adult/child €6/4, temporary exhibition
€4.50/3, combination ticket €8/5.50, free from
3pm Sun & 1st Sun of the month; ⊙10am-8pm
Tue-Sun; Ⓜ Glòries) Barcelona's design museum lies inside a monolithic contemporary
building with geometric facades and a rather brutalist appearance that's nicknamed
la grapadora (the stapler) by locals. Inside
it houses a dazzling collection of ceramics,
decorative arts and textiles, and is a must
for anyone interested in the design world.

★ Top Tip
Audioguides – including some tailored
to children – are available at La Sagrada
Família for an additional fee.

Tree-lined La Rambla

La Rambla

Barcelona's most famous street is both tourist magnet and a window into Catalan culture, with arts centres, theatres and intriguing architecture. The middle is a broad pedestrian boulevard, crowded daily with a wide cross-section of society. A stroll here is pure sensory overload, with souvenir hawkers, buskers, pavement artists and living statues part of the ever-changing street scene.

Great For...

ⓘ Need to Know

(Map p250; Ⓜ Catalunya, Liceu, Drassanes)

The Rambla stroll, from Plaça de Catalunya to Plaça del Portal de la Pau, is 1.5km.

★ **Top Tip**

Things have improved in recent years, but pickpockets still prey on head-in-air tourists along here.

History

La Rambla takes its name from a seasonal stream (derived from the Arabic word for sand, *raml*) that once ran here. From the early Middle Ages, it was better known as the Cagalell (Stream of Shit) and lay outside the city walls until the 14th century. Monastic buildings were then built and, subsequently, mansions of the well-to-do from the 16th to the early 19th centuries. Unofficially, La Rambla is divided into five sections, which explains why many know it as Las Ramblas.

La Rambla de Canaletes

The section of La Rambla north of Plaça de Catalunya is named after the **Font de Canaletes** (Map p250; La Rambla; Ⓜ Catalunya), an inconspicuous turn-of-the-20th-century drinking fountain, the water of which supposedly emerges from what were once known as the springs of Canaletes. It used to be said that *barcelonins* 'drank the waters of Les Canaletes'. Nowadays, people claim that anyone who drinks from the fountain will return to Barcelona, which is not such a bad prospect. Delirious football fans gather here to celebrate whenever the city's principal team, FC Barcelona, wins a cup or league title (ie often).

La Rambla dels Estudis

La Rambla dels Estudis, from Carrer de la Canuda south to Carrer de la Portaferrissa, was formerly home to a twittering bird market, which closed in 2010 after 150 years in operation.

Església de Betlem

Just north of Carrer del Carme, this **church** (Map p250; ☑93 318 38 23; www.mdbetlem.net; Carrer d'en Xuclà 2; ⊙8.30am-1.30pm & 6-9pm; Ⓜ Liceu) was constructed in baroque style for the Jesuits in the late 17th and early 18th centuries to replace an earlier church destroyed by fire in 1671. Fire was a bit of a theme for this site: the church was once considered the most splendid of Barcelona's few baroque offerings, but leftist arsonists torched it in 1936.

Palau Moja

Looming over the eastern side of La Rambla, **Palau Moja** (Map p250; ☑93 316 27 40; https://palaumoja.com; Carrer de Portaferrissa 1; ⊙10am-9pm, cafe 9.30am-midnight Mon-Fri, 11am-midnight Sat & Sun; Ⓜ Liceu) 𝗙𝗥𝗘𝗘 is a neoclassical building dating from the second half of the 18th century. Its clean, classical lines are best appreciated from across La Rambla. Unfortunately, interior access is limited, as it houses mostly government offices.

La Rambla de Sant Josep

From Carrer de la Portaferrissa to Plaça de la Boqueria, La Rambla de Sant Josep (named after a 16th-century convent that was located there) is lined with flower stalls, which give it the alternative name La Rambla de les Flors.

Palau de la Virreina

The **Palau de la Virreina** (Map p250; La Rambla 99; Ⓜ Liceu) is a grand 18th-century rococo mansion (with some neoclassical elements) that houses a municipal arts/entertainment information and ticket office run by the *ajuntament* (town hall). It was built by Manuel d'Amat i de Junyent, the corrupt captain general of Chile (a Spanish colony that included the silver mines of Potosí), and is a rare example of such a post-baroque building in Barcelona. It's home to the **Centre de la Imatge** (Map p250; ☑93 316 10 00; http://ajuntament.barcelona.cat/lavirreina/ca/; ⊙noon-8pm Tue-Sun; Ⓜ Liceu), which has rotating photography exhibits. Admission prices vary.

TRABANTOS/SHUTTERSTOCK ©

Mosaïc de Miró

At Plaça de la Boqueria, where four side streets meet just north of Liceu metro station, you can walk all over a Miró – the colourful **mosaic** (Map p250; Plaça de la Boqueria; MLiceu) in the pavement, with one tile signed by the artist. Miró chose this site as it's near the house where he was born on the Passatge del Crèdit. The mosaic's bold colours and vivid swirling forms are instantly recognisable to Miró fans, though plenty of tourists stroll right over it without realising.

La Rambla dels Caputxins

La Rambla dels Caputxins, named after a former monastery, runs from Plaça de la Boqueria to Carrer dels Escudellers. The latter street is named after the potters' guild, founded in the 13th century, whose members lived and worked here. On the western side of La Rambla is the **Gran Teatre del Liceu** (Map p250; 93 485 99 00; www.liceubarcelona.cat; La Rambla 51-59; tours 45min adult/concession/child under 7yr €9/7.50/free, 25min €6/5/free; 45min tours hourly 2-6pm Mon-Fri, from 9.30am Sat, 25min tours 1.30pm Mon-Sat; MLiceu). To the southeast is the entrance to the palm-shaded Plaça Reial. Below this point La Rambla gets seedier, with the occasional strip club and peep show.

La Rambla de Santa Mònica

The final stretch of La Rambla widens out to approach the Mirador de Colom overlooking Port Vell. La Rambla here is named after the Convent de Santa Mònica, which once stood on the western flank of the street and has since been converted into the **Centre d'Art Santa Mònica** (Map p250; 93 567 11 10; http://artssantamonica. gencat.cat; La Rambla 7; 11am-9pm Tue-Sat, to 5pm Sun; MDrassanes) FREE, a cultural centre that mostly exhibits modern multimedia installations.

What's Nearby?

Basílica de Santa Maria del Pi
Church

(Map p250; 93 318 47 43; www.basilicadelpi. com; Plaça del Pi; adult/concession/child under 7yr €4/3/free; 10am-6pm; MLiceu) This striking 14th-century church is a classic of Catalan Gothic, with an imposing facade, a wide interior and a single nave. The simple decor in the main sanctuary contrasts with the gilded chapels and exquisite stained-glass windows that bathe the interior in ethereal light. The beautiful rose window above its entrance is one of the world's largest. Occasional concerts are staged here (classical guitar, choral groups and chamber orchestras).

Plaça Reial

Plaça Reial Square

(Map p250; MLiceu) One of the most photogenic squares in Barcelona, and certainly its liveliest. Numerous restaurants, bars and nightspots lie beneath the arcades of 19th-century neoclassical buildings, with a buzz of activity at all hours.

Via Sepulcral Romana Archaeological Site

(Map p250; ☎93 256 21 22; www.muhba.cat; Plaça de la Vila de Madrid; adult/concession/child €2/1.50/free; ⊙11am-2pm Tue & Thu, to 7pm Sat & Sun; MCatalunya) Along Carrer de la Canuda, a block east from the top end of La Rambla, is a sunken garden where a series of Roman tombs lies exposed. A smallish display in Spanish and Catalan by the tombs explores burial and funerary rites and customs. A few bits of pottery (including a burial amphora with the skeleton of a three-year-old Roman child) accompany the display.

Mirador de Colom Viewpoint

(Columbus Monument; ☎93 285 38 32; www.barcelonaturisme.com; Plaça del Portal de la Pau; adult/child €6/4; ⊙8.30am-8.30pm; MDrassanes) High above the swirl of traffic on the roundabout below, Columbus keeps permanent watch, pointing vaguely out to the Mediterranean from this Corinthian-style iron column built for the 1888 Universal Exhibition. Zip up 60m in a lift for bird's-eye views back up La Rambla and across Barcelona's ports.

★ **Top Tip**

Take an early morning stroll and another late at night to sample La Rambla's many moods.

RADU BERCAN/SHUTTERSTOCK ©

Mercat de la Boqueria

Barcelona's most central produce market, the Mercat de la Boqueria, provides one of the greatest sound, smell and colour sensations in Europe, and is housed in a building every bit as impressive. It spills over with the rich and varied colours of plentiful fruit and vegetable stands, and seemingly limitless varieties of sea critters, cheeses and meats.

Great For...

ⓘ Need to Know

(Map p250; 📞93 318 20 17; www.boqueria. info; La Rambla 91; ⏰8am-8.30pm Mon-Sat; Ⓜ Liceu)

★ **Top Tip**
Stallholders aren't here for tourists: give way to purchasers and ask permission before taking photos.

KIEV.VICTOR/SHUTTERSTOCK ©

The Historic Market

Some chronicles place a market here as early as 1217. As much as it has become a modern-day attraction, this has always been the place where locals come to shop.

Between the 15th and 18th centuries, a pig market known as Mercat de la Palla (Straw Market) stood here; it was considered part of a bigger market extending to Plaça del Pi. What we now know as La Boqueria didn't come to exist until the 19th century, when the local authorities decided to build a structure that would house fishmongers and butchers, as well as fruit and vegetable sellers. The iron Modernista gate was constructed in 1914.

Many of Barcelona's top restaurateurs buy their produce here, although nowadays it's no easy task getting past the seething crowds of tourists to snare a slippery slab of sole or a tempting piece of *queso de cabra* (goat's cheese).

What to Try?

La Boqueria is dotted with several unassuming places to eat, and eat well, with stallholders opening up at lunchtime. Whether you eat here or you're self-catering, it's worth trying some of Catalonia's gastronomic specialities, such as *bacallà salat* (dried salted cod), which usually comes in an *esqueixada*, a tomato, onion and black olive salad with frisée lettuce; *calçots* (a cross between a leek and an onion), which are chargrilled and the insides eaten as a messy whole; *cargols* (snails), a Catalan staple that is best eaten baked as *cargols a la llauna* (snails sautéed in a tin); *peus de porc* (pig's trotters), which

are often stewed with snails; or *percebes* (goose-necked barnacles). Much loved across Spain, these crustaceans look like witches' fingers and are eaten with a garlic and parsley sauce.

Fish Market

While stalls aimed at tourists make tentative inroads, the fish market in the market's geographical centre is the guardian of tradition. Razor clams and red prawns, salmon, sea bass and swordfish, all almost as fresh as when it was caught; so much so that there's scarcely a fishy aroma to inhale. Barcelona's love affair with fish and seafood starts here.

☑ Don't Miss

Picking up fresh produce for a beach picnic.

Juanito

Juanito encapsulates the spirit of the market and features in a thousand tourist snaps. Head barman at Bar Pinotxo (p137) for more than four decades, resplendent in waistcoat and bow tie, and unfailingly warm in many languages and none, he cajoles his staff, greets passers-by and announces the daily specials in the finest Barcelona tradition of food as performance.

Joan

The family-run Joan La Llar del Pernil (p159) is our pick of the numerous purveyors of *jamón* (cured Spanish-style ham; *pernil* in Catalan) scattered around the market. Stall owner Joan knows his *jamón*, cheerfully regaling passers-by with lessons in the dark arts of cured meats as he cuts another thin slice and hands it over to try.

Quim

The food at **El Quim** (Map p250; ☎93 301 98 10; www.elquimdelaboqueria.com; Mercat de la Boqueria; mains €16-21; ☺noon-4pm Mon, 7am-4pm Tue-Thu, 7am-5pm Fri & Sat; ⓂLiceu), buried in the heart of the market, is as fresh as the market produce. Quim himself serves a dazzling array of dishes, but he does particularly wonderful things with eggs: *tortilla de patatas* (Spanish omelette), fried eggs with squid, or with foie gras. Pull up a stool.

What's Nearby?

Antic Hospital de la Santa Creu   Historic Building

(Former Hospital of the Holy Cross; Map p249; www.barcelonaturisme.com; Carrer de l'Hospital 56; ☺9am-10pm; ⓂLiceu) FREE Behind La Boqueria stands this building, which was once the city's main hospital. Begun in 1401, it functioned until the 1930s and was considered one of the best in Europe in its medieval heyday – it is famously the place where Antoni Gaudí died in 1926. Today it houses the **Biblioteca de Catalunya** and the **Institut d'Estudis Catalans** (Institute for Catalan Studies). The hospital's Gothic chapel, **La Capella** (☎93 256 20 44; www.bcn.cat/lacapella; ☺noon-8pm Tue-Sat, 11am-2pm Sun & holidays) FREE, shows temporary exhibitions.

Chandelier inside Casa Batlló

Casa Batlló

One of the strangest residential buildings in Europe, Casa Batlló is Gaudí at his hallucinatory best. To some, Casa Batlló appears like a mythical creature, frozen in place. It has numerous intriguing design elements, both on the striking exterior and in the dream-like, exuberant interior. This is one of three notable Modernista buildings in this landmark block.

Great For...

ℹ Need to Know

(Map p254; ☎93 216 03 06; www.casabatllo. es; Passeig de Gràcia 43; adult/child €28/ free; ⏱9am-9pm, last admission 8pm; ⓂPasseig de Gràcia)

★ **Top Tip**

Make a return visit after sunset to see the facade illuminated in all its glory.

The building is remarkable in every respect. Casa Batlló and neighbouring Casa Amatller and Casa Lleó Morera were all renovated between 1898 and 1906; together, they demonstrate Modernisme's eclecticism.

Facade

To Salvador Dalí it resembled 'twilight clouds in water'. Others see a more-than-passing resemblance to the impressionist masterpiece *Water Lilies* by Claude Monet. A Rorschach blot for the imagination, Casa Batlló's facade is exquisite and whimsical, sprinkled with fragments of blue, mauve and green tiles, and studded with wave-shaped window frames and mask-like balconies.

Roof

Casa Batlló's roof, with the twisting chimney pots so characteristic of Gaudí's structures, is the building's grand crescendo. The eastern end represents Sant Jordi (St George) and the Dragon; one local name for Casa Batlló is the *casa del drac* (house of the dragon). The ceaseless curves of coloured tiles have the effect of making the building seem like a living being.

Sala Principal

The staircase wafts you to the 1st floor, where everything swirls in the main salon: the ceiling twists into a whirlpool-like vortex around its sun-like lamp; the doors, window and skylights are dreamy waves of wood and coloured glass in mollusc-like shapes. The sense of light and space here is extraordinary thanks to the wall-length window onto Passeig de Gràcia.

Back Terrace

Opening onto an expansive L'Eixample patio, Casa Batlló's back terrace is like a fantasy garden in miniature. It's a place where flowerpots take on strange forms and where the accumulation of *trencadís*

> ✕ **Take a Break**
> Tapas 24 (p145), a modern basement tapas joint, opens all day.

(broken ceramic pieces) – a mere 330 of them on the building's rear facade – has the effect of immersing you in a kaleidoscope.

Manzana de la Discordia

Despite the Catalanisation of most Barcelona street names since 1980, this stretch of Passeig de Gràcia (Manzana de la Discordia) is still known by its Spanish name to preserve a pun on *manzana,* which means 'block' and 'apple'. In Greek mythology, the original Apple of Discord was tossed onto Mt Olympus by Eris (Discord), with orders that it be given to the most beautiful goddess, sparking jealousies that were the catalyst for the Trojan War.

What's Nearby?

Casa Amatller   Architecture

(Map p254; ☎93 461 74 60; www.amatller.org; Passeig de Gràcia 41; adult/child 1hr guided tour

Facade of Casa Batlló from Passeig de Gràcia

€17/8.50, 40min multimedia tour €14/7, with 20min chocolate tasting €17/10; ⊙11am-6pm; ⓂPasseig de Gràcia) One of Puig i Cadafalch's most striking bits of Modernista fantasy, Casa Amatller combines Gothic window frames with a stepped gable borrowed from Dutch urban architecture. But the busts and reliefs of dragons, knights and other characters dripping off the main facade are pure caprice.

Casa Lleó Morera   Architecture

(Map p254; Passeig de Gràcia 35; ⓂPasseig de Gràcia) Domènech i Montaner's 1905 contribution to the Manzana de la Discordia, with Modernista carving outside and a bright, tiled lobby in which floral motifs predominate, is perhaps the least odd-looking of the three main buildings on the block. The 1st floor is open to the public (by guided tour only), so you can appreciate the giddy with swirling sculptures, rich mosaics and whimsical decor.

Fundació Antoni Tàpies   Gallery

(Map p254; ☎93 487 03 15; www.fundaciotapies. org; Carrer d'Aragó 255; adult/child €7/5.60; ⊙10am-7pm Tue-Sun; ⓂPasseig de Gràcia) This is both a pioneering Modernista building (completed in 1885) and the major collection of leading 20th-century Catalan artist Antoni Tàpies, a man known for his esoteric work. Tàpies died in 2012 but left behind a powerful painting collection and a foundation that promotes contemporary artists.

☑ Don't Miss

Before going inside Casa Batlló, take a look at the pavement. Each paving piece carries stylised images of an octopus and a starfish, designs that Gaudí originally cooked up for Casa Batlló.

Museu Nacional d'Art de Catalunya

From across Barcelona, the flamboyant neobaroque silhouette of the Palau Nacional can be seen on the slopes of Montjuïc. It houses a vast and formidable collection of mostly Catalan art, from the early Middle Ages to the early 20th century.

Great For...

☑ Don't Miss

The fantastic assemblage of Romanesque frescoes from churches around Catalonia.

Romanesque Masterpieces

The Romanesque art section is considered the most important concentration of early medieval art in the world. Rescued from neglected country churches across northern Catalonia in the early 20th century, the collection consists of 21 frescoes, woodcarvings and painted altar frontals (low-relief wooden panels that were the forerunners of the elaborate altarpieces that adorned later churches). The insides of several churches have been recreated and the frescoes – in some cases fragmentary, in others extraordinarily complete and alive with colour – have been placed as they were when in situ.

The first of the two most striking frescoes, in Sala 7, is a magnificent image of Christ in Majesty painted around 1123. Based on the text of the Apocalypse, the

BRIAN KINNEY/SHUTTERSTOCK ©

❶ Need to Know

(MNAC; Map p256; ☎93 622 03 76; www. museunacional.cat; Mirador del Palau Nacional; adult/child €12/free, after 3pm Sat & 1st Sun of month free, rooftop viewpoint only €2; ⊙10am-8pm Tue-Sat, to 3pm Sun May-Sep, to 6pm Tue-Sat Oct-Apr; ☐55, ⓂEspanya)

✕ Take a Break

On-site, there's high-end Oleum (p149), a cafeteria and a rooftop bar with great vistas.

★ Top Tip

The Articket pass gives discounts for six museums (including MNAC).

fresco depicts Christ enthroned with the world at his feet. He holds a book open with the words *Ego Sum Lux Mundi* (I am the Light of the World) and is surrounded by the four evangelists. The images were taken from the apse of the Església de Sant Climent de Taüll in northwest Catalonia. Nearby in Sala 9 are frescoes painted around the same time in the nearby Església de Santa Maria de Taüll. This time the central image taken from the apse is of the Virgin Mary and Christ Child. These images were not mere decoration but tools of instruction in the basics of Christian faith for the local population – try to set yourself in the mind of the average medieval citizen: illiterate, ignorant, fearful and in most cases eking out a subsistence living. These images transmitted the basic personalities and tenets of the faith and were accepted at face value by most.

Gothic Collection

Opposite the Romanesque collection on the ground floor is the museum's Gothic art section. In these halls you can see Catalan Gothic painting and works from other Spanish and Mediterranean regions. Look out especially for the work of Bernat Martorell in Sala 25 and Jaume Huguet in Sala 26. Among Martorell's works you'll find images of the martyrdom of St Vincent and St Llúcia. Huguet's *Consagració de Sant Agustí*, in which St Augustine is depicted as a bishop, is dazzling in its detail.

Cambó Bequest & the Thyssen-Bornemisza Collection

As the Gothic collection draws to a close, you pass through two separate and equally eclectic private collections. The Cambó Bequest, donated by Francesc Cambó, spans the history of European painting between the 14th century and the beginning of the

19th century. The Thyssen-Bornemisza Collection presents a selection of European painting and sculpture produced between the 13th and the 18th centuries, on loan to the MNAC by the Museo Thyssen-Bornemisza in Madrid. The Thyssen-Bornemisza Collection's highlight is Fra Angelico's *Madonna of Humility*, whereas the Cambó Bequest holds wonderful works by masters Veronese, Titian and Canaletto. Cranach, El Greco, Rubens and even Gainsborough also feature; the collection's finale includes works by Francisco de Goya.

Modern Catalan Art

On the next floor, the collection turns to modern art, mainly but not exclusively Catalan. This collection is arranged thematically: Modernisme, Noucentisme, Art and the Civil War and so on. Among the many highlights:

an early Salvador Dalí painting *(Portrait of My Father)*, Juan Gris' collage-like paintings, the brilliant portraits of Marià Fortuny, and 1930s call-to-arms posters against the Francoist onslaught (nearby you'll find photos of soldiers and bombed-out city centres). There are works by Modernista painters Ramon Casas and Santiago Rusiñol, as well as Catalan luminary Antoni Tàpies.

Also on show are items of Modernista furniture and decoration, which include a mural by Ramon Casas (the artist and Pere Romeu on a tandem bicycle) that once adorned the legendary bar and restaurant Els Quatre Gats (p142).

Fresco Strippers

Among the little-known curiosities inside MNAC, you'll find a video (in Sala 3) depicting the techniques used by the

Poble Espanyol

'Fresco Strippers' to preserve the great Romanesque works. The Stefanoni brothers, Italian art restorers, brought the secrets of *strappo* (stripping of frescoes from walls) to Catalonia in the early 1900s. The Stefanoni would cover frescoes with a sheet of fabric, stuck on with a glue made of cartilage. When dry, this allowed the image to be stripped off the wall and rolled up. For three years the Stefanoni roamed the Pyrenean countryside, stripping churches and chapels and sending the rolls back to Barcelona, where they were eventually put back up on walls and inside purpose-built church apses to reflect how they had appeared in situ.

★ Did You Know?

An emblematic building, the Palau Nacional was built for the 1929 World Exhibition and restored in 2005.

CATARINA BELOVA/SHUTTERSTOCK ©

What's Nearby?

Museu d'Arqueologia de Catalunya   Museum

(MAC; Map p256; ☑93 423 21 49; www.mac. cat; Passeig de Santa Madrona 39-41; adult/child €5.50/free; ◷9.30am-7pm Tue-Sat, 10am-2.30pm Sun; ☐55, ⓂPoble Sec) This archaeology museum, housed in what was the Graphic Arts palace during the 1929 World Exhibition, covers Catalonia and cultures from elsewhere in Spain. Items range from copies of pre-Neanderthal skulls to lovely Carthaginian necklaces and jewel-studded Visigothic crosses.

Museu Etnològic   Museum

(Map p256; ☑93 424 68 07; http://ajuntament. barcelona.cat/museuetnologic; Passeig de Santa Madrona 16-22; adult/child €5/free, 4-8pm Sun & 1st Sun of month free; ◷10am-7pm Tue-Sat, to 8pm Sun; ☐55) Barcelona's ethnology museum presents an intriguing permanent collection that delves into the rich heritage of Catalonia. Exhibits cover origin myths, religious festivals, folklore and the blending of the sacred and the secular. (Along those lines, don't miss the Nativity scene with that quirky Catalan character *el caganer*, aka 'the crapper'.)

Poble Espanyol   Cultural Centre

(Map p256; www.poble-espanyol.com; Avinguda de Francesc Ferrer i Guàrdia 13; adult/child €14/7; ◷9am-8pm Mon, to midnight Tue-Thu & Sun, to 3am Fri, to 4am Sat; ☐13, 23, 150, ⓂEspanya) Welcome to Spain! All of it! This 'Spanish Village' is both a cheesy souvenir hunters' haunt and an intriguing scrapbook of Spanish architecture built for the Spanish crafts section of the 1929 World Exhibition. You can meander from Andalucía to the Balearic Islands in the space of a couple of hours, visiting surprisingly good copies of Spain's characteristic buildings.

★ Top Tip

Be sure to take in MNAC's fine views from the terrace just in front of the museum. It draws crows around sunset.

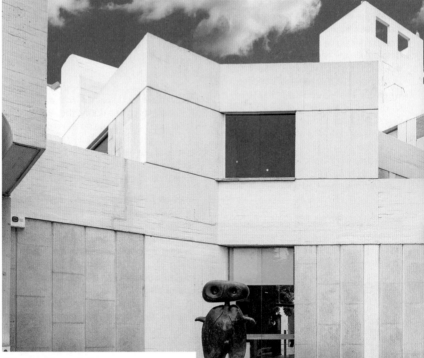

Fundació Joan Miró

Joan Miró, the city's best-known 20th-century artistic progeny, bequeathed this art foundation to his home town in 1971. Its light-filled buildings are crammed with seminal works.

Great For...

☑ **Don't Miss**

Miró's masterworks in Rooms 18 and 19.

Sert's Temple to Miró's Art

Designed by Josep Lluís Sert, this shimmering white temple to one of Spain's artistic luminaries is considered one of the world's most outstanding museum buildings. The architect designed it after spending many of Franco's dictatorship years in the USA as the head of the School of Design at Harvard University. The foundation rests amid the greenery of the mountains and holds the greatest single collection of Miró's work, containing around 220 of his paintings, 180 sculptures, some textiles and more than 8000 drawings spanning his entire life. Only a small portion is ever on display.

The Collection

The exhibits give a broad impression of Miró's artistic development. The first couple of rooms (11 and 12) hold various works,

ALIONABIRUKOVA/SHUTTERSTOCK ©

**Fundació
Joan Miró**

Estació
Parc
Montjuïc

Jardins de
Laribal

Av de Miramar

ℹ️ Need to Know

(Map p256; 📞93 443 94 70; www.fmirobcn.
org/ca/; Parc de Montjuïc; adult/child €12/
free; ⏱10am-8pm Tue, Wed, Fri & Sat, to 9pm
Thu, to 3pm Sun; 🚌55, 150, 🚇Paral·lel)

✕ Take a Break

The museum has a restaurant and terrace bar. Nearby, **La Font del Gat** (Map
p256; 📞93 289 04 04; www.lafontdelgat.com;
Passeig de Santa Madrona 28; 3-course meal
€16; ⏱10am-6pm Tue-Fri, noon-6pm Sat &
Sun; 🚌55) has high-end Catalan cuisine.

★ Top Tip

Pay €5 for the multimedia guide,
with commentary and background
information.

including a giant tapestry in his trademark
primary colours. Along the way, you'll pass
Mercury Fountain by Alexander Calder, a
rebuilt work that was originally built for the
1937 Paris Fair and represented Spain at
the Spanish Republic's Pavilion. Room 13, a
basement space called Espai 13, leads you
downstairs to a small room for temporary
exhibitions.

After Room 13, climb back up the stairs
then descend again to two other basement
rooms, 14 and 15. Together labelled Hom-
enatge a Joan Miró (Homage to Joan Miró),
this space is dedicated to photos of the
artist, a 15-minute video on his life and a
series of works from some of his contemporaries, including Henry Moore, Antoni
Tàpies, Eduardo Chillida, Yves Tanguy and
Fernand Léger.

Returning to the main level, you'll find
Room 16, the Sala Joan Prats, with works
spanning the early years until 1919. Here
you can see how the young Miró moved
away, under surrealist influence, from
relative realism (for instance his 1917
painting *Ermita de Sant Joan d'Horta*, with
obvious Fauvist influences) toward his own
unique style that uses primary colours and
morphed shapes symbolising the moon,
the female form and birds.

This theme is continued upstairs in
Room 17, the Sala Pilar Juncosa (named
after his wife), which covers his surrealist years of 1932 to 1955. Rooms 18
and 19 contain the central highlights of
the collection: masterworks of the years
1956 to 1983. Room 20 holds a series of
paintings done on paper. Room 21 hosts a
selection of the private Katsuta collection
of Miró works from 1914 to 1974. Room 22

rounds off the permanent exhibition with some major paintings and bronzes from the 1960s and '70s. The museum library contains Miró's personal book collection.

The Garden

Outside on the eastern flank of the museum is the Jardí de les Escultures, a small garden with various pieces of modern sculpture. The green areas surrounding the museum, together with the garden, are perfect for a picnic in the shade, after a hard day's sightseeing.

What's Nearby?

L'Anella Olímpica   Area
(Map p256; www.estadiolimpic.cat; Avinguda de l'Estadi; 🚌13, 150) **FREE** L'Anella Olímpica (Olympic Ring) is the group of installa-

tions built for the main events of the 1992 Olympics. They include the Piscines Bernat Picornell (p208), where the swimming and diving events were held, and the Estadi Olímpic.

**Estadi Olímpic
Lluís Companys**   Stadium
(Map p256; 📞93 426 20 89; www.estadiolimpic. cat; Passeig Olímpic 15-17; ⊘8am-8pm May-Sep, 10am-6pm Oct-Apr; 🚌13, 150) **FREE** The Estadi Olímpic was the main stadium of Barcelona's Olympic Games. If you saw the Olympics on TV, the 65,000-capacity stadium may seem surprisingly small. So might the Olympic flame holder into which an archer spectacularly fired a flaming arrow during the opening ceremony. The stadium was opened in 1929 and restored for the 1992 Olympics. It is open to the public when it's not in use for sporting events or concerts.

Castell de Montjuïc

Museu Olímpic i de l'Esport
Museum

(Map p256; ☏93 292 53 79; www.museu olimpicbcn.cat; Avinguda de l'Estadi 60; adult/child €5.80/free; ☺10am-8pm Tue-Sat, to 2.30pm Sun Apr-Sep, 10am-6pm Tue-Sat, to 2.30pm Sun Oct-Mar; ☒55, 150) The Museu Olímpic i de l'Esport is an information-packed interactive museum dedicated to the history of sport and the Olympic Games. Pick up tickets and wander down a ramp that snakes below ground level. It is lined with displays on the history of sport, starting with the ancients.

✗ Take a Break
Enjoy a picnic in the shady sculpture garden, or head to the terraced gardens at Jardins de Laribal (p126).

VITALYEDUSH/GETTY IMAGES ©

Castell de Montjuïc
Fortress

(Map p256; ☏93 256 44 45; http://ajuntament. barcelona.cat/castelldemontjuic; Carretera de Montjuïc 66; adult/child €5/3, after 3pm Sun & 1st Sun of month free; ☺10am-8pm Apr-Oct, to 6pm Nov-Mar; ☒150, ☒Telefèric de Montjuïc, Castell de Montjuïc) This forbidding *castell* (castle or fort) dominates the southeastern heights of Montjuïc and enjoys commanding views over the Mediterranean. It dates, in its present form, from the late 17th and 18th centuries. For most of its dark history, it has been used to watch over the city and as a political prison and killing ground.

Teleférico del Puerto
Cable Car

(Map p256; ☏93 430 47 16; www.telefericode barcelona.com; Avinguda de Miramar; one way/return €11/16.50; ☺10.30am-8pm Jun–mid-Sep, 10.30am-7pm Mar-May & mid-Sep–Oct, 11am 5.30pm Nov-Feb; ☒150) The quickest way from the beach to the mountain is via the cable car that runs between Torre de Sant Sebastiá in La Barceloneta and the Miramar stop on Montjuïc (from mid-June to mid-September only). From Estació Parc Montjuïc, the separate **Telefèric de Montjuïc** (Map p256; ☏93 328 90 03; www.telefericdemontjuic.cat; adult/child one way €8.20/6.50; ☺10am-9pm Jun-Sep, to 7pm Mar-May & Oct, to 6pm Nov-Feb) cable car carries you to the Castell de Montjuïc via the mirador (lookout point).

MUHBA Refugi 307
Historic Site

(Map p256; ☏93 256 21 22; http://ajuntament. barcelona.cat/museuhistoria; Carrer Nou de la Rambla 175; adult/child incl tour €3.40/free; ☺tours in English 10.30am Sun; ☒Paral·lel) Part of the Museu d'Història de Barcelona (MUHBA), this shelter dates back to the days of the Spanish Civil War. Barcelona was the city most heavily bombed from the air during the war and had more than 1300 air-raid shelters. Local citizens started digging this one under a fold of Montjuïc in March 1937. Reserve ahead for compulsory tours as places are limited.

Detail of the church tower

La Catedral

The richly decorated Gothic main facade of Barcelona's central place of worship, laced with gargoyles and stone intricacies, sets it quite apart from other churches in Barcelona.

Great For...

☑ Don't Miss

The *claustre* (cloister) and its 13 geese, plus the views from the roof.

The treasure of the Barri Gòtic, the cathedral was built between 1298 and 1460, though the facade was added in 1870.

Interior

The interior is a broad, soaring space divided into a central nave and two aisles by lines of elegant, slim pillars. The cathedral was one of the few churches in Barcelona spared by the anarchists in the civil war, so its ornamentation, never overly lavish, is intact.

Coro

In the middle of the central nave is the late-14th-century, exquisitely sculpted timber *coro* (choir stalls). The coats of arms on the stalls belong to members of the Barcelona chapter of the Order of the Golden Fleece. Emperor Charles V presided over the order's meeting here in 1519.

GENNADY STETSENKO/SHUTTERSTOCK ©

❶ Need to Know

(Map p250; 📞93 342 82 62; www.catedral
bcn.org; Plaça de la Seu; donation entrance
€7, choir €3, roof €3; ⏰8am-12.45pm & 5.45-
7.30pm Mon-Fri, 8am-8pm Sat & Sun, entry
by donation 1-5.30pm Mon, 1-5pm Sat, 2-5pm
Sun; Ⓜ Jaume I)

✕ Take a Break

A couple of minutes' walk away, Els
Quatre Gats (p142) makes for an
architecturally splendid pit stop.

★ Top Tip

Pay the 'donation entrance' to avoid the
crowds and appreciate the building's
splendour in relative peace.

Crypt

A broad staircase before the main altar
leads you down to the crypt, which contains
the tomb of Santa Eulàlia, one of Barcelona's two patron saints and more affectionately known as Laia. The reliefs on the
alabaster sarcophagus recount some of her
tortures and, along the top strip, the remov-
al of her body to its present resting place.

Sant Crist de Lepant

In the first chapel on the right from the
northwest entrance, the main Crucifixion
figure above the altar is Sant Crist de
Lepant. It is said Don Juan's flagship bore
it into battle at Lepanto and that the figure
acquired its odd stance by dodging an
incoming cannonball. Left from the main
entrance is the baptismal font where, according to one story, six Native Americans

brought to Europe by Columbus after his
first voyage of accidental discovery were
bathed in holy water.

Roof

For a bird's-eye view (mind the poo) of
medieval Barcelona, visit the cathedral's
roof and tower by taking the lift from the
Capella de les Animes del Purgatori near
the northeast transept.

Claustre

From the southwest transept, exit via the
partly Romanesque door (one of the few
remnants of the present church's predecessor) to the leafy *claustre*, with its fountains
and flock of 13 geese. The geese supposedly
represent the age of Santa Eulàlia at the
time of her martyrdom and have, generation after generation, been squawking here
since medieval days. One of the cloister
chapels commemorates 930 priests,
monks and nuns killed during the civil war.

In the northwest corner of the cloister is the **Capella de Santa Llúcia** (Map p250; ⊘8am-7.30pm Mon-Fri, to 8pm Sat & Sun) **FREE**, one of the few reminders of Romanesque Barcelona (although the interior is largely Gothic). Originally it was the chapel for the adjacent Palau Episcopal.

Casa de l'Ardiaca

Upon exiting the Capella de Santa Llúcia, wander across the lane into the 16th-century **Casa de l'Ardiaca** (Arxiu Històric; Map p250; Carrer de Santa Llúcia 1; ⊘9am-8.45pm Mon-Fri, 10am-8pm Sat Sep-Jun, 9am-7.30pm Jul & Aug; MJaume I) **FREE**, which houses the city's archives. Stroll around the supremely serene courtyard, cooled by trees and a fountain. It was renovated by Lluís Domènech i Montaner in 1902, when the building was owned by the lawyers' college. Domènech i Montaner also designed the postal slot, which is adorned with swallows and a tortoise, said to represent the swiftness of truth and the plodding pace of justice. You can get a good glimpse of a stout Roman wall in here. In fact, the lower part of the entire northwest wall of the Casa de l'Ardiaca is of Roman origin – you can also make out part of the first arch of a Roman aqueduct. Upstairs, you can look down into the courtyard and across to La Catedral.

Palau Episcopal

Across Carrer del Bisbe is the 17th-century **Palau Episcopal** (Palau del Bisbat, Bishop's Palace; Map p250; Carrer del Bisbe; MJaume I). Virtually nothing remains of the original 13th-century structure. The Roman city's

Courtyard of Casa de l'Ardiaca

northwest gate was here and you can see the lower segments of the Roman towers that stood on either side of the gate at the base of the Palau Episcopal and Casa de l'Ardiaca.

What's Nearby?

Temple d'August Ruins

(Map p250; 93 256 21 22; www.muhba.cat; Carrer del Paradis 10; 10am-7pm Tue-Sat, to 8pm Sun, to 2pm Mon; Jaume I) FREE Opposite the southeast end of La Catedral, narrow

Carrer del Paradis leads towards Plaça de Sant Jaume. Inside No 10, an intriguing building with Gothic and baroque touches, are four columns and the architrave of Barcelona's main Roman temple, dedicated to Caesar Augustus and built to worship his imperial highness in the 1st century AD.

Museu Diocesà/
Gaudí Exhibition Center Museum

(Casa de la Pia Almoina; Map p250; 93 315 22 13; www.gaudiexhibitioncenter.com; Plaça de la Seu 7; adult/concession/child under 8yr €15/12/ free; 10am-6pm Nov-Feb, to 8pm Mar-Oct; Jaume I) Next to the cathedral, the Diocesan Museum has a handful of exhibits on Gaudí (including a fascinating documentary on his life and philosophy) on the upper floors. There's also a sparse collection of medieval and Romanesque religious art, usually supplemented by a temporary exhibition or two.

> **☑ Don't Miss**
>
> Outside La Catedral there's always some kind of entertainment, from *sardana* dancing (Catalonia's folk dance) on weekends to periodic processions and open-air markets; street musicians are never far away.

Palau del Lloctinent Historic Site

(Map p250; Carrer dels Comtes; 10am-2pm & 4-8pm Mon-Sat; Jaume I) FREE This converted 16th-century palace has a peaceful courtyard worth wandering through. Have a look upwards from the main staircase to admire the extraordinary timber *artesonado,* a sculpted ceiling made to seem like the upturned hull of a boat. Temporary exhibitions, usually related in some way to the archives, are often held here.

Roman Walls Ruins

(Map p250; Jaume I) From Plaça del Rei it's worth a detour to see the two best surviving stretches of Barcelona's Roman walls, which once boasted 78 towers (as much a matter of prestige as of defence). One section is on the southern side of Plaça de Ramon Berenguer el Gran, with the Capella Reial de Santa Àgata atop. The other is a little further south, by the northern end of Carrer del Sotstinent Navarro.

VIKTOR GLADKOV/SHUTTERSTOCK ©

> **✕ Take a Break**
>
> For exquisite dishes from the East, head to nearby Koy Shunka (p142).

Park Güell

Park Güell is where Gaudí turned his hand to landscape gardening. It's a strange, enchanting place, where this iconic Modernista's passion for natural forms really took flight.

Great For...

☑ **Don't Miss**

The undulating tiled bench with views across the city.

City Park

Park Güell originated in 1900, when Count Eusebi Güell bought the tree-covered hillside of El Carmel (then outside Barcelona) and hired Gaudí to create a miniature city of houses for the wealthy, surrounded by landscaped grounds. The project was a commercial flop and was abandoned in 1914 – but not before Gaudí had created, in his inimitable manner, steps, a plaza, two gatehouses and 3km of roads and walks. In 1922 the city bought the estate for use as a public park. The park became a Unesco World Heritage site in 2004. The idea was based on the English 'garden cities', much admired by Güell, hence the spelling of 'Park'.

Just inside the main entrance on Carrer d'Olot, immediately recognisable by the

❶ Need to Know

(Map p254; ☎93 409 18 31; www.parkguell.
cat; Carrer d'Olot 7; adult/child €8/5.60;
⏱8am-9.30pm May-Aug, to 8.30pm Apr,
Sep & Oct, to 6.30pm Nov-Mar; 🚌24, 92,
Ⓜ Lesseps, Vallcarca)

✕ Take a Break

It's a spectacular picnic setting, but
bring supplies with you as there's nowhere to stock up nearby.

★ Top Tip

The walk from metro stop Lesseps is
signposted. From the Vallcarca stop, it
is marginally shorter and the uphill trek
eased by escalators. Buses 24 and 92
drop you at an entrance near the top of
the park.

two Hansel-and-Gretel gatehouses, is the
park's Centre d'Interpretació, in the Pavelló
de Consergeria, which is a typically curvaceous former porter's home that hosts a
display on Gaudí's building methods and
the history of the park. There are superb
views from the top floor.

Much of the park is still wooded, but it's
laced with pathways. The best views are
from the cross-topped Turó del Calvari in
the southwest corner.

Sala Hipóstila

The steps up from the entrance, guarded
by a mosaic dragon/lizard (a copy of which
you can buy in many central souvenir
shops), lead to the Sala Hipóstila (aka
the Doric Temple). This forest of 88 stone
columns – some leaning like mighty trees

bent by the weight of time – was originally
intended as a market. To the left curves a
gallery, the twisted stonework columns and
roof of which give the effect of a cloister
beneath tree roots – a motif repeated in
several places in the park. On top of the
Sala Hipóstila is a broad open space. Its
centrepiece is the Banc de Trencadís, a
tiled bench curving sinuously around its
perimeter, which was designed by one
of Gaudí's closest colleagues, architect
Josep Maria Jujol (1879–1949). With Gaudí,
however, there is always more than meets
the eye. This giant platform was designed
as a kind of catchment area for rainwater
washing down the hillside. The water is
filtered through a layer of stone and sand
and it drains down through the columns to
an underground cistern.

Casa-Museu Gaudí

The spired house above and to the right of the entrance is the **Casa-Museu Gaudí** (Map p254; ☎93 219 38 11; www.casamuseu gaudi.org; Park Güell, Carretera del Carmel 23a; adult/child €5.50/free; ⏰9am-8pm Apr-Sep, 10am-6pm Oct-Mar; ☎24, 92, 116, ⓜLesseps), where Gaudí lived for almost the last 20 years of his life (1906–26). It contains furniture he designed (including items that once lived in La Pedrera, Casa Batlló and Casa Calvet) along with other memorabilia. The house was built in 1904 by Francesc Berenguer i Mestres as a prototype for the 60 or so houses that were originally planned here.

What's Nearby?

Gaudí Experience   Museum

(Map p254; ☎93 285 44 40; www.gaudiexperi encia.com; Carrer de Larrard 41; adult/child €9/7.50; ⏰10.30am-7pm Apr-Sep, to 5pm Oct-Mar; ⓜLesseps) The 'Gaudí Experience' is a fun-filled Disney-style look at the life and work of Barcelona's favourite son, just a stone's throw from Park Güell. There are models of his buildings and achingly modern interactive exhibits and touchscreens, but the highlight is the stomach-churning 4D presentation in its tiny screening room. Not recommended for the frail or children aged under six years.

Casa Vicens

Turó de la Rovira
Viewpoint

(Bunkers del Carmel; Map p254; ☎93 256 21 22; www.museuhistoria.bcn.cat; Carrer de Marià Labèrnia; ⊙museum 10am-2pm Wed, to 3pm Sat & Sun; ☒V17, 119) **FREE** For a magnificent view over the city that's well off the beaten path, head to the neighbourhood of El Carmel and make the ascent up the hill known as Turó de la Rovira to the Bunkers del Carmel viewpoint. Above the weeds and dusty hillside you'll find the old concrete platforms that were once part of anti-aircraft battery during the Spanish Civil War (postwar it was a shanty town until the early 1990s, and it has lain abandoned since then).

Casa Vicens
Museum

(☎93 348 42 58; www.casavicens.org; Carrer de les Carolines 18-24; adult/child €16/14, guided tour per person additional €3; ⊙10am-8pm, last tour 7.30pm; ℍFontana) A Unesco-listed masterpiece, Casa Vicens was first opened regularly to the public in 2017. The angular, turreted 1885-completed private house created for stock and currency broker Manuel Vicens i Montaner was Gaudí's inaugural commission, when the architect was aged just 30. Tucked away west of Gràcia's main drag, the richly detailed facade is awash with ceramic colour and shape. You're free to wander through at your own pace but 30-minute guided tours (available in English) bring the building to life.

As was frequently the case, Gaudí sought inspiration from the past, in this case the rich heritage of building in the Mudéjar-style brick, typical in those parts of Spain reconquered from the Moors. Mudéjar architecture was created by those Arabs and Berbers allowed to remain in Spain after the Christian reconquests.

The renovated building is accessible for visitors with limited mobility (including wheelchairs). Temporary exhibitions are mounted alongside permanent displays covering the building's history. Allow time for a drink at the cafe in the garden.

★ **Top Tip**

One-hour guided tours of Park Güell, in multiple languages including English, take place year-round and cost €7 (plus park admission); prebook online.

EGROY/SHUTTERSTOCK ©

✕ **Take a Break**

Before or after making the trip up to the park, stop off at La Panxa del Bisbe (p139) for deliciously creative tapas and good wines.

★ **Top Tip**

Go first thing in the morning or late in the day to beat the worst of the crowds.

Players tunnel at Camp Nou

Camp Nou

A pilgrimage site for football fans from around the world, Camp Nou, home to FC Barcelona, is one of the sport's most hallowed grounds. While you should do your utmost to attend a live match, the museum and stadium tour offered by the Camp Nou Experience is also a must for football fans.

Great For...

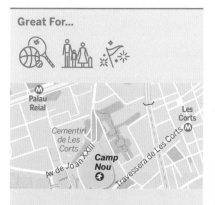

❶ Need to Know

(Map p256; ☎ 902 189 900; www.fc barcelona.com; Gate 9, Avinguda de Joan XXIII; Camp Nou Experience adult/child €25/20; ☺ 9.30am-7.30pm Apr-Sep, 10am-6.30pm Mon-Sat, to 2.30pm Sun Oct-Mar; Ⓜ Palau Reial)

★ **Top Tip**
No need to wait in line – purchase tour tickets from vending machines at Gate 9.

FC Barcelona

FC Barcelona, or 'Barça', is a name that resounds around the world to the point of being an ambassador for the region of Catalonia; it is a club deeply associated with Catalans and even Catalan nationalism. The team was long a rallying point when other aspects of Catalan culture were suppressed. The club openly supported Catalonia's drive towards autonomy in 1918, and in 1921 the club's statutes were drafted in Catalan. The pro-Catalan leanings of the club and its siding with the republic during the Spanish Civil War earned reprisals from the government. Club president Josep Sunyol was murdered by Franco's soldiers in 1936, and the club building was bombed in 1938.

In 1968 club president Narcís de Carreras uttered the now famous words, *El Barça: més que un club* ('more than a club'), which became the team's motto – and emphasised its role as an anti-Franco symbol and catalyst for change in the province and beyond. Today Barça is one of the world's most admired teams, with membership at around 170,000 in recent years.

Camp Nou Experience

The Camp Nou Experience begins in FC Barcelona's museum, which provides a high-tech view into the club. Massive touchscreens allow visitors to explore arcane aspects of the legendary team. You can also watch videos of particularly artful goals. Displays delve into the club's history, its social commitment and connection to Catalan identity, and in-depth stats of

FC Barcelona match

on-field action. Sound installations include the club's anthem (with translations in many languages) and the match-day roar of the amped-up crowds.

The museum's highlights are the photo section, the goal videos and the views out over the stadium. You can admire the golden boots (in at least one case literally) of great goal scorers of the past and learn about the greats who have played for the club over the years, including Maradona, Ronaldinho, Cruyff, Kubala and many others. A special area is devoted to Lionel Messi, generally considered to be the world's greatest current footballer.

> ✕ **Take a Break**
> There's a handful of open-air eating spots just inside the gates (but outside the stadium).

Stadium

Gazing out across Camp Nou is an experience in itself. The stadium, built in 1957 and enlarged for the 1982 World Cup, is one of the world's biggest, holding almost 100,000 people. The club has a world-record membership of 173,000. After renovations that will last until 2022 (the stadium will remain open throughout), it will have a capacity of 105,000.

The self-guided tour of the stadium takes in the team's dressing rooms, heads out through the tunnel, on to the pitch and winds up in the presidential box. You'll also get to visit the TV studio, the press room and the commentary boxes. Set aside about 2½ hours for the whole visit.

To take the tour, enter at Gate 9.

Getting to a Game

Tickets to FC Barcelona matches are available at Camp Nou (at gates 9 and 15), online (through FC Barcelona's official website), and at various city locations. Tourist offices sell them – the main office (p239) at Plaça de Catalunya is a centrally located option – as do FC Botiga stores. Tickets can cost anything from €39 to upwards of €250, depending on the seat and match. Tickets for matches against Real Madrid (a match-up known as *el clásico*) are very difficult to come by.

If you attend a game, go early so you'll have ample time to find your seat (this stadium is massive) and soak up the atmosphere.

You will almost definitely find scalpers lurking near the ticket windows. They are often club members and can sometimes get you in at a significant reduction. Don't pay until you are safely seated.

CHRISTIAN BERTRAND/GETTY IMAGES ©

> ☑ **Don't Miss**
> A live match, or if not, the museum's footage of the team's best goals.

Skyward view of La Pedrera

La Pedrera

This undulating beast is a madcap Gaudí masterpiece, built from 1905 to 1910 as a combined apartment and office block. Formally called Casa Milà after the businessman who commissioned it, it is better known as La Pedrera (the Quarry) because of its uneven grey stone facade, which ripples around the corner of Carrer de Provença.

Great For...

❶ Need to Know

(Casa Milà; Map p254; ☎902 202 138; www. lapedrera.com; Passeig de Gràcia 92; adult/ child €25/15; ❀9am-8.30pm Mar-Oct, to 6.30pm Nov-Feb; ⓂDiagonal)

★ Top Tip

For a few extra euros, a 'Premium' ticket means you don't have to queue.

History

Pere Milà had married the older – and far richer – Roser Guardiola, the widow of Josep Guardiola, and he clearly knew how to spend his wife's money. When commissioned to design this apartment building, Gaudí wanted to top anything else done in L'Eixample. Milà was one of the city's first car owners and Gaudí built a parking space into the building, itself a first.

Facade

The natural world was one of the most enduring influences on Gaudí's work, and La Pedrera's undulating grey stone facade evokes a cliff-face sculpted by waves and wind. The wave effect is emphasised by elaborate wrought-iron balconies that bring to mind seaweed washed up on the shore.

Roof Terrace

Gaudí's blend of mischievous form with ingenious functionality is evident on the roof, with its clusters of chimneys, stairwells and ventilation towers that rise and fall atop the structure's wave-like contours like giant medieval knights. Some are unadorned, others are decorated with *trencadís* (ceramic fragments) and even broken cava bottles. The deep patios, which Gaudí treated like interior facades, flood the apartments with natural light.

Espai Gaudí

With 270 gracious parabolic arches, the Espai Gaudí (the attic) feels like the fossilised ribcage of some giant prehistoric beast. At one point, 12 arches come together to form a palm tree. Watch out also for the strange optical effect of the mirror and hanging sculpture on the east side.

✕ **Take a Break**
Classy **La Bodegueta Provença** (✆93 215 17 25; www.provenca.labodegueta.cat; Carrer de Provença 233; ⊙7am-1.45am Mon-Fri, 8am-1.45am Sat, 1pm-12.45am Sun; 🛜; ☒FGC Provença) serves first-rate tapas and wines by the glass.

Apartment

Below the attic, the apartment (El Pis de la Pedrera) spreads out. Bathed in evenly distributed light, twisting and turning with the building's rippling distribution, the labyrinthine apartment is Gaudí's vision of domestic bliss. In the ultimate nod to flexible living, the apartment has no load-bearing walls: the interior walls could thus be moved to suit the inhabitants' needs.

What's Nearby?

Casa de les Punxes   Architecture
(Casa Terrades; Map p254; ✆93 016 01 28; www.casadelespunxes.com; Avinguda Diagonal 420; audioguide tour adult/child €12.50/11.25, guided tour €20/17; ⊙9am-8pm; Ⓜ Diagonal) Puig i Cadafalch's Casa Terrades is better known as the Casa de les Punxes (House of Spikes) because of its pointed turrets. This

The marvellous roof terrace

apartment block, completed in 1905, looks like a fairy-tale castle and has the singular attribute of being the only fully detached building in L'Eixample.

Museu Egipci   Museum

(Map p254; www.museuegipci.com; Carrer de València 284; adult/child €11/5; ☺10am-8pm Mon-Sat, to 2pm Sun mid-Jun–early Oct & Dec, 10am-2pm & 4-8pm Mon-Fri, to 8pm Sat, to 2pm Sun Jan–mid-Jun & early Oct-Nov; MPasseig de Gràcia) Hotel magnate Jordi Clos has spent much of his life collecting ancient Egyptian artefacts, brought together in this private museum. It's divided into different thematic areas (the pharaoh, religion, funerary practices, mummification, crafts etc) and boasts an interesting variety of exhibits.

Fundació Suñol   Gallery

(Map p254; ☎93 496 10 32; www.fundaciosunol. org; Passeig de Gràcia 98; adult/child €4/free; ☺11am-2pm & 4-8pm Mon-Fri, 4-8pm Sat; MDiagonal) Rotating exhibitions of portions of this private collection of mostly 20th-century art (some 1200 works in total) offer anything from Man Ray's photography to sculptures by Alberto Giacometti. Over two floors, the collection mainly features Spanish artists (anyone from Picasso to Jaume Plensa) along with a sprinkling of international artists.

Església de la Puríssima Concepció I Assumpció de Nostra Senyora   Church

(Map p254; ☎93 457 65 52; www.parroquia concepciobcn.org; Carrer de Roger de Llúria 70; ☺7.30am-1pm & 5-9pm Mon-Sat, 7.30am-2pm & 5-9pm Sun; MPasseig de Gràcia) Transferred stone by stone from the old centre between 1871 and 1888, this 14th-century church has a pretty 16th-century cloister with a peaceful garden.

Museu Picasso

Picasso's itchy feet and his extraordinary artistic output mean that his works fill several museums in Europe. Though his best-known works aren't here, the setting alone, in five contiguous medieval stone mansions, makes the Museu Picasso unique. The pretty courtyards, galleries and staircases preserved in these buildings are as delightful as the collection inside.

Great For...

❶ Need to Know

(Map p250; 📞93 256 30 00; www.museu picasso.bcn.cat; Carrer de Montcada 15-23; adult/concession/under 16yr all collections €14/7.50/free, permanent collection €11/7/ free, temporary exhibitions vary, 6-9.30pm Thu & 1st Sun of month free; ⏱9am-7pm Tue-Wed & Fri-Sun, to 9.30pm Thu; Ⓜ Jaume I)

★ **Top Tip**

Queues here can be very long; the people strolling to the front booked online. Be them.

The permanent collection is housed in Palau Aguilar, Palau del Baró de Castellet and Palau Meca, all dating to the 14th century. The 18th-century Casa Mauri, built over medieval remains (even some Roman leftovers have been identified), and the adjacent 14th-century Palau Finestres accommodate temporary exhibitions. The first three of these buildings are particularly splendid.

History of the Museum

Allegedly it was Picasso himself who proposed the museum's creation, to his friend and personal secretary Jaume Sabartés, a Barcelona native, in 1960. Three years later, the 'Sabartés Collection' was opened, since a museum bearing Picasso's name would have been met with censorship –

Picasso's opposition to the Franco regime was well known. The Museu Picasso we see today opened in 1983. It originally held only Sabartés' personal collection of Picasso's art and a handful of works hanging at the Barcelona Museum of Art, but the collection gradually expanded with donations from Salvador Dalí and Sebastià Junyer Vidal, among others, though most artworks were bequeathed by Picasso himself. His widow, Jacqueline Roque, also donated 41 ceramic pieces and the *Woman with Bonnet* painting after Picasso's death.

Sabartés' contribution and years of service are honoured with an entire room devoted to him, including Picasso's famous Blue Period portrait of Sabartés wearing a ruff.

The cloister of the Palau Aguilar

Collection

This collection concentrates on the artist's formative years, yet there is enough material from subsequent periods to give you a thorough impression of the man's versatility and genius. Above all, you come away feeling that Picasso was the true original, always one step ahead of himself (and everyone else, of course) in his search for new forms of expression. The collection includes more than 3500 artworks, largely pre-1904, which is apt considering the artist spent his formative creative years in Barcelona.

It is important, however, not to expect a parade of his well-known works, or even

PIG3/SHUTTERSTOCK ©

works representative of his best-known periods. The holdings at the museum reflect Picasso's years in Barcelona and elsewhere in Spain, and what makes this collection truly impressive – and unique among the many Picasso museums around the world – is the way in which it displays his extraordinary talent at such a young age. Faced with the technical virtuosity of a painting such as *Ciència i caritat* (Science and Charity), for example, it is almost inconceivable that such a work could have been created by the hands of a 15-year-old. Some of his self-portraits and the portraits of his parents, which date from 1896, are also evidence of his precocious talent.

Las Meninas through the Prism of Picasso

From 1954 to 1962, Picasso was obsessed with the idea of researching and 'rediscovering' the greats, in particular Velázquez. In 1957 he created a series of renditions of the latter's masterpiece *Las Meninas,* now displayed in rooms 12–14. It is as though Picasso has looked at the original Velázquez painting through a prism reflecting all the styles he had worked through until then, creating his own masterpiece in the process. This is a wonderful opportunity to see *Las meninas* in its entirety, in this beautiful space.

Ceramics

What is also special about the Museu Picasso is its showcasing of his work in lesser-known mediums. The last rooms contain engravings and some 40 ceramic pieces completed throughout the latter years of his unceasingly creative life. You'll see plates and bowls decorated with simple, single-line drawings of fish, owls and other animal shapes, typical of Picasso's daubing on clay.

What's Nearby?

Parc de la Ciutadella   Park

(Map p250; Passeig de Picasso; ⊙8am-9pm May-
Sep, to 7pm Oct-Apr; 🚻; MArc de Triomf) Come
for a stroll, a picnic, a visit to the zoo or to
inspect Catalonia's regional parliament, but
don't miss a visit to this, the most central
green lung in the city. Parc de la Ciutadella
is perfect for winding down.

Museu de Cultures
del Món   Museum

(Map p250; 📞93 256 23 00; http://museu
culturesmon.bcn.cat; Carrer de Montcada 12;
adult/concession/under 16yr €5/3.50/free,
temporary exhibition €2.20/1.50/free, 3-8pm Sun
& 1st Sun of month free; ⊙10am-7pm Tue-Sat, to
8pm Sun; MJaume I) The Palau Nadal and the
Palau Marquès de Llió, which once housed
the Museu Barbier-Mueller and the Museu

Tèxtil respectively, reopened in 2015 to the
public as the site of a new museum, the
Museum of World Cultures. Exhibits from
private and public collections, including
many from the Museu Etnològic on Montjuïc, take the visitor on a trip through the
ancient cultures of Africa, Asia, the Americas
and Oceania. There's a combined ticket
with Museu Egipci (p79) and the Museu
Etnològic (p59) for €12.

Castell dels
Tres Dragons   Architecture

(Parc de la Ciutadella; MArc de Triomf) The Passeig de Picasso side of Parc de la Ciutadella
is lined by several buildings constructed
for, or just before, the Universal Exhibition
of 1888. The medieval-looking caprice at
the top end is the most engaging. Known
as the Castell dels Tres Dragons (Castle

Castell dels Tres Dragons

of the Three Dragons), it long housed the Museu de Zoologia, which has since been transferred to the Fòrum area.

Espai Santa Caterina
Archaeological Site

(Map p250; ☎93 256 21 22; www.museuhistoria. bcn.cat; Plaça de Joan Capri; ⊙7.30am-3.30pm Mon-Sat; Ⓜ Jaume I) FREE The Mercat de Santa Caterina's 1848 predecessor was built over the remains of the demolished 15th-century Gothic Monestir de Santa Caterina, a powerful Dominican monastery. A small section of the church foundations is glassed over in one corner as an archaeo-

---

★ Did You Know?

Picasso's full name is Pablo Diego José Francisco de Paula Juan Nepomuceno María de los Remedios Cipriano de la Santísima Trinidad Ruiz y Picasso.

PITK/SHUTTERSTOCK ©

logical reminder (with explanatory panels) – the Espai Santa Caterina.

Born Centre de Cultura i Memòria
Historic Building

(Map p250; ☎93 256 68 51; http://elborncultura imemoria.barcelona.cat; Plaça Comercial 12; centre free, exhibition spaces adult/concession/ under 16yr €4.40/3/free; ⊙10am-8pm Tue-Sun Mar-Oct, to 7pm Tue-Sat, to 8pm Sun Nov-Feb; Ⓜ Jaume I) Launched to great fanfare in 2013, as part of the events held for the tercentenary of the Catalan defeat in the War of the Spanish Succession, this cultural space is housed in the former Mercat del Born, a handsome 19th-century structure of slatted iron and brick. Excavation in 2001 unearthed remains of whole streets flattened to make way for the much-hated *ciutadella* (citadel) – these are now on show on the exposed subterranean level.

Carrer de Montcada
Street

(Map p250; Ⓜ Jaume I) An early example of town planning, this medieval high street was driven towards the sea from the road that in the 12th century led northeast from the city walls. It was the city's most coveted address for the merchant classes. The bulk of the great mansions that remain today mostly date to the 14th and 15th centuries.

Fundació Gaspar
Gallery

(Map p250; ☎93 887 42 48; Carrer de Montcada 25; adult/concession/under 12yr €8/5/free; ⊙10am-8pm Tue-Fri & Sun, to 9.30pm Sat; Ⓜ Jaume I) Set in a stunning Gothic *palau* next to the Museu Picasso, the Fundació Gaspar opened in November 2015 with the intention of complementing the works of other galleries and museums around town by bringing contemporary artists who have yet to exhibit here or whose work explores new concepts and styles.

★ Top Tip

The Carnet del Museu Picasso annual pass (€15) allows multiple entries. Buy from a separate ticket desk.

Walking Tour: Hidden Treasures in the Barri Gòtic

This scenic walk will take you back in time, from the early days of Roman-era Barcino to the medieval era.

Start: La Catedral
Distance: 1.5km
Duration: 1½ hours

Classic Photo: The Gothic main facade of La Catedral

1 Before entering the cathedral, look at the three Picasso friezes on the building facing the square. Next, wander through the magnificent **La Catedral** (p64).

2 Pass through the city gates; turn right into **Plaça de Sant Felip Neri** (Map p250). The shrapnel-scarred church was damaged by pro-Franco bombers in 1938.

3 Head west to the looming 14th-century **Església de Santa Maria del Pi** (p46), famed for its magnificent rose window.

4 Follow the curving road to pretty **Plaça Reial** (p47). Flanking the fountain are Gaudí-designed lamp posts.

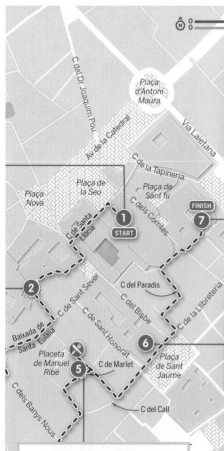

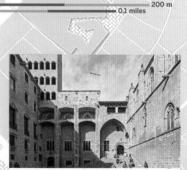

7 The final stop is picturesque **Plaça del Rei** (Map p250). The former palace located here houses a superb history museum, with significant Roman ruins.

6 Cross Plaça de Sant Jaume and turn left after Carrer del Bisbe. You'll pass the entrance to **Temple d'August** (p67), a ruined roman temple with four columns hidden in a small courtyard.

5 Nearby is El Call, the medieval Jewish quarter. Here you'll find **Sinagoga Major** (Map p250), one of Europe's oldest synagogues.

Take a Break...
In the heart of El Call, **Alcoba Azul** (p139) is atmospheric.

Replica of Don Juan of Austria's Flagship

Museu Marítim

The mighty Reials Drassanes (Royal Shipyards) are an extraordinary piece of civilian architecture. From here, Don Juan of Austria's flagship galley was launched to lead a joint Spanish-Venetian fleet into the momentous Battle of Lepanto against the Turks in 1571. Today, the broad arches shelter the Museu Marítim, the city's seafaring-history museum and one of Barcelona's most intriguing institutions.

Great For...

ⓘ Need to Know

(☎93 342 99 20; www.mmb.cat; Avinguda de les Drassanes; adult/child €10/5, free from 3pm Sun; ☉10am-8pm; ⓜDrassanes)

★ **Top Tip**

Your ticket is valid for the **Pailebot de Santa Eulàlia** (www.mmb.cat; Moll de la Fusta; adult/child €3/1, free with Museu Marítim ticket; ◷10am-8.30pm Tue-Sun; Ⓜ Drassanes), docked nearby.

Royal Shipyards

The shipyards were, in their heyday, among the greatest in Europe. Begun in the 13th century and completed by 1378, the long, arched bays (the highest arches reach 13m) once sloped off as slipways directly into the water, which lapped the seaward side of the Drassanes until at least the end of the 18th century. Shipbuilding was later moved to southern Spain and the Drassanes became a barracks for artillery.

Replica of Don Juan of Austria's Flagship

The centre of the shipyards is dominated by a full-sized replica (made in the 1970s) of Don Juan of Austria's flagship. A clever audiovisual display aboard the vessel brings to life the ghastly existence of the slaves, prisoners and volunteers who, at full steam, could haul this vessel along at 9 knots. They remained chained to their seats, four to an oar, at all times. Here they worked, drank (fresh water was stored below decks, where the infirmary was also located), ate, slept and went to the loo. You could smell a galley like this from miles away.

Exhibitions

Fishing vessels, old navigation charts, models and dioramas of the Barcelona waterfront make up the rest of this engaging museum. Temporary exhibitions are also held (an intriguing show on the history of explorations in Antarctica was held here in 2014). Following major renovations completed in 2017, it has a greatly expanded collection with multimedia exhibits evoking more of Spain's epic history on the high seas.

Submarines

In the courtyard, you can have a look at a life-size replica of the *Ictíneo I*, one of the

world's first submarines. It was invented and built in 1858 by Catalan polymath Narcis Monturiol, and was operated by hand-cranked propellers turned by friends of Monturiol who accompanied him on dozens of successful short dives (two hours maximum) in the harbour. He later developed an even larger submarine (*Ictíneo II*) powered by a combustion engine that allowed it to dive to 30m and remain submerged for seven hours. Despite impressive demonstrations to awestruck crowds he never attracted the interest of the navy and remains largely forgotten today.

What's Nearby?

L'Aquàrium   Aquarium
(Map p250; 93 221 74 74; www.aquariumbcn. com; Moll d'Espanya; adult/child €20/15, dive €300, sleeping with sharks €90; 10am-9.30pm

Passeig Marítim de la Barceloneta

✖ **Take a Break**
The pleasant museum cafe offers courtyard seating, set lunches and a small assortment of bites.

Jul & Aug, shorter hours Sep-Jun; MDrassanes)
It is hard not to shudder at the sight of
a shark gliding above you, displaying its
toothy, wide-mouthed grin. But this, the
80m shark tunnel, is the highlight of one
of Europe's largest aquariums. It has the
world's best Mediterranean collection and
plenty of colourful fish from as far off as the
Red Sea, the Caribbean and the Great Bar-
rier Reef. All up, some 11,000 fish (including
a dozen sharks) of 450 species reside here.

Museu d'Història
de Catalunya   Museum

(Museum of the History of Catalonia; Map p250;
☑93 225 47 00; www.mhcat.cat; Plaça de Pau
Vila 3; adult/child €4.50/3.50, last Tue of the
month Oct-Jun free; ☺10am-7pm Tue & Thu-Sat,
to 8pm Wed, to 2.30pm Sun; MBarceloneta)
Inside the Palau de Mar, this worthwhile
museum takes you from the Stone Age

through to the early 1980s. It is a busy
hotchpotch of dioramas, artefacts, videos,
models, documents and interactive bits:
all up, an entertaining exploration of 2000
years of Catalan history. Signage is in
Catalan/Spanish.

Passeig Marítim
de la Barceloneta   Waterfront

(MBarceloneta, Ciutadella Vila Olímpica) On La
Barceloneta's seaward side are the first of
Barcelona's beaches, which are popular on
summer weekends. The Passeig Marítim de
la Barceloneta, a 1.25km promenade from
La Barceloneta to Port Olímpic, is a haunt for
strollers and runners, with cyclists zipping
past on a separate path nearby.

☑ Don't Miss

The replica of Don Juan of Austria's
flagship.

FRANK GEHRY'S EL PEIX D'OR (GOLDFISH SCULPTURE) SPATULETAIL/SHUTTERSTOCK ©

View of the Central Hall's parabolic dome

LUCIANO MORTULA - LGM/SHUTTERSTOCK ©

Palau Güell

This extraordinary neo-Gothic mansion, one of few major buildings of that era raised in the old city, is a magnificent example of the early days of Gaudí's fevered architectural imagination.

Great For...

☑ **Don't Miss**

The music room, the basement stables and the tiled chimney pots.

Gaudí & Güell

Gaudí built the palace just off La Rambla in the late 1880s for his wealthy and faithful patron, the industrialist Eusebi Güell. Without his support it is unlikely Gaudí would have left a fraction of the creative legacy that is now so celebrated, but at the time was viewed with deep suspicion by much of Catalan society. Although a little sombre compared with some of his later whims, the Palau is still a characteristic riot of styles and materials. After the civil war, the police occupied it and tortured political prisoners in the basement. The building was then abandoned, leading to its long-term disrepair. It finally reopened in 2012 after lengthy renovations.

The roof's tiled mosaics and chimney pots

ALEKSANDAR TODOROVIC/SHUTTERSTOCK ©

ⓘ Need to Know

(Map p250; 📞93 472 57 71; www.palauguell.
cat; Carrer Nou de la Rambla 3-5; adult/
concession/child under 10yr incl audioguide
€12/€9/free, 1st Sun of month free; 🕙10am-
8pm Tue-Sun Apr-Oct, to 5.30pm Nov-Mar;
ⓂDrassanes)

✗ Take a Break

Nearby **Bar Cañete** (📞93 270 34 58;
www.barcanete.com; Carrer de la Unió 17;
tapas from €4.50; 🕙1pm-midnight Mon-Sat;
📶; ⓂLiceu) has great modern tapas.

★ Top Tip

Book online to avoid the queue and
ensure you visit at your preferred time.

Building

The ground floor was once the coach
house, and the basement, with squat
mushroom-shaped brick pillars, is where
the horses were stabled. Back upstairs,
admire the elaborate wrought iron of the
main doors from the splendid vestibule and
the grand staircase lined with sandstone
columns. Up another floor are the main hall
and its annexes; check out the rosewood
coffered ceilings and the gallery behind
trelliswork, from where the family could spy
on their guests as they arrived.

Central to the structure is the magnificent music room with a rebuilt organ
played during opening hours; the choir
would sing from the mezzanine up on the
other side. Alongside the alcove containing
the organ is another that opened out to
become the family chapel, with booths to

seat nobility and, above them, the servants.
The main hall is a parabolic pyramid – each
wall an arch stretching up three floors and
coming together to form a dome, giving
a magnificent sense of space in what is a
surprisingly narrow building, constructed
on a site of just 500 sq metres.

Above the main floor are the family
rooms, which are sometimes labyrinthine
and dotted with piercings of light or grand,
stained-glass windows. The bright, diapha-
nous attic used to house the servants' quarters but now houses a detailed exhibition on
the history and renovation of the building.
The roof is a tumult of tiled mosaics and
fanciful chimney pots. The audioguide
(included) is worth getting not only for the
detailed description of the architecture, but
also for the pieces of music and its photo-
graphic illustrations (displayed on screen)
of the Güell family's life.

MACBA

Designed by Richard Meier and opened in 1995, MACBA (Museu d'Art Contemporani de Barcelona) has become the city's foremost contemporary art centre, with captivating exhibitions for the serious art lover.

The ground and 1st floors of this great white bastion of contemporary art are generally given over to exhibitions from the gallery's own collections. There are some 3000 pieces centred on three periods: post-WWII; around 1968; and the years since the fall of the Berlin Wall in 1989, right up until the present day.

Permanent Collection

The permanent collection is on the ground floor and dedicates itself to Spanish and Catalan art from the second half of the 20th century, with works by Antoni Tàpies, Joan Brossa and Miquel Barceló, among others, though international artists, such as Paul Klee, Bruce Nauman and John Cage, are also represented.

The gallery, across two floors, is dedicated to temporary visiting exhibitions that are

Great For...

☑ **Don't Miss**

The permanent collection dedicated to 20th-century Spanish and Catalan art.

KARSOL/SHUTTERSTOCK ©

❶ Need to Know

(Museu d'Art Contemporani de Barcelona; Map p249; ☑93 412 08 10; www.macba.cat; Plaça dels Àngels 1; adult/concession/child under 14yr €10/8/free; ◷11am-7.30pm Mon & Wed-Fri, 10am-9pm Sat, 10am-3pm Sun & holidays; Ⓜ Universitat)

✕ Take a Break

Modernista Casa Almirall (p179) is a stunning nearby bar, perfect for a cool beer.

★ Top Tip

Unlike most Barcelona museums, MACBA is open on Mondays.

almost always challenging and intriguing. MACBA's 'philosophy' is to do away with the old model of a museum where an artwork is a spectacle and to create a space where art can be viewed critically, so the exhibitions are usually tied in with talks and events. This is food for the brain as well as the eyes.

Capella MACBA

Across the square in front, where the city's skateboarders gather, the renovated 400-year-old Convent dels Àngels houses the Capella MACBA, where MACBA regularly rotates selections from its permanent collection. The Gothic framework of the one-time convent-church remains intact.

Fringe Attractions

The library and auditorium stage regular concerts, talks and events, all of which are either reasonably priced or free. The exten-sive art bookshop is fantastic for stocking up on art and art theory books, as well as quirky gifts and small design objects.

What's Nearby?

Centre de Cultura Contemporània de Barcelona   Gallery

(CCCB; Map p249; ☑93 306 41 00; www.cccb.org; Carrer de Montalegre 5; adult/concession/child under 12yr for 1 exhibition €6/4/free, 2 exhibitions €8/6/free, Sun 3-8pm free; ◷11am-8pm Tue-Sun; Ⓜ Universitat) A complex of auditoriums, exhibition spaces and conference halls opened here in 1994 in what had been an 18th-century hospice, the Casa de la Caritat. The courtyard, with a vast glass wall on one side, is spectacular. With 4500 sq metres of exhibition space in four separate areas, the centre hosts a constantly chang-ing program of exhibitions, film cycles and other events.

Basílica del Sagrat Cor de Jesús (p99)

Tibidabo

Framing the north end of the city, the forest-covered mountain of Tibidabo, which tops out at 512m, is the highest peak in Serra de Collserola. Aside from the superb views from the top, highlights include an 80 sq km park, an old-fashioned amusement park, a telecommunications tower with viewing platform, and a looming basilica, visible from many parts of the city.

Great For...

Parc de la Collserola

Ctra del Vallvidrera al Tibidabo

⊙ **Tibidabo**

Funicular del Tibidabo

ℹ Need to Know

See Getting There (p100)

★ **Top Tip**

Pack a picnic and make a day of it, staying for sunset cocktails at a bar with a view.

Tibidabo gets its name from the devil, who, trying to tempt Christ, took him to a high place and said, in Latin: '*Haec omnia tibi dabo si cadens adoraberis me*' ('All this I will give you if you fall down and worship me').

Parc de la Collserola

Barcelonins needing an escape from the city without heading far seek out this extensive park in the hills. It's a great place to hike and bike, and it has plenty of cafes and snack bars. Pick up a map from one of the information centres (such as the Carretera de l'Església 92 location, close to the Baixador de Vallvidrera FGC train station).

The park has a smattering of country chapels (some Romanesque), the ragged ruins of the 14th-century Castellciuro castle in the west, various lookout points and, to the north, the 15th-century Can Coll, a grand farmhouse. It's used as an environmental education centre where you can see how richer farmers lived around the 17th to 19th centuries. You can also learn about one of Barcelona's great 19th-century writers at the **Vil·la Joana** (☑93 256 21 00; www.museuhistoria.bcn.cat; Carretera de l'Església 104; ☉10am-2pm Thu, to 5pm Sat, Sun & holidays; ▨FGC Baixador de Vallvidrera) FREE. This historic villa is where Catalonia's revered writer Jacint Verdaguer lived in the final days of his life before his death on 10 July 1902. Displays pay homage to Verdaguer's legacy and his impact on literature in Catalonia and beyond.

Torre de Collserola

Sir Norman Foster designed the 288m-high **Torre de Collserola** (☑93 406 93 54; www.torredecollserola.com; Carretera de Vallvidrera al Tibidabo; adult/child €5.60/3.30; ☉hours vary, closed Jan & Feb; ▨111, ▨Funicular de Vallvidrera) telecommunications tower, which was completed in 1992. An external

glass lift whisks you to the visitors' observation area, 115m up, from where there are some magnificent views – extending up to 70km on a clear day. All of Barcelona's TVs and radios receive transmissions from here, and repeater stations across Catalonia are also controlled from this tower.

Parc d'Atraccions

The reason most *barcelonins* come up to Tibidabo is for some thrills at this **funfair** (☑93 211 79 42; www.tibidabo.cat; Plaça de Tibidabo 3-4; adult/child €28.50/10.30; ☉closed Jan & Feb; ▨T2A, ▨Funicular del Tibidabo), close to the top funicular station. Here you'll find whirling high-speed rides and high-tech 4D cinema, as well as old-fashioned amusements including an old steam train and the Museu d'Autòmats,

Roller coaster at Parc d'Atraccions

✕ **Take a Break**
Grab a drink with a view at Mirablau (p178) by the funicular.

with automated puppets dating as far back as 1880. Check the website for seasonal opening times.

Basílica del Sagrat Cor de Jesús

Above Tibidabo's top funicular station, this landmark **basílica** (Basílica of the Sacred Heart of Jesus; 📞93 417 56 86; www.templotibidabo.es; Plaça de Tibidabo; lift €3.50; ⏰11am-7pm; 🚌T2A, 🚡Funicular del Tibidabo) **FREE** is meant to be Barcelona's answer to Paris' Sacré-Cœur. Built from 1902 to 1961 with some Modernista influence, it's certainly as visible as its Parisian counterpart, and even more vilified by aesthetes. It's actually two churches, one on top of the other. The top one is surmounted by a giant statue of Christ and has a lift to take you to the roof for the panoramic (and often wind-chilled) views.

Stargazing

Inaugurated in 1904, the Modernista **Observatori Fabra** (📞93 417 57 36; www.fabra.cat; Carretera del Observatori; tour €2, night observation €15-25; ⏰tours 11am-2pm Sun, night observation by reservation Fri & Sat Oct-Jun; 🚉FGC Avinguda Tibidabo), 415m above sea level, is still a functioning scientific foundation. On certain evenings visitors can observe the stars through its grand old telescope (check the website for the latest schedule). Visits, generally in Catalan or Spanish, must be prebooked. From mid-June to mid-September, **Sopars amb Estrelles** (dinner under the stars; 📞93 327 01 21; www.sternalia.com; Carretera del Observatori;

☑ Don't Miss

A break-from-the-city stroll in the Parc de la Collserola.

SHLER/SHUTTERSTOCK ©

meal & observatory packages €71-125.50; ⊙mid-Jun–mid-Sep; ✈🚻) offers an evening of high-end dining and astronomy.

Gran Hotel La Florida

Hemingway is among the guests to have stayed at this magnificent 1920s-built **property** (☎93 259 30 00; www.hotellaflorida.com; Carretera de Vallvidrera al Tibidabo 83-93; d/f/ste from €233.50/347.50/497.50; 🅿❄🤍🏊; 🛏111), which only received its first guests in the 1950s and had a designer makeover this century. Amenities include indoor and outdoor swimming pools, a spa and two restaurants. Its location atop Tibidabo provides jaw-dropping views. Public areas are lined with original works by local artists.

Getting There

To reach the basilica and amusement park, take an FGC train to Avinguda Tibidabo. Outside Avinguda Tibidabo station, hop on the *tramvia blau,* which runs past fancy Modernista mansions to Plaça del Doctor Andreu (one way €5.50, 15 minutes, every 15 or 30 minutes 10am to 7.30pm daily late June to early September, 10am to 6.15pm Saturday, Sunday and holidays early September to late June; hours can vary). Bus 196 runs the same route. From Plaça del Doctor Andreu, the Tibidabo funicular railway climbs to the top of the hill (return €7.70, five minutes). Departures start around 10am and run every 15 minutes until shortly after the Parc d'Atraccions' closing time. Start queuing well before the funicular stops running, as places are limited.

An alternative is bus T2A, the 'Tibibús', from Plaça de Catalunya to Plaça de Tibidabo (€3, 30 minutes, every 30 to 50 minutes on Saturday, Sunday and holidays March to December, and hourly from 10.15am Monday to Friday late June to early September).

For Parc de la Collserola, take an FGC train to Baixador de Vallvidrera. Alternatively, you can stop one station earlier at Peu del Funicular and ride to the top via the Funicular Vallvidrera.

Bus 111 runs between Tibidabo and Vallvidrera (passing in front of the Torre de Collserola).

What's Nearby?

Bellesguard   Architecture
(☎93 250 40 93; www.bellesguardgaudi.com; Carrer de Bellesguard 16; adult/child €9/free; ⊙10am-3pm Tue-Sun; 🚇FGC Avinguda Tibidabo) This Gaudí masterpiece was rescued from obscurity and opened to the public in 2013. Built between 1900 and 1909, this private residence (still owned by the original Guilera family) has a castle-like appearance with crenellated walls of stone and brick, narrow stained-glass windows, elaborate ironwork and a soaring turret mounted by a Gaudían cross. It's a fascinating work that combines both Gothic and Modernista elements.

The basilica's statues overlook the amusement park

Guided tours in English (€16 per person) take place on weekends at 11am. At other times, you can visit the interior of the building and the grounds with an audio-guide that gives historical background.

The downside: it's a long walk to a train station, though many buses pass near (including bus 22 and bus 58 from Plaça de Catalunya). Be sure to call before making the trek out – Bellesguard sometimes closes for private events.

Parc de la Creueta del Coll   Park
(Passeig de la Mare de Déu del Coll 77; ☺10am-9pm Apr-Oct, to 7pm Nov-Mar; 🚌92, 129, N5, Ⓜ Penitents) A favourite with families, this refreshing public park has a meandering, splashing lake pool, along with swings, showers and a snack bar. Only the pool closes outside summer. The park is set inside a deep crater left by long years of stone quarrying, with an enormous concrete sculpture, Elogio del agua (In Praise of Water) by Eduardo Chillida, suspended on one side. Views of the city and Tibidabo extend from the hilly trails.

Enter from Passeig de la Carrer Mare de Déu del Coll, a 1km walk east from the Penitents metro station.

★ **Did You Know?**

Tibidabo is the setting for one of Spain's best-loved rock songs, Cadillac solitario, by legendary local singer Loquillo and his band Los Trogloditas.

KONSTANTIN TRONIN/SHUTTERSTOCK ©

Museu-Monestir de Pedralbes

Dating from medieval times, this atmospheric convent is now a museum of monastic life. Perched at the top of busy Avinguda de Pedralbes in what was once unpeopled countryside, the monastery remains a divinely quiet corner of Barcelona and is full of architectural treasures. Adjoining the monastery is the sober church, an excellent example of Catalan Gothic.

Great For...

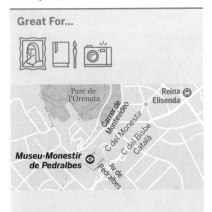

❶ Need to Know

(☎93 256 34 34; http://monestirpedralbes.
bcn.cat; Baixada del Monestir 9; adult/child
€5/free, after 3pm Sun free; ⊙10am-5pm
Tue-Fri, to 7pm Sat, to 8pm Sun Apr-Sep,
10am-2pm Tue-Fri, to 5pm Sat & Sun Oct-Mar;
🚍63, 68, 75, 78, H4, 🚆FGC Reina Elisenda)

★ **Top Tip**

To make the most of your visit, be sure to pick up an audioguide, which gives crucial historical details.

Cloister & Chapel

The architectural highlight is the large, elegant, three-storey cloister, a jewel of Catalan Gothic, built in the early 14th century. Following its course to the right, stop at the first chapel, the Capella de Sant Miquel, the murals of which were done in 1346 by Ferrer Bassá, one of Catalonia's earliest documented painters. A few steps on is the ornamental grave of Queen Elisenda, who founded the convent. It is curious, as it is divided in two: the side in the cloister shows her dressed as a penitent widow, while the other part, an alabaster masterpiece inside the adjacent church, shows her dressed as queen.

Refectory & Sleeping Quarters

As you head around the ground floor of the cloister, you can peer into the restored refectory, kitchen, stables, stores and a reconstruction of the infirmary – all giving a good idea of convent life. Eating in the refectory must not have been a whole lot of fun, judging by the inscriptions around the walls exhorting *Silentium* (Silence) and *Audi Tacens* (Listen and Keep Quiet).

Upstairs is a grand hall that was once the *dormidor* (sleeping quarters). It was lined with tiny night cells, but they were long ago removed. Today this space is graced by a modest collection of the monastery's art, especially Gothic devotional works, and furniture.

Giant tree display at CosmoCaixa

Parc de l'Orenata

A little-visited park lies just behind the Museu-Monestir de Pedralbes. Set amid woodlands, the compact oak- and pine-filled Parc de l'Orenata has fine lookouts and the ruins of an old castle. On weekends families arrive for pony rides and short rides

> ★ **Did You Know?**
>
> The monastery's different rooms are grouped around the three-storey Gothic cloister and include the chapel, dormitory, refectory, kitchen, infirmary, storerooms, abbey room and chapter house.

> ☑ **Don't Miss**
>
> Ferrer Bassá's murals, the three-storey Gothic cloister or the refectory's admonishing inscriptions.

---

on a mini locomotive. To get there, take the stairs leading past the monastery and continue uphill along Carrer de Montevideo.

What's Nearby?

CosmoCaixa   Museum

(Museu de la Ciència; ☏93 212 60 50; www.cosmocaixa.com; Carrer d'Isaac Newton 26; adult/child €4/free, guided tours from €2, planetarium €4; ⊘10am-8pm Tue-Sun; ☐60, 196) Kids (and kids at heart) are fascinated by displays here and this science museum remains one of the city's most popular attractions. The single greatest highlight is the re-creation of over 1 sq km of flooded **Amazon Rainforest** (Bosc Inundat). More than 100 species of Amazon flora and fauna (including anacondas, colourful poisonous frogs and caimans) prosper in this unique, living diorama in which you can even experience a tropical downpour.

In another original section, the Mur Geològic, seven great chunks of rock (90 metric tons in all) have been assembled to create a **Geological Wall**.

These and other displays on the lower 5th floor (the bulk of the museum is underground) cover many fascinating areas of science, from fossils to physics, and from the alphabet to outer space. To gain access to other special sections, such as the **Planetari** (Planetarium), check for guided visits. Most of these activities are interactive and directed at children, and cost €4. The planetarium has been adapted so that people with visual and hearing impairments may also enjoy it.

Outside, there's a nice stroll through the extensive Plaça de la Ciència, whose modest garden flourishes with Mediterranean flora.

> ✗ **Take a Break**
>
> A kilometre northeast, next door to Sarrià's pretty 18th-century church, cheery **Santamasa** (www.santamasarestaurant.com; Carrer Major de Sarrià 97; mains €6.50-13; ⊘8am-midnight Mon-Fri, 9am-midnight Sat & Sun; ☐FGC Reina Elisenda) is open all day.

Palau de la Música Catalana

This concert hall is a high point of Barcelona's Modernista architecture: a symphony in tile, brick, sculpted stone and stained glass conceived as a temple for the Catalan Renaixença (Renaissance).

Great For...

☑ Don't Miss

The principal facade's mosaics and columns, and the foyer and pillars in the restaurant.

Built by Domènech i Montaner between 1905 and 1908 for the Orfeó Català musical society, the *palau* (palace) was built with the help of some of the best Catalan artisans of the time, in the cloister of the former Convent de Sant Francesc. Since 1990 it has undergone several major changes.

Facade

The *palau*, like a peacock, shows off much of its splendour on the outside. Take in the principal facade with its mosaics, floral capitals and the sculpture cluster representing Catalan popular music.

Interior

Wander inside the foyer and restaurant areas to admire the spangled, tiled pillars. Best of all, however, is the richly colourful auditorium upstairs, with its ceiling of

CCAT82/SHUTTERSTOCK ©

ⓘ Need to Know

(Map p254; ☎93 295 72 00; www.palau
musica.cat; Carrer de Palau de la Música 4-6;
adult/concession/under 10yr €18/15/free;
⊙guided tours 10am-3.30pm, to 6pm Easter,
Jul & Aug; Ⓜ Urquinaona)

✕ Take a Break

Le Cucine Mandarosso (☎93 269 07
80; www.lecucinemandarosso.com; Carrer de
Verdaguer i Callís 4; mains €12-14, menú del
día €12; ⊙1.30-4pm, 9pm-midnight Tue-Sat,
1.30-4.30pm, 9pm-midnight Sun; Ⓜ Urquinaona) for Italian comfort food.

★ Top Tip

Book tours online if visiting in summer.

blue-and-gold stained glass and shimmering skylight that looks like a giant, crystal-
line, downward-thrusting nipple. Above a
bust of Beethoven on the stage towers a
wind-blown sculpture of Wagner's Valkyries
(Wagner was top of the Barcelona charts at
the time it was created). This can only be
savoured on a guided tour or by attending a
performance – either is highly recommended. Admission is by tour only and tickets
can be bought up to a week in advance
by phone or online. Space is limited to a
maximum of 55 people.

Performances

This is the city's most traditional venue
for classical and choral music, although
it has a wide-ranging program, including
flamenco, pop and – particularly – jazz.
Just being here for a performance (p200)
is an experience. Sip a pre-concert tipple in
the foyer, its tiled pillars all a-glitter.

Controversial History

The original Modernista creation, now a
World Heritage site, did not meet with universal approval in its day. The doyen of Catalan literature, Josep Pla, did not hesitate
to condemn it as 'horrible' (although few
share his sentiments today). Domènech i
Montaner himself was also in a huff – he
failed to attend the opening ceremony in
response to unsettled bills.

The *palau* was at the centre of a
fraud scandal from 2009 to 2012, as its
president, Felix Millet, who subsequently
resigned, admitted to having siphoned off
millions of euros of its funds. He and his
partner were ordered to repay the embez-
zled money to the *palau* in March 2012.

Charcuterie selection

Foodie Trails in La Ribera

Gourmands and gastronomes will be thoroughly beguiled by the choice in La Ribera, home to a fabulous market and gourmet shops offering all sorts of delicacies. It's almost impossible to walk into its enticing pedestrian zone and come out without having tried, tasted or bought something.

Great For...

ℹ Need to Know

Buying cooked meats and meat products? The Spanish phrase for 'vacuum pack' is *'envasar al vacío'*.

★ **Top Tip**
Get to the market early; it's far more interesting in the morning.

Mercat de Santa Caterina — Market

(Map p250; ☎93 319 57 40; www.mercat santacaterina.com; Avinguda de Francesc Cambó 16; ⊙7.30am-3.30pm Mon, Wed & Sat, to 8.30pm Tue, Thu & Fri, closed afternoons Jul & Aug; Ⓜ Jaume I) Come shopping for your tomatoes at this extraordinary-looking produce market, designed by Enric Miralles and Benedetta Tagliabue to replace its 19th-century predecessor. Finished in 2005, it is distinguished by its kaleidoscopic and undulating roof, held up above the bustling produce stands, restaurants, cafes and bars by twisting slender branches of what look like grey steel trees.

Museu de la Xocolata — Museum

(☎93 268 78 78; www.museuxocolata.cat; Carrer del Comerç 36; adult/concessions/under 7yr €6/5/free; ⊙10am-7pm Mon-Sat, to 3pm Sun;

🚻; Ⓜ Arc de Triomf) Chocoholics have a hard time containing themselves in this museum dedicated to the fundamental foodstuff – particularly when faced with tempting displays of cocoa-based treats in the cafe at the exit. The displays trace the origins of chocolate, its arrival in Europe and the many myths and images associated with it.

Kids and grown-ups can join guided tours and occasionally take part in chocolate-making and tasting sessions, especially at weekends.

Hofmann Pastisseria — Food

(Map p250; ☎93 268 82 21; www.hofmann-bcn. com; Carrer dels Flassaders 44; ⊙9am-2pm & 3.30-8pm Mon-Thu, 9am-2pm & 3.30-8.30pm Fri & Sat, 9am-2.30pm Sun; Ⓜ Barceloneta) With its painted wooden cabinets, this bite-sized gourmet patisserie, linked to the prestigious Hofmann cooking school, has an air of

Entrance to Mercat de Santa Caterina

timelessness. Choose from jars of delicious chocolates, the renowned croissants (in various flavours) and more dangerous pastries, and an array of cakes and other sweet treats.

Casa Gispert
Food

(Map p250; ☑93 319 75 35; www.casagispert. com; Carrer dels Sombrerers 23; ☺10am-8.30pm Mon-Sat; Ⓜ Jaume I) The wonderful, atmospheric and wood-fronted Casa Gispert has been toasting nuts and selling all manner of dried fruit since 1851. Pots and jars piled high on the shelves contain an unending variety of crunchy tidbits: some roasted, some honeyed, all of them moreish. Your order is shouted over to the till, along

> ☑ **Don't Miss**
> The Mercat de Santa Caterina: what a place.

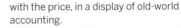

with the price, in a display of old-world accounting.

La Botifarreria
Food

(Map p250; ☑93 319 91 23; www.labotifarreria. com; Carrer de Santa Maria 4; ☺8.30am-2.30pm & 5-8.30pm Mon-Sat; closed Aug; Ⓜ Jaume I) Say it with a sausage! Although this delightful deli sells all sorts of goodies, the mainstay is an astounding variety of handcrafted sausages – the *botifarra*. Not just the regular pork variety either – these sausages are stuffed with anything from green pepper and whisky to apple curry.

El Magnífico
Coffee

(Map p250; ☑93 319 60 81; www.cafeselmagni fico.com; Carrer de l'Argenteria 64; ☺9.30am-8pm Mon-Sat; Ⓜ Jaume I) All sorts of coffee has been roasted here since the early 20th century. The variety of coffee (and tea) available is remarkable – and the aromas hit you as you walk in.

Vila Viniteca
Wine

(Map p250; ☑93 777 70 17; www.vilaviniteca.es; Carrer dels Agullers 7; ☺8.30am-8.30pm Mon-Sat; Ⓜ Jaume I) One of the best wine stores in Barcelona (and there are a few...), this place has been searching out the best local and imported wines since 1932. On a couple of November evenings it organises what has become an almost riotous wine-tasting event in Carrer dels Agullers and surrounding lanes, at which cellars from around Spain present their young new wines.

Olisoliva
Food

(Map p250; ☑93 268 14 72; Mercat de Santa Caterina; ☺9.30am-3.30pm Mon, Wed & Sat, to 7pm Tue, to 8pm Thu & Fri; Ⓜ Jaume I) Inside the Mercat de Santa Caterina, this simple, glassed-in store is stacked with olive oils and vinegars from all over Spain. Taste some of the products before deciding.

Sans i Sans
Drinks

(Map p250; ☑93 310 25 18; www.sansisans.com; Carrer de l'Argenteria 59; ☺10am-8pm Mon-Sat; Ⓜ Jaume I) This exquisite tea shop is run by the same people who run El Magnífico across the road.

JOAN_BAUTISTA/SHUTTERSTOCK ©

The museum's underground ruins

Museu d'Història de Barcelona

This fascinating Barri Gòtic museum takes you back through the centuries to the foundations of Roman Barcino. It's an impressive display of archaeology and most intriguing to wander in the city's underground.

Great For...

☑ **Don't Miss**

The public laundry and the winemaking stores.

At the museum, you'll stroll amid extensive ruins of the town that flourished here following its founding by Emperor Augustus around 10 BC. Equally impressive is the setting inside the former Palau Reial Major (Grand Royal Palace), among the key locations of medieval princely power in Barcelona.

Casa Padellàs

Enter through Casa Padellàs, just south of Plaça del Rei. Casa Padellàs was built for a 16th-century noble family in Carrer dels Mercaders and moved here, stone by stone, in the 1930s. It has a courtyard typical of Barcelona's late-Gothic and baroque mansions, with a graceful external staircase up to the 1st floor. Today it leads to a restored Roman tower and a section of Roman wall (the exterior of which faces Plaça Ramon

ⓘ Need to Know

(MUHBA; Map p250; ☎93 256 21 00; www.
museuhistoria.bcn.cat; Plaça del Rei; adult/
concession/child €7/5/free, 3-8pm Sun & 1st
Sun of month free; ⏰10am-7pm Tue-Sat, to
2pm Mon, to 8pm Sun; Ⓜ Jaume I)

★ Top Tip

Entry includes admission to other
MUHBA-run sites, such as Domus de
Sant Honorat (p115).

✖ Take a Break

Stop by La Granja (p142) for a hot chocolate and another glimpse of Roman
walls.

de Berenguer el Gran), as well as a section
of the house set aside for temporary
exhibitions.

Underground Ruins

Below ground is a remarkable walk through
about 4 sq km of excavated Roman and
Visigothic Barcelona. After the display on
the typical Roman *domus* (villa), you reach
a public laundry. (Outside in the street
were containers for people to urinate into,
as the urine was used as disinfectant.) You
pass more laundries and dyeing shops, a
6th-century public cold-water bath and
more dye shops. As you hit the Cardo Minor
(a main street), you turn right then left
and reach various shops dedicated to the
making of *garum*. This paste, a favourite
food across the Roman Empire, was made
of mashed-up fish intestines, eggs and

blood. Occasionally prawns, cockles and
herbs were added to create other flavours.
Further on are fish-preserve stores. Fish
were sliced up (and all innards removed for
making *garum*), laid in alternate layers, using salt for preservation, and sat in troughs
for about three weeks before being ready
for sale and export.

Next come remnants of a 6th- to
7th-century church and episcopal buildings, followed by winemaking stores, with
ducts for allowing the must to flow off, and
ceramic, round-bottomed *dolia* for storing
and ageing wine. Ramparts then wind
around and upward, past remains of the
gated patio of a Roman house, the medieval
Palau Episcopal (Bishops' Palace) and into
two broad vaulted halls with displays on
medieval Barcelona.

In Columbus' Footsteps

You eventually emerge at a hall and ticket office set up on the north side of Plaça del Rei. To your right is the Saló del Tinell, the banqueting hall of the royal palace and a fine example of Catalan Gothic (built 1359–70). Its broad arches and bare walls give a sense of solemnity that would have made an appropriate setting for Fernando and Isabel to hear Columbus' first reports of the New World. The hall is sometimes used for temporary exhibitions, which may cost extra and mean that your peaceful contemplation of its architectural majesty is somewhat obstructed.

Chapel

As you leave the *saló,* you come to the 14th-century Capella Reial de Santa Àgata, the palace chapel. Outside, a spindly bell tower rises from the northeast side of Plaça del Rei. Inside, all is bare except for the 15th-century altarpiece and the magnificent *techumbre* (decorated timber ceiling). The altarpiece is considered to be one of Jaume Huguet's finest surviving works.

Out to the Square

Head down the fan-shaped stairs into Plaça del Rei and look up to observe the Mirador del Rei Martí (lookout tower of King Martin), built in 1555, long after the king's death. It is part of the Arxiu de la Corona d'Aragón (General Archive of the Crown of Aragon); the magnificent views over the old city are now enjoyed only by a privileged few.

Plaça del Rei near an entrance to MUHBA

What's Nearby?

Palau de la Generalitat   Historic Building

(Map p250; http://presidencia.gencat.cat; Plaça de Sant Jaume; ⊘2nd & 4th weekend of month; MJaume I) Founded in the early 15th century, the Palau de la Generalitat is open on limited occasions only (one-hour guided tours on the second and fourth weekends of the month, plus open-door days). The most impressive of the ceremonial halls is the Saló de Sant Jordi (Hall of St George), named after the region's patron saint. To see inside, book on the website.

Marc Safont designed the original Gothic main entrance on Carrer del Bisbe. The modern main entrance on Plaça de Sant Jaume is a late-Renaissance job with neoclassical leanings. If you wander by in the evening, squint up through the windows into the Saló de Sant Jordi and you will get some idea of the sumptuousness of the interior.

Normally you will have to enter from Carrer de Sant Sever. The first rooms you pass through are characterised by low, vaulted ceilings. From here you head upstairs to the raised courtyard known as the Pati dels Tarongers, a modest Gothic orangery (open about once a month for concert performances of the palace's chimes). The 16th-century Sala Daurada i de Sessions, one of the rooms leading off the patio, is a splendid meeting hall lit up by huge chandeliers. Still more imposing is the Renaissance Saló de Sant Jordi, the murals of which were added last century – many an occasion of pomp and circumstance takes place here. Finally, you descend the staircase of the Gothic Pati Central to leave by what was originally the building's main entrance.

Domus de Sant Honorat   Archaeological Site

(Map p250; ☎93 256 21 00; www.museuhistoria. bcn.cat; Carrer de la Fruita 2; adult/concession/ child €2/1.50/free, 1st Sun of month free; ⊘10am-2pm Sun; MJaume I) The remains of a Roman *domus* have been unearthed and opened to the public. The house (and vestiges of three small shops) lies close to the Roman forum and the owners were clearly well off. Apart from providing something of an idea of daily Roman life through these remains, the location also contains six medieval grain silos installed during the period when this was the Jewish quarter, El Call.

The whole site is housed in the mid-19th-century Casa Morell. So, in an unusual mix, one gets a glimpse of three distinct periods in history in the same spot.

ANDREW HASSON/ALAMY STOCK PHOTO ©

✗ **Take a Break**

For microbrews and vegan burgers check out **Cat Bar** (www.catbarcat.com; Carrer de la Bòria 17; mains €6.50-8.50; ⊘1-10pm Thu-Mon) in El Born.

Basílica de Santa Maria del Mar

At one end of Passeig del Born stands the apse of Barcelona's finest Catalan Gothic church, Santa Maria del Mar (Our Lady of the Sea). Its construction started in 1329, with Berenguer de Montagut and Ramon Despuig as the architects. Famously the parishioners themselves gave up their time to help construct the church, particularly the stevedores from the nearby port.

Great For...

ℹ Need to Know

(Map p250; ☎93 310 23 90; www.santamaria delmarbarcelona.org; Plaça de Santa Maria del Mar; €8 1-5pm (incl guided tour); ⊙9am-8.30pm Mon-Sat, 10am-8pm Sun; MJaume I)

★ **Top Tip**

Use the website www.classictic.com and filter by venue to find upcoming concerts here.

Main Sanctuary

The pleasing unity of form and symmetry of the church's central nave and two flanking aisles owed much to the rapidity with which the church was built – a mere 54 years, which must be a record for a major European house of worship. The slender, octagonal pillars create an enormous sense of lateral space bathed in the light of stained glass.

People's Church

Its construction started in 1329, with Berenguer de Montagut and Ramon Despuig as the architects in charge. During construction the city's *bastaixos* (porters) spent a day each week carrying on their backs the stone required to build the church from royal quarries in Montjuïc.

Their memory lives on in reliefs of them in the main doors and stone carvings elsewhere in the church. The walls, the side chapels and the facades were finished by 1350, and the entire structure was completed in 1383.

Interior

The exterior gives an impression of sternness, and the narrow streets surrounding it are restrictive and claustrophobic. It may come as a (pleasant) surprise then to find a spacious and light interior.

Even before anarchists gutted the church in 1909 and again in 1936, Santa Maria always lacked superfluous decoration. Gone are the gilded chapels that weigh heavily over so many Spanish churches, while the splashes of colour high above the nave are subtle – unusually and beautifully

View of the basilica's spacious and light interior

so. It all serves to highlight the church's fine proportions, purity of line and sense of space. Keep an ear out for music recitals, often baroque and classical.

Old Flame

Opposite Basílica de Santa Maria del Mar's southern flank, an eternal flame burns brightly over an apparently anonymous sunken square. This is El Fossar de les Moreres (The Mulberry Cemetery), the site of a Roman cemetery. It's also where Catalan resistance fighters were buried after the siege of Barcelona ended in defeat in September 1714; it is for them that the flame burns.

☑ Don't Miss
The church's architects in memorial stone relief.

STEVE LOVEGROVE/SHUTTERSTOCK ©

What's Nearby?

Museu Europeu d'Art Modern
Museum

(MEAM; Map p250; ☎93 319 56 93; www.meam. es; Carrer Barra de Ferro 5; adult/concession/ under 10yr €9/7/free; ◉10am-8pm Tue-Sun; ⓂJaume I) The European Museum of Modern Art opened in 2011 in the Palau Gomis, a handsome 18th-century mansion around the corner from the Museu Picasso. The art within is strictly representational (the 'Modern' of the name simply means 'contemporary') and is mostly from young Spanish artists, though there are some works from elsewhere in Europe.

Casa Llotja de Mar
Architecture

(La Llotja; Map p250; ☎93 547 88 49; www. casallotja.com; Passeig d'Isabel II 1; ◉10am-2pm Mon-Fri; ⓂBarceloneta) FREE The centrepiece of the city's medieval stock exchange (more affectionately known as La Llotja) is the fine Gothic Saló de Contractacions (Transaction Hall), built in the 14th century. Pablo Picasso and Joan Miró attended the art school that was housed in the Saló dels Cònsols from 1849.

These and five other halls were encased in a neoclassical shell in the 18th century. The stock exchange was in action until well into the 20th century and the building remains in the hands of the city's chamber of commerce. Visitors can only see the courtyard and a handful of rooms except during special events.

Barcelona Head
Sculpture

(Map p250; Passeig de Colom; ⓂBarceloneta) An icon by the waterfront, this eye-catching 15m-high primary-coloured sculpture was designed by famous American pop artist Roy Lichtenstein for the 1992 Olympics.

✖ Take a Break
Admire the church's western facade with tapas and drinks at La Vinya del Senyor (p185).

Photovoltaic solar panel, Zona de Banys

TTABOGRAPHY/SHUTTERSTOCK ©

Exploring El Fòrum

Once an urban wasteland, this area has seen dramatic changes since the turn of the millennium, with sparkling buildings, open plazas and waterfront recreation areas.

Great For...

☑ **Don't Miss**

Fraternitat, a sculpture dedicated to the hundreds executed here during the Franco years.

Edifici Fòrum

The most striking architectural element of the Fòrum area is the eerily blue, triangular *2001: A Space Odyssey*–style Edifici Fòrum building by Swiss architects Herzog & de Meuron, which houses the Museu Blau. The facades look like sheer cliff faces, with angular crags cut into them as if by divine laser. Grand strips of mirror create fragmented reflections of the sky.

Museu Blau

Set inside the futuristic Edifici Fòrum, the **Museu Blau** (Blue Museum; ☏93 256 60 02; www.museuciencies.cat; adult/child €6/free, free from 3pm Sun & 1st Sun of month; ⊘10am-7pm Tue-Sat, to 8pm Sun Mar-Sep, to 6pm Tue-Fri, to 7pm Sat, to 8pm Sun Oct-Feb) takes visitors on a journey across the natural world. Multimedia and interactive exhibits explore

Abstract view of Museu Blau's ceiling

ℹ️ Need to Know

(Ⓜ️El Maresme Fòrum)

✕ Take a Break

The **Centre Comercial Diagonal Mar**
(☎️93 567 76 37; www.diagonalmarcentre.es;
Avinguda Diagonal 3; 🕐9.30am-10pm Mon-
Sat Jun-Sep, 9am-9pm Mon-Sat Oct-May; Ⓜ️El
Maresme Fòrum) is a shopping centre with
lots of eating options.

★ Top Tip

Take a bike out here to best explore the
area.

topics like the history of evolution, the
earth's formation and the great scientists
who have helped shape human knowledge. There are also specimens from the
animal, plant and mineral kingdoms – plus
dinosaur skeletons – all rather dramatically
set amid the sprawling 9000 sq metres of
exhibition space.

Sinuous Steel

Next door to Edifici Fòrum, Josep Lluís
Mateo's high-tech Centre de Convencions
Internacional de Barcelona (CCIB) is a mas-
sive work in steel with intriguing contours.

Zona de Banys

A 300m stroll east from the Edifici Fòrum
is the Zona de Banys, a popular summer
attraction for families with kayaks and bikes
available for rent, diving lessons, and other
activities. This tranquil seawater swimming

area was won from the sea by the creation
of massive cement-block dykes. At its
northern end, like a great rectangular
sunflower, an enormous photovoltaic panel
turns its face up to the sun to power the
area with solar energy. Along with another
set of solar panels in the form of porticoes,
it generates enough electricity for 1000
households.

Port Fòrum

Just behind the Zona de Banys spreads
Port Fòrum, Barcelona's third marina. The
area is unified by an undulating esplanade
and walkways (with wheelchair access)
that are perfect for walking, bikes and
skateboards. In summer, a weekend
amusement park sets up with all the usual
suspects: rides, shooting galleries, snack
stands, inflatable castles and dodgem cars.

Parc de Diagonal Mar

This park, designed by Enric Miralles, contains pools, fountains, a didactic botanical
walk (with more than 30 species of trees
and other plants) and modern sculptures.

Museu Frederic Marès

One of the wildest collections of historical curios lies inside this vast medieval complex, once part of the royal palace of the counts of Barcelona.

Great For...

☑ **Don't Miss**

Displays from the collector's cabinet.

The building holding the museum is an intriguing one. A rather worn coat of arms on the wall indicates that it was also, for a while, the seat of the Spanish Inquisition in Barcelona.

Sculpture

Frederic Marès i Deulovol (1893–1991) was a rich sculptor, traveller and obsessive collector. He specialised in medieval Spanish sculpture, huge quantities of which are displayed in the basement and on the ground and 1st floors – including some lovely polychrome wooden sculptures of the Crucifixion and the Virgin. Among the most eye-catching pieces is a reconstructed Romanesque doorway with four arches, taken from a 13th-century country church in the Aragonese province of Huesca.

EQROY/SHUTTERSTOCK ©

❶ Need to Know

(Map p250; ☑93 256 35 00; www.museu mares.bcn.cat; Plaça de Sant lu 5; adult/ concession/child €4.20/2.40/free, 3-8pm Sun & 1st Sun of month free; ⊙10am-7pm Tue-Sat, 11am-8pm Sun; Ⓜ Jaume I)

✕ Take a Break

The museum's likeable summer cafe is the handiest place for refreshments.

★ Top Tip

This museum is very close to the cathedral (p64): kill two birds with one stone.

Collector's Cabinet

The top two floors comprise the 'collector's cabinet', a mind-boggling array of knick-knacks, including medieval weaponry, finely carved pipes, delicate ladies' fans, intricate 'floral' displays made of seashells and 19th-century daguerreotypes and photographs. A room that once served as Marès' study and library is now crammed with sculptures.

The shady courtyard houses a pleasant summer cafe (Cafè de l'Estiu).

What's Nearby?

Plaça de Sant Jaume Square

(Map p250; Ⓜ Liceu, Jaume I) In the 2000 or so years since the Romans settled here, the area around this (often remodelled) square, which started life as the forum, has been the focus of Barcelona's civic life. This is still the central staging area for Barcelona's traditional festivals. Facing each other across the square are the seat of Catalonia's regional government, the Palau de la Generalitat (p115), on the north side, and the town hall, or **Ajuntament** (Casa de la Ciutat; Map p250; ☑93 402 70 00; www.bcn.cat; ⊙10.30am-1.30pm Sun) **FREE** to the south.

Palau Centelles Architecture

(Map p250; Baixada de Sant Miquel 8; Ⓜ Jaume I) A rare 15th-century gem, Palau Centelles is on the corner of Baixada de Sant Miquel. You can wander into the fine Gothic-Renaissance courtyard if the gates are open.

Walking Tour: Modernisme in L'Eixample

Catalan modernism (Modernisme) abounds in Barcelona's L'Eixample district. This walk introduces you to the movement's main form of expression: architecture.

Start: Casa Calvet
Distance: 4km
Duration: One hour

5 Completed in 1912, **Casa Thomas** was one of Domènech i Montaner's earlier efforts; the wrought-iron decoration is magnificent.

4 Casa Comalat, built in 1911 by Salvador Valeri, shows Gaudí's influence on the main facade, with its wavy roof and bulging balconies.

3 Puig i Cadafalch let his imagination loose on **Casa Serra** (1903–08), a neo-Gothic whimsy now home to government offices.

Verdaguer

Av Diagonal

L'EIXAMPLE

C de Còrsega

C del Rosselló

C de Mallorca

C de Roger de Llúria

Plaça de Joan Carles I

Diagonal

Av Diagonal

C del Rosselló

Pg de Gràcia

C de Provença

C de Pau Claris

Diagonal

C de Provença

C de Mallorca

Rambla de Catalunya

Passeig de Gràcia

Passeig de Gràcia

C d'Aragó

Pg de Gràcia

Jardins de la Reina Victòria

Classic Photo: Striking view of **Casa Comalat** (Stop 4) from Avinguda Diagonal.

7 Puig i Cadafalch's **Casa Macaya** (1901) features the typical playful, pseudo-Gothic decoration that characterises many of the architect's projects.

6 Casa Llopis i Bofill, designed by Antoni Gallissà in 1902, has a particularly striking graffiti-covered facade.

Take a Break...
It's worth seeking out **Casa Amalia** (p146) for hearty Catalan cooking.

2 Casa Enric Batlló, today part of the Comtes de Barcelona hotel, was completed in 1896 by Josep Vilaseca.

1 Antoni Gaudí's most conventional contribution to L'Eixample is **Casa Calvet** (p148), built in 1900. Inside, admire the staircase from the swanky restaurant.

Map labels:
- 400 m / 0.2 miles
- Pg de Sant Joan
- Verdaguer (M)
- Av Diagonal
- FINISH
- Plaça de Mossèn Jacint Verdaguer
- SANT GERVASI
- C de València
- Pg de Sant Joan
- C d'Aragó
- C de Bailén
- C de Girona
- Gran Via de les Corts Catalanes
- C de Casp
- START
- Via Laietana
- Ronda de Sant Pere
- Plaça de Joan Carles I
- Urquinaona (M) d'Urquinaona

1 YURY DMITRIENKO/SHUTTERSTOCK © CSP/SHUTTERSTOCK © 5 STEFANO PATERNA/ALAMY STOCK PHOTO © 7 MERITXELL TORNE/SHUTTERSTOCK ©

Susanna al Bany sculpture in Jardins de Joan Maragall

Gardens of Montjuïc

The hillside overlooking the centre and port is a gem. Exploring verdant Montjuïc on foot, along the numerous forest paths that zigzag through gardens, is one of Barcelona's great pleasures.

Great For...

☑ **Don't Miss**

The attractive watercourses of Jardins de Laribal.

Jardí Botànic
Gardens

(Map p256; www.museuciencies.cat; Carrer del Doctor Font i Quer 2; adult/child €3.50/free, after 3pm Sun & 1st Sun of month free; ⏱10am-7pm Apr-Sep, to 5pm Oct-Mar; ☐55, 150) This botanical garden is dedicated to Mediterranean flora and has a collection of some 40,000 plants across 1500 species, including many that thrive in areas with a climate similar to that of the Mediterranean, such as the Canary Islands, North Africa, Australia, California, Chile and South Africa.

Jardins de Laribal
Gardens

(Map p256; Passeig de Santa Madrona 2; ⏱10am-sunset; ☐55) **FREE** Opened in 1922, the Jardins de Laribal comprise a combination of terraced gardens linked by paths and stairways. The pretty sculpted watercourses along some of the stairways were inspired by Granada's palace of El Alhambra.

Taking a break among the foliage

Gardens of Montjuïc

ⓘ Need to Know

Getting up here by the Teleférico del Puerto (p63) is both quick and spectacular.

✕ Take a Break

The museums have cafes, but this is real picnic territory.

★ Top Tip

It's worth being up here in the late afternoon; the sunsets can be spectacular.

Jardins de Mossèn Cinto de Verdaguer   Gardens

(Map p256; http://ajuntament.barcelona.cat/ecologiaurbana; Avinguda Miramar 30; ⊙10am-sunset; 🚌55, 150) **FREE** Near the Estació Parc Montjuïc funicular/Teleféric station are the ornamental Jardins de Mossèn Cinto de Verdaguer. These sloping, verdant gardens are home to various kinds of bulbs and aquatic plants. Many of the bulbs (some 80,000) have to be replanted every year. The aquatic plants include lotus and water lilies.

Jardins de Mossèn Costa i Llobera   Gardens

(Map p256; http://ajuntament.barcelona.cat/ecologiaurbana; Carretera de Miramar 38; ⊙10am-sunset; 🚡Transbordador Aeri, Miramar) **FREE** Above the thundering traffic of the main road to Tarragona, the Jardins de Mossèn Costa i Llobera have a good collection of tropical and desert plants – including a veritable forest of cacti (Europe's largest collection), with some species reaching over 5m in height.

Jardins de Joan Maragall   Gardens

(Map p256; Avinguda dels Montanyans 48; ⊙10am-3pm Sat & Sun; Ⓜ Plaça Espanya) **FREE** Lovely but little visited, this garden's lush lawns, ornamental fountains, photogenic sculptures and a neo-classical palace (the Spanish royal family's residence in Barcelona) set it apart from the other green spaces on Montjuïc.

Jardins del Mirador   Gardens

(Map p256; http://ajuntament.barcelona.cat/ecologiaurbana; Carretera de Montjuïc; ⊙10am-sunset; 🚡Teleféric de Montjuïc, Mirador) **FREE** From the Jardins del Mirador, opposite the Estació Mirador, you have expansive views over the port of Barcelona.

Jardins de Joan Brossa   Gardens

(Map p256; Plaça de la Sardana; ⊙10am-sunset; 🚡Teleféric de Montjuïc, Mirador) **FREE** Set on the site of a former amusement park, these gardens contain many Mediterranean species, from cypresses to pines and a few palms.

DINING OUT

From tapas to world-renowned restaurants

Dining Out

Barcelona has a celebrated food scene fuelled by a combination of world-class chefs, imaginative recipes and magnificent ingredients fresh from farms and the sea. Catalan culinary masterminds like Ferran and Albert Adrià, and Carles Abellán have become international icons, reinventing the world of haute cuisine, while classic old-world Catalan recipes continue to earn accolades in dining rooms and tapas bars across the city.

Traditional Catalan recipes showcase the great produce of the Mediterranean. Classic dishes also feature unusual pairings (seafood with meat, fruit with fowl) such as cuttlefish with chickpeas, cured ham with caviar, rabbit with prawns, or goose with pears. Great Catalan restaurants can be found in nearly every neighbourhood around town.

In This Section

Price Ranges & Tipping

The following price ranges represent the average cost of a main course:

€ less than €12

€€ €12–€20

€€€ over €20

A service charge is rarely included in the bill. Catalans and other Spaniards are not overwhelming tippers. If you are particularly happy, 5% is generally fine.

Gràcia & Park Güell
Hip and characterful
tapas bars and taverns
(p138)

**Camp Nou, Pedralbes
& La Zona Alta**
Culinary gems well worth the trip
(p136)

**La Sagrada Família
& L'Eixample**
Some of Barcelona's
best restaurants
(p145)

La Ribera
Atmospheric and
avant-garde restaurants
(p143)

*Port
Olímpic*

El Raval
Classic, budget and
artful newcomers
(p137)

**La Rambla &
Barri Gòtic**
Both touristy and
well-respected eateries
(p139)

**Barceloneta &
the Waterfront**
Top choice for
seafood and paella
(p134)

**Montjuïc, Poble Sec
& Sant Antoni**
Historic taverns, famed tapas bars,
new trendsetters
(p148)

*Port
Vell*

*Mediterranean
Sea*

Useful Phrases

The bill, please. *La cuenta, por favor.* la kwen·ta por fa·vor.

I'd/We'd like... *Quería/ queríamos...* ke·ria/ ke·ria·mos

A dish of... chicken *Una de... pollo* oo·na de... pol·yo

I'm allergic to... *Tengo alergia a...* ten·go al·er·hi·ya a

I don't eat... meat *No como... carne* No ko·mo... kar·ne

Very good, thank you! *Muy rico, gracias!* Mwee ri·ko gra·thyas!

Classic Dishes

Calçots Barbecued leek/spring onion cross.

Escalivada Grilled and cooled sliced vegetables with oil.

Esqueixada Salad of salt cod with vegetables and beans.

Botifarra amb mongetes Pork sausage with white beans.

Cargols/Caracoles Snails, often stewed with rabbit.

Fideuà Like seafood paella, but with vermicelli noodles.

The Best...

Experience Barcelona's top restaurants and cafes

By Budget: €

La Cova Fumada (p134) Barceloneta hole-in-the-wall with excellent small plates.

Bormuth (p143) Tasty tapas in an old-city setting.

La Plata (p139) A humble but well-loved bodega that serves just three plates.

For Architecture

Els Quatre Gats (p142; pictured above) Finely crafted interiors in a building where Picasso once supped.

Casa Calvet (p147) A stylish restaurant set in an early Gaudí building.

Enigma (p149) Dazzlingly modern in its design; tricky to get a reservation.

For Tapas

El 58 (p134) French-owned space on the newly hip Rambla del Poblenou.

Quimet i Quimet (p148) Mouth-watering morsels served to a standing crowd.

Palo Cortao (p149) A buzzy Poble Sec option with outstanding sharing plates.

Bar Pinotxo (p137) Pull up a bar stool at this legendary Boqueria joint.

Tapas 24 (p145) Everyone's favourite gourmet tapas bar.

For Brunch

Federal (p148) Excellent brunches and a small roof terrace.

En Aparté (p143) French restaurant serving tasty brunch dishes.

Milk (p140) Serves brunch daily (till 4.30pm).

Benedict (p140) The clue is in the name, but there's more besides.

Copasetic (p145) Vintage-filled cafe with weekend brunch.

Cafes

Bar del Convent (p145) Great terrace in a former cloister.
Café Godot (p139) Friendly and easy-going, with tasty snacks and mains.
Federal (p140) Unnervingly hip, but the food is excellent and the service friendly.
La Granja (p142) Best place in town for a hot chocolate.
La Nena (p138) Kid-friendly cafe in Gràcia.

For Nueva Cocina Catalana

Disfrutar (p147; pictured above) Set up by three alumni of El Bulli, this is one to watch.
Cinc Sentits (p147) Serves a magnificent tasting menu of the freshest, highest-quality ingredients.
Tickets (p149) Avant-garde gastronomy from Albert Adrià.

For Catalan

Vivanda (p136) Magnificent Catalan cooking with year-round garden dining.
La Panxa del Bisbe (p139) Creative sharing plates on a quiet Gràcia street.
Cafè de l'Acadèmia (p140) High-quality dishes that never disappoint.
Can Culleretes (p140) The city's oldest restaurant, with great-value traditional dishes.

☆ Top Choices for Vegetarians

Sésamo (p137) Upbeat and welcoming veggie tapas extravaganza.
Aguaribay (p134) First-rate prix fixe lunches and a small but well-executed evening à la carte menu.
Cereria (p141) Pizzas and galettes in an old-fashioned setting.
Flax & Kale (p137) Vast, colourful salads and a truly creative approach.
Rasoterra (p141) Airy vegetarian charmer in Barri Gòtic.

⊗ Barceloneta & the Waterfront

El 58 · Tapas €

(Le cinquante huit; Rambla del Poblenou 58; tapas €3.50-12; ☻1.30-11pm Tue-Sat, to 4pm Sun; Ⓜ Llacuna) This French-Catalan place serves imaginative, beautifully prepared tapas dishes: codfish balls with romesco sauce, scallop ceviche, *tartiflette* (cheese, ham and potato casserole), salmon tartare. Solo diners can take a seat at the marble-topped front bar. The back dining room with its exposed brick walls, industrial light fixtures and local artworks is a lively place to linger over a long meal.

La Cova Fumada · Tapas €

(☏93 221 40 61; Carrer del Baluard 56; tapas €4-12; ☻9am-3.15pm Mon-Wed, 9am-3.15pm & 6-8.15pm Thu & Fri, 9am-1pm Sat; Ⓜ Barceloneta) There's no sign and the setting is decidedly downmarket, but this tiny, buzzing, family-run tapas spot always packs in a crowd. The secret? Mouthwatering *pulpo* (octopus), calamari, sardines, *bombas* (meat and potato croquettes served with alioli) and grilled *carxofes* (artichokes) cooked in the open kitchen. Everything is amazingly fresh.

Can Maño · Seafood €

(Carrer del Baluard 12; mains €7-15; ☻8-11pm Mon, 8.30am-4pm & 8-11pm Tue-Fri, 8.30am-4pm Sat; Ⓜ Barceloneta) It may look like a dive, but you'll need to be prepared to wait before being squeezed in at a packed table for a raucous night of *raciones* (full-plate-size tapas serving) over a bottle of cloudy white *turbio* (Galician wine) at this family-run stalwart. The seafood is abundant, with first-rate squid, prawns and fish served at rock-bottom prices.

Aguaribay · Vegetarian €

(☏93 300 37 90; www.aguaribay-bcn.com; Carrer del Taulat 95; mains €7.50-13; ☻1-4pm Mon-Wed, 1-4pm & 8.30-11pm Thu-Sat, 1-4.30pm Sun; ☒; Ⓜ Llacuna) 🌿 Polished Aguaribay serves a small well-executed à la carte menu by night: miso and smoked tofu meatballs, soba noodles with shiitake mushrooms, and seasonal vegetables with rich black rice, along with craft beers and biodynamic wines. At lunchtime, stop in for the prix fixe lunch specials, which change daily. All ingredients are organic; vegan and gluten-free options abound.

Isla Tortuga · Tapas €€

(Map p250; ☏93 198 40 74; www.encompania delobos.com/en/isla-tortuga; Carrer de Llauder 1; tapas €3-9.50, mains €11-18; ☻noon-midnight; 🛜; Ⓜ Barceloneta) Stripped timbers, bare bricks and a namesake *tortuga* (turtle) above the bar create a stylised castaway feel in this chic space. Seasonally changing menus incorporate over 20 contemporary tapas dishes (eg vodka-steamed clams, stingray with black butter, grilled octopus with kalamata tapenade, kimchi-stuffed Padrón peppers) along with tacos (Peking duck, crackling prawn, marinated rib) and several varieties of paella.

Minyam · Seafood €€

(☏93 348 36 18; www.facebook.com/minyam cisco; Carrer de Pujades 187; tapas €2-9.50, mains €15-25; ☻12.30pm-midnight Tue-Thu, to 2am Fri & Sat, to 5pm Sun; 🛱; Ⓜ Poblenou) Billowing with smoke beneath a tajine-like metal lid, smouldering herbs infuse the rice of Minyam's signature *vulcanus* (smoked seafood paella with squid ink). Tapas dishes at this stylish, contemporary El Poblenou restaurant are equally inventive and include asparagus fritters, oysters with sea urchin and lemon, fried anchovies, and prawn tortillas. Crayons and paper are provided for kids.

Can Recasens · Catalan €€

(☏93 300 81 23; www.facebook.com/can recasens; Rambla del Poblenou 102; mains €8-21; ☻8.30am-1.30pm & 5-11.45pm Mon, to 1am Tue-Thu, to 3am Fri, 9am-1pm & 9pm-3am Sat, 9pm-1am Sun; Ⓜ Poblenou) One of El Poblenou's most romantic settings, Can Recasens hides a warren of warmly lit rooms full of oil paintings, flickering candles, fairy lights and baskets of fruit. The food is outstanding, with a mix of salads, smoked meats, fondues, and open sandwiches topped with delicacies like wild mushrooms and brie, *escalivada* (grilled vegetables) and gruyere, and spicy chorizo.

Green Spot   Vegetarian €€

(Map p250; ☑93 802 55 65; www.encompania
delobos.com/en/the-green-spot; Carrer de la
Reina Cristina 12; mains €10-15; ☺12.30pm-
midnight Mon-Fri, from 1pm Sat & Sun; ✈; MBarceloneta) Purple carrot salad with papaya and
feta, aubergine and courgette tacos, buck-
wheat and spinach *spätzle* (hand-rolled egg
noodles), sweet potato gnocchi with black
truffle, and hemp pizza with cashew cheese
and asparagus are among the inventive
vegetarian, vegan and gluten-free dishes
presented in a stylish, minimalist dining
room with vaulted ceilings.

Barraca   Seafood €€

(☑93 224 12 53; www.tribuwoki.com; Passeig
Marítim de la Barceloneta 1; mains €16-21.50;
☺12.30-11pm; ✈; MBarceloneta) 🍴 This
buzzing space has mesmerising views over
the Mediterranean – a key reference point
in the all-organic dishes served here. Start
off with a cauldron of chilli-infused clams,
cockles and mussels before moving on to
the lavish rice dishes. Vegetarian options
are plentiful and it's one of the few places in
Barcelona serving a vegan paella.

Oaxaca   Mexican €€€

(Map p250; ☑93 018 06 59; www.oaxacacuina
mexicana.com; Pla de Palau 19; mains €22-32;
☺1-4pm & 8pm-midnight; ✈; MBarceloneta)
Chef Joan Bagur trained in Mexico for a
decade under traditional cooks, and has his
own garden of Mexican plants, which supplies ingredients for culinary creations like
coyoacán (roast corn with chilli ash) and *co-
chinita pibil* (slow-roasted pork tacos). Hefty
tables are made from Mexican hardwoods
and original Mexican art lines the walls.

La Barra de Carles
Abellán   Seafood €€€

(☑93 760 51 29; www.carlesabellan.com/
mis-restaurantes/la-barra; Passeig Joan de Borbó
19; tapas €5-8.50, mains €24-36; ☺1.30-4pm &
8-11pm; MBarceloneta) Catalan chef Carles
Abellán's stunning glass-encased, glossy-
tiled restaurant celebrates seafood in tapas
such as pickled octopus, mini anchovy
omelettes and fried oyster with salmon roe.
Even more showstopping are the mains:
grilled razor clams with *ponzu* citrus sauce,
squid filled with spicy poached egg yolk,
stir-fried sea cucumber, and lush lobster
paella with smoked prawns.

Grilled vegetable dish with olives and capers

Can Solé   Seafood €€€

(📞93 221 50 12; http://restaurantcansole.
com; Carrer de Sant Carles 4; mains €17-39;
⏰1-4pm & 8-11pm Tue-Thu, 1-4pm & 8.30-11pm
Fri & Sat, 1-4pm Sun; Ⓜ Barceloneta) Behind
imposing wooden doors, this elegant
restaurant with white-clothed tables and
white-jacketed waiters has been serving
seafood since 1903, and is now run by the
fourth generation of owners. Freshly landed
seafood stars in traditional dishes such
as *arròs caldòs* (rice broth with squid and
langoustines) and *zarzuela* (casserole with
ground almonds, saffron, garlic, tomatoes,
mussels, fish and white wine).

Torre d'Alta
Mar   Mediterranean €€€

(📞93 221 00 07; www.torredealtamar.com; Torre
de Sant Sebastià, Passeig de Joan de Borbó 88;
mains €34.50-44, 7-/9-course menus €80/96,
€112/135 with wine; ⏰1-3.30pm Tue-Thu,
1-3.30pm & 7.30-11pm Fri & Sat; 🚌V15, 39,
Ⓜ Barceloneta) Head 75m skyward to the top
of the 1929-built Teleférico del Puerto (p63)
cable-car tower Torre de Sant Sebastià, and
take a ringside seat for 360-degree views of
the harbour, beaches, city and mountains.
Menu highlights include salt-baked red
prawns, suckling Iberian pig, and squid and
bluefish stew.

Can Ros   Seafood €€€

(📞93 221 45 79; www.canros.cat; Carrer del Almirall Aixada 7; mains €15-29; ⏰1-4pm & 7-11pm
Tue-Sun; Ⓜ Barceloneta) The fifth generation
is now at the controls of this immutable
seafood favourite, which first opened in
1908. In a restaurant where the decor
is a reminder of simpler times, there's a
straightforward guiding principle: juicy
fresh fish cooked with a light touch.

⊗ Camp Nou, Pedralbes
& La Zona Alta

A Contraluz   Mediterranean €€

(📞93 203 06 58; www.acontraluz.com; Carrer
del Milanesat 19; mains €15-27; ⏰1.30-4pm &
8.30pm-midnight Mon-Sat, 1.30-4pm Sun; 🚉FGC

Les Tres Torres) The most magical place to
dine at this romantic restaurant is in the
bougainvillea-draped, tree-filled garden,
reached by an arbour. Olive-crusted monkfish with caramelised fennel, black paella
with squid and clams, and suckling pig with
fig jam are all outstanding choices.

Aspic   Cafe, Deli €€

(📞93 200 04 35; www.aspic.es; Avinguda de
Pau Casals 24; dishes €9-19.50; ⏰cafe 11am-
1.30pm & 6-8.30pm Tue-Sat, 11am-4pm Sun, deli
9am-8pm Tue-Sat, to 4pm Sun, bar to midnight
Tue-Sat, to 4pm Sun; 🚇⏰; 🚉T1, T2, T3 Francesc
Macià) Luxury ingredients (smoked salmon,
premium charcuterie and cheeses, high-
grade olive oils and carefully chosen Spanish wines) are utilised at the flagship cafe
of this Barcelona caterer in stunning dishes
like local carrelet fish with cockle foam and
broccoli purée. The attached deli is perfect
for picking up items for a gourmet picnic in
nearby Jardins del Poeta Eduard Marquina.

Vivanda   Catalan €€

(📞93 203 19 18; www.vivanda.cat; Carrer Major de
Sarrià 134; sharing plates €9-21; ⏰1.30-3.30pm
& 8.30-11pm Tue-Sat, 1.30-3.30pm Sun; 🚉FGC
Reina Elisenda) With a menu designed by
acclaimed Catalan chef Jordi Vilà, diners are
in for a treat at this Sarrià classic. Changing
dishes showcase seasonal fare, such as
eggs with truffles, rice with cuttlefish, and
artichokes with romesco sauce. Hidden
behind the restaurant is the tree-shaded
terrace.

El Asador de Aranda   Spanish €€

(📞93 417 01 15; www.asadordearanda.net;
Avinguda del Tibidabo 31; tapas €6-16.50, mains
€15-22.50; ⏰1-4.30pm & 8-11.30pm; 🚇; 🚉FGC
Avinguda Tibidabo) Set in a striking Modernista building, complete with stained-glass
windows, Moorish-style brick arches and
elaborate ceilings, El Asador de Aranda's
most popular seats are on the landscaped
terrace. You'll find a fine assortment of
tapas for sharing, though the speciality
is the meat (roast lamb, spare ribs, beef),
prepared in a wood oven.

La Balsa
Mediterranean €€€

(📞93 211 50 48; www.labalsarestaurant.com; Carrer de la Infanta Isabel 4; mains €20-28; ⏰1.30-3.30pm & 8.30-10.30pm Tue-Sat, 1.30-3.30pm Sun; 🚇; 🚉FGC Avinguda Tibidabo) With its grand ceiling and the scented gardens that surround the main terrace dining area, La Balsa is one of the city's premier dining addresses. The seasonally changing menu is a mix of traditional Catalan and creative expression (suckling pig with melon; cod confit with prune compote).

Via Veneto
Gastronomy €€€

(📞93 200 72 44; www.viaveneto.es; Carrer de Ganduxer 10; mains €28-52.50; ⏰1-4pm & 8-11.45pm Mon-Fri, 8-11.45pm Sat, closed Aug; 🚉FGC La Bonanova) Dalí was a regular in this high-society restaurant after it opened in 1967, and you can still dine at his favourite table today. The oval mirrors, orange-rose tablecloths, leather chairs and fine cutlery set the stage for intricate dishes such as smoked oysters with minced black bread, red mullet with chargrilled onion leaves.

⊗ El Raval

Sésamo
Vegetarian €

(Map p249; 📞93 441 64 11; Carrer de Sant Antoni Abat 52; mains €9-13; ⏰7pm-midnight Tue-Sun; 🚇🍴; 🚇Sant Antoni) Widely held to be the best veggie restaurant in the city (admittedly not as great an accolade as it might be elsewhere), Sésamo is a cosy, fun place. The menu is mainly tapas, and most people go for the seven-course tapas menu (€25, wine included), but there are a few more substantial dishes.

Granja M Viader
Cafe €

(Map p250; 📞93 318 34 86; www.granjaviader. cat; Carrer d'en Xuclà 6; ⏰9am-1pm & 5-9pm Mon-Sat; 🚇Liceu) For more than a century, people have been coming here for hot chocolate with whipped cream (ask for a *suís*) ladled out in this classically Catalan milk bar. In 1931, the Viader clan invented Cacaolat, a bottled chocolate milk drink, with iconic label design. The interior here is delightfully old-fashioned and the atmosphere always lively.

🍽 Seafood Heaven

There is a wealth of restaurants specialising in seafood. Not surprisingly Barceloneta, which lies near the sea, is packed with eateries of all shapes and sizes doling out decadent paellas, cauldrons of bubbling molluscs, grilled catches of the day and other delights. Nearest the sea, you'll find pricier open-air places with Mediterranean views; plunge into the narrow lanes to find the real gems, including bustling family-run places that serve first-rate plates at great prices.

Bar Pinotxo
Tapas €€

(Map p250; 📞93 317 17 31; www.pinotxobar.com; Mercat de la Boqueria; mains €9-17; ⏰7am-4pm Mon-Sat; 🚇Liceu) Bar Pinotxo is arguably La Boqueria's, and even Barcelona's, best tapas bar. The ever-charming owner, Juanito, might serve up chickpeas with pine nuts and raisins, a soft mix of potato and spinach sprinkled with salt, soft baby squid with cannellini beans, or a quivering cube of caramel-sweet pork belly.

Flax & Kale
Vegetarian €€

(Map p249; 📞93 317 56 64; www.teresacarles. com/fk/; Carrer dels Tallers 74; mains €13-18; ⏰9.30am-11.30pm Mon-Fri, from 10am Sat & Sun; 🚇🍴; 🚇Universitat) A far cry from the veggie restaurants of old, Flax & Kale marks a new approach (for Barcelona, at least) that declares that going meat-free does not mean giving up on choice, creativity or style. There are gluten-free and vegan options, and dishes include tacos with guacamole, aubergine and sour cashew cream, or Penang red curry.

Can Lluís
Catalan €€

(Map p249; 📞93 441 11 87; www.restaurantcan lluis.cat; Carrer de la Cera 49; mains €14-16; ⏰1.30-4pm & 8.30-11.30pm Mon-Sat; 🚇Sant Antoni) Three generations have kept this spick-and-span old-time classic in business since 1929. Beneath the olive-green beams in the back dining room you can see the spot where an anarchist's bomb went off in

👍 Top Tapas Plates

If you opt for *tapes*/tapas, it is handy to recognise some of the common items:

bombes/bombas large meat and potato croquettes

boquerons/boquerones white anchovies in vinegar – delicious and tangy

carxofes/alcachofas artichokes

gambes/gambas prawns, either done *al all/al ajillo* (with garlic), or *a la plantxa/plancha* (grilled)

navalles/navajas razor clams

patates braves/patatas bravas potato chunks bathed in a slightly spicy tomato sauce, sometimes mixed with mayonnaise

pop a feira/pulpo a la gallega tender boiled octopus with paprika

truita de patates/tortilla de patatas potato-filled omelette; one with vegetables is a *tortilla de verduras*

xampinyons/champiñones mushrooms

1946, killing the then owner. The restaurant is still going strong, however, with particularly good seafood dishes and a *menú del día* for €10.90.

Suculent   Catalan €€€

(Map p250; ☑93 443 65 79; www.suculent.com; Rambla del Raval 43; tasting menus €45-75; ☺1-4pm & 8-11.30pm Wed-Sun; ☎; MLiceu) Celebrity chef Carles Abellán adds to his stable with this old-style bistro, which showcases the best of Catalan cuisine. From the cod brandade to the oxtail stew with truffled sweet potato, only the best ingredients are used. There is no à la carte, just four different tasting menus to choose from.

🚫 Gràcia & Park Güell

Bar Bodega Quimet   Tapas €

(☑93 218 41 89; Carrer de Vic 23; tapas €3-11.50; ☺10am-11.30pm Mon-Fri, noon-11.30pm Sat & Sun; MFontana) A remnant from a bygone age, Bar Bodega Quimet is a delightfully atmospheric bar, with old bottles lining the walls, marble tables and a burnished wooden bar. The list of tapas and seafood is almost exhaustive, while another house speciality is *torrades* – huge slabs of toasted white bread topped with cured meats, fresh anchovies and sardines.

Chivuo's   Burgers €

(☑93 218 51 34; www.chivuos.com; Carrer del Torrent de l'Olla 175; burgers €7-9; ☺1-5pm & 7pm-midnight Mon-Sat; MFontana) Burgers and craft beers make a fine pair at this buzzing den. A mostly local crowd comes for huge burgers (served rare unless you specify otherwise) with house-made sauces – best ordered with fluffy, golden-fried *fritas* (chips). Mostly Catalan and Spanish brews, including excellent offerings from Barcelona-based Edge Brewing, Catalan Brewery, Napar and Garage Beer, rotate on the eight taps.

La Empanaderia de Gràcia   Empanadas €

(Map p254; Carrer de Francisco Giner 60; empanadas €1.95; ☺noon-4pm & 5.30-10pm; ⬛FGC Gràcia) For a cheap, filling snack, this corner empanaderia is a brilliant bet, serving scrumptious stuffed pastries. Each day, 20 different varieties are available: savoury flavours might include pumpkin and mozzarella, pear and goats cheese, hummus, celery and Roquefort or spicy beef and olive, while sweet styles span banana and honey to apple and cinnamon.

La Nena   Cafe €

(Map p254; ☑93 285 14 76; www.facebook.com/chocolaterialanena; Carrer de Ramon i Cajal 36; dishes €2-4.50; ☺8.30am-10.30pm Mon-Fri, 9am-10.30pm Sat & Sun; ⬤; MFontana) At this delightfully chaotic space, indulge in cups of *suïssos* (rich hot chocolate) served with a plate of heavy homemade whipped cream and *melindros* (spongy sweet biscuits), desserts and a few savoury dishes (including crêpes). The place is strewn with books, and you can play with the board games on the shelves.

La Panxa del Bisbe · Tapas €€

(Map p254; ☑93 213 70 49; Carrer del Torrent de les Flors 158; tapas €8.50-15, tasting menus €28-36; ☺1.30-3.30pm & 8.30pm-midnight Tue-Sat; Ⓜ Joanic) With low lighting and an artfully minimalist interior, the 'Bishop's Belly' serves creative tapas that earn high praise from the mostly local crowd. Feast on prawn-stuffed courgette flowers, grilled octopus with green chilli and watermelon, and slow-roasted lamb with mint couscous. Top off the meal with a bottle of wine such as an Albariño white from Galicia.

El Glop · Catalan €€

(Map p254; ☑93 213 70 58; www.elglop.com; Carrer de Sant Lluís 24; mains €8-20; ☺1pm-midnight Mon-Fri, noon-midnight Sat & Sun; Ⓜ Joanic) This raucous restaurant is decked out in country Catalan fashion, with gingham tablecloths and no-nonsense, slap-up meals. The secret is hearty portions of simple dishes, such as *cordero a la brasa* (grilled lamb), *paella de pescado y marisco* (fish and seafood paella) and appetisers like *berenjenas rellenas* (stuffed aubergines) or *calçots* in winter.

Café Godot · International €€

(Map p254; ☑93 368 20 36; www.cafegodot.com; Carrer de Sant Domènec 19; mains €10-18.50; ☺10am-1am Mon-Fri, 11am-2am Sat & Sun; Ⓜ Fontana) A stylish space of exposed brick, timber and tiles, opening to a garden out back, Godot is a relaxing place with an extensive menu, from white-wine-steamed mussels and scallops with Thai-style green curry to duck confit with lentils and spinach. Brunch is an American-style affair with eggs, crispy bacon and fluffy pancakes.

Con Gracia · Fusion €€€

(Map p254; ☑93 238 02 01; www.congracia.es; Carrer de Martínez de la Rosa 8; tasting menus €65, with wine €95; ☺7-11pm Tue-Sat; Ⓜ Diagonal) This teeny hideaway (seating about 20 in total) is a hive of originality, producing delicately balanced Mediterranean cuisine with Asian touches. On offer is a regularly changing surprise tasting menu or the set 'traditional' one (both six courses), with

dishes such as squid stuffed with *jamón ibérico* (cured ham) and black truffle, and sake-marinated tuna with walnut pesto.

Botafumeiro · Seafood €€€

(☑93 218 42 30; www.botafumeiro.es; Carrer Gran de Gràcia 81; mains €22-59; ☺noon-1am; Ⓜ Fontana) This temple of Galician shellfish has long been a magnet for VIPs visiting Barcelona. You can bring the price down by sharing a few *medias raciones* (large tapas plates) to taste a range of marine offerings, followed by mains like spider crab pie, squid ink paella or grilled spiny lobster.

Roig Robí · Catalan €€€

(Map p254; ☑93 218 92 22; www.roigrobi.com; Carrer de Sèneca 20; mains €21-36; ☺1.30-4pm & 8.30-11.30pm Mon-Fri, 8.30-11.30pm Sat; Ⓟ; Ⓜ Diagonal) At this altar to refined traditional cooking, the seasonally changing menu serves as a showcase for beautifully presented creations with local and organic ingredients. Start off with tomato crème with Gorgonzola ice cream, before moving on to outstanding seafood rice dishes, salt-baked market-fresh fish or slow-roasted Pyrenees lamb.

⊗ La Rambla & Barri Gòtic

La Plata · Tapas €

(Map p250; ☑93 315 10 09; www.barlaplata.com; Carrer de la Mercè 28; tapas €2.50-5; ☺9am-3.30pm & 6.30-11.30pm Mon-Sat; Ⓜ Jaume I) Tucked away on a narrow lane near the waterfront, La Plata is a humble but well-loved bodega that serves just three plates: *pescadito frito* (small fried fish), *butifarra* (sausage) and tomato salad. Add in the drinkable, affordable wines and you have the makings of a fine pre-dinner tapas spot.

Alcoba Azul · Mediterranean €

(Map p250; ☑93 302 81 41; Carrer de Sant Domènec del Call 14; mains €6-10; ☺6pm-midnight; ☎; Ⓜ Jaume I) Peel back the centuries inside this remarkably atmospheric watering hole, with medieval walls, low ceilings, wooden floors and flickering candles. Grab one of the seats at the tiny bar in front or slide into one of the table booths at the back, where you can enjoy good wines by the glass, satisfying plates of stuffed peppers, salads, *tostas* (sandwiches) and blood sausage with caramelised onions.

Milk
International €

(Map p250; ☑93 268 09 22; www.milkbarcelona. com; Carrer d'en Gignàs 21; mains €9-12; ⏰9am-2am Mon-Thu & Sun, to 2.30am Fri & Sat; 🛜; Ⓜ Jaume I) Also known to many as an enticing cocktail spot, Irish-run Milk's key role for Barcelona night owls is providing morning-after brunches (served till 4.30pm). Tuck into pancakes, eggs Benedict and other hangover dishes in a cosy lounge-like setting complete with ornate wallpaper, framed prints on the wall and cushion-lined seating. The musical selection is also notable.

Federal
Cafe €

(Map p250; ☑93 280 81 71; www.federalcafe.es; Passatge de la Pau 11; mains €7-10; ⏰9am-11pm Mon-Thu, to 11.30pm Fri & Sat, to 5pm Sun; 🛜; Ⓜ Drassanes) Don't be intimidated by the industrial chic, the sea of open MacBooks or the stack of design mags – this branch of the Poble Sec Federal mothership is incredibly welcoming, with healthy, hearty and good-value food. Choose a salad and a topping (poached eggs, strips of chicken) or a yellow curry, say, and follow it up with a moist slab of carrot cake.

Benedict
Brunch €

(Map p250; ☑93 250 75 11; www.benedictbcn. com; Carrer d'en Gignás 23; mains €10-11; ⏰9am-4pm Mon, 9am-4pm & 7pm-2am Tue-Fri, 9am-2.30am Sat & Sun; 🛜; Ⓜ Jaume I) As the name suggests, brunch is the main event at friendly little Benedict, with eggs prepared every which way and an option for the full English fry-up. There's also a list of hand-made burgers and club sandwiches, and in the evening various tapas are served, along with onion rings, deep-fried brie, chicken wings and other American favourites.

Xurreria
Churros €

(Map p250; ☑93 318 76 91; Carrer dels Banys Nous 8; cone €1.20; ⏰7am-1.30pm & 3.30-8.15pm Mon-Fri, 7am-2pm & 3.30-8.30pm Sat &

Sun; Ⓜ Jaume I) It doesn't look much from the outside, but this brightly lit street joint is Barcelona's best spot for paper cones of piping-hot churros – long batter sticks fried and sprinkled with sugar and best enjoyed dunked in hot chocolate.

La Vinateria del Call
Spanish €

(Map p250; ☑93 302 60 92; www.lavinateriadel call.com; Carrer de Sant Domènec del Call 9; raciones €7-12; ⏰7.30pm-1am; 🛜; Ⓜ Jaume I) In a magical setting in the former Jewish quarter, this tiny jewel-box of a restaurant serves up tasty Iberian dishes including Galician octopus, cider-cooked chorizo and the Catalan *escalivada* (roasted peppers, aubergine and onions) with anchovies. Portions are small and made for sharing, and there's a good and affordable selection of wines.

Cafè de l'Acadèmia
Catalan €€

(Map p250; ☑93 319 82 53; Carrer dels Lledó 1; mains €15-20; ⏰1-3.30pm & 8-11pm Mon-Fri; 🛜; Ⓜ Jaume I) Expect a mix of traditional Catalan dishes with the occasional creative twist. At lunchtime, local city hall workers pounce on the *menú del día* (€15.75). In the evening it is rather more romantic, as low lighting emphasises the intimacy of the beamed ceiling and stone walls.

Belmonte
Tapas €€

(Map p250; ☑93 310 76 84; Carrer de la Mercè 29; tapas €4-10, mains €13-14; ⏰8pm-midnight Tue-Fri, 1-3.30pm & 8pm-midnight Sat Jul-Oct, 7.30pm-midnight Tue-Thu, 1-3.30pm & 7.30pm-midnight Fri & Sat Nov-Jun; 🛜; Ⓜ Jaume I) This tiny tapas joint in the southern reaches of Barri Gòtic whips up beautifully prepared small plates – including an excellent *truita* (tortilla), rich *patatons a la sal* (salted new potatoes with romesco sauce) and tender *carpaccio de pop* (octopus carpaccio). Wash it down with the homemade *vermut* (vermouth).

Can Culleretes
Catalan €€

(Map p250; ☑93 317 30 22; www.culleretes.com; Carrer d'en Quintana 5; mains €10-18; ⏰1.30-3.45pm & 8-10.45pm Tue-Sat, 1.30-3.45pm Sun; 🛜; Ⓜ Liceu) Founded in 1786, Barcelona's oldest restaurant is still going strong, with tourists and locals flocking here to enjoy its rambling interior, old-fashioned tile-filled decor and enormous helpings of traditional Catalan food, including fresh seafood and sticky stews.

Pla   Fusion €€

(Map p250; ☑93 412 65 52; www.restaurantpla. cat; Carrer de la Bellafila 5; mains €17-23; ⏰1.30-5.30pm & 7-11.30pm Sun-Thu, to midnight Fri & Sat; 🛜; Ⓜ Jaume I) One of Gòtic's long-standing favourites, Pla is a stylish, romantically lit medieval dining room where the cooks churn out such temptations as oxtail braised in red wine, seared tuna with oven-roasted peppers, and polenta with seasonal mushrooms.

Rasoterra   Vegetarian €€

(Map p250; ☑93 318 69 26; www.rasoterra.cat; Carrer del Palau 5; platillos €6-10, lunch menu €13; ⏰1-4pm & 7-11pm Tue-Sun; 🛜🌿; Ⓜ Jaume I) Slow food advocates at Rasoterra cook up first-rate vegetarian dishes in a Zen-like setting with tall ceilings, low-playing jazz and fresh flowers on the tables. The creative, globally influenced menu changes regularly

and might feature Vietnamese-style coconut pancakes with tofu and vegetables, beluga lentils with basmati rice, and pear and goat cheese quesadillas. Good vegan and gluten-free options.

Ocaña   International €€

(Map p250; ☑93 676 48 14; www.ocana.cat; Plaça Reial 13; mains €9.50-16; ⏰noon-2am Sun-Thu, to 2.30am Fri & Sat; 🛜; Ⓜ Liceu) A flamboyant but elegantly designed space of high ceilings, chandeliers and plush furnishings, Ocaña blends late-night carousing with serious eating. The Spanish and Catalan dishes are given a creative and successful twist, and are now complemented on Thursday, Friday and Saturday nights with a superb selection of Mexican dishes.

Cerería   Vegetarian €€

(Map p250; ☑93 301 85 10; Baixada de Sant Miquel 3; mains €8-15; ⏰1-11pm Tue-Sat, to 6pm Sun; 🛜🌿; Ⓜ Jaume I) Black-and-white marble floors, a smattering of old wooden tables and ramshackle displays of musical instruments lend a certain bohemian charm to this small vegetarian restaurant. The

Gambas al ajillo (Prawns with garlic)

KANKITTI CHUPAYOONG/SHUTTERSTOC ©

pizzas are delicious and feature organic ingredients – as do the flavourful galettes, dessert crêpes and bountiful salads. Vegan options too.

Opera Samfaina   Catalan €€

(Map p250; 📞93 481 78 71; www.operasamfaina. com; La Rambla 51; mains €11-15, Odissea tasting menu adult/child under 12yr €33/€20; 🕑6pm-midnight Mon-Wed, to 1am Thu & Fri, 1pm-1am Sat, 1pm-midnight Sun; MLiceu) A surreal sensory experience deep in the bowels of the Liceu opera house. Enter through the Vermuteria, a tenebrous tapas bar, and then either head to the Odissea – a shared table, surrounded by audiovisuals – for a tasting menu of traditional Catalan dishes; or down to the Opera Prima, a dreamlike labyrinth of wine and tapas bars and psychedelic installations.

Koy Shunka   Japanese €€€

(Map p250; 📞93 412 79 39; www.koyshunka. com; Carrer de Copons 7; tasting menu €89-132; 🕑1.30-3pm & 8.30-11pm Tue-Sat, 1.30-3pm Sun; MUrquinaona) Down a narrow lane north of the cathedral, Koy Shunka opens a portal to exquisite dishes from the East – mouthwatering sushi, sashimi, seared Wagyu beef and flavour-rich seaweed salads are served alongside inventive fusion dishes such as steamed clams with sake or tempura of scallops and king prawns with Japanese mushrooms. Don't miss the house speciality of tender *toro* (tuna belly).

Els Quatre Gats   Catalan €€€

(Map p250; 📞93 302 41 40; www.4gats.com; Carrer de Montsió 3; mains €23-29; 🕑1-4pm & 7pm-1am; MUrquinaona) Once the lair of Barcelona's Modernista artists, Els Quatre Gats is a stunning example of the movement, inside and out, with its colourful tiles, geometric brickwork and wooden fittings. The restaurant is not quite as thrilling as its setting, though you can just have a coffee and a croissant in the cafe at the front.

Caelum   Cafe €

(Map p250; 📞93 302 69 93; Carrer de la Palla 8; 🕑10am-8.30pm Mon-Fri, to 9pm Sat & Sun; 📶; MLiceu) Centuries of heavenly gastronomic

tradition from across Spain are concentrated in this exquisite medieval space in the heart of the city. The upstairs cafe is a dainty setting for decadent cakes and pastries, while descending into the underground chamber with its stone walls and flickering candles is like stepping into the Middle Ages.

Cafè de l'Òpera   Cafe €

(Map p250; 📞93 317 75 85; www.cafeoperabcn. com; La Rambla 74; 🕑8am-2am; 📶; MLiceu) Opposite the Gran Teatre del Liceu is La Rambla's most traditional cafe. Operating since 1929 and still popular with operagoers, it is pleasant enough for an early evening libation or, in the morning, coffee and croissants. Head upstairs for a seat overlooking the busy boulevard, and try the house speciality, the *cafè de l'Òpera* (coffee with chocolate mousse).

La Granja   Cafe €

(Map p250; 📞93 302 69 75; Carrer dels Banys Nous 4; 🕑9am-9pm; 📶; MJaume I) This long-running cafe serves up thick, rich cups of chocolate, in varying formats, but it doesn't make its own churros. Buy them a few doors down at Xurreria (p140) and bring them here for the perfect combo of churros dipped in chocolate.

Salterio   Cafe €

(Map p250; 📞93 302 50 28; Carrer de Sant Domènec del Call 4; 🕑noon-1am; 📶; MJaume I) A wonderfully photogenic candlelit spot tucked down a tiny lane in El Call, Salterio serves Turkish coffee, authentic mint teas and snacks amid stone walls, incense and ambient Middle Eastern music. If hunger strikes, try the *sardo* (grilled flat-bread covered with pesto, cheese or other toppings).

Čaj Chai   Cafe €

(Map p250; 📞93 301 95 92; www.cajchai.com; Carrer de Sant Domènec del Call 12; 🕑10.30am-10pm; MJaume I) Inspired by Prague's bohemian tearooms, this bright and buzzing cafe in the heart of the old Jewish quarter is a tea connoisseur's paradise. Čaj Chai stocks around 200 teas from China, India, Korea, Japan, Nepal, Morocco and beyond. It's a much-loved local haunt.

La Ribera

Euskal Etxea — Tapas €

(Map p250; 93 310 21 85; www.euskaletxea
taberna.com; Placeta de Montcada 1; tapas €2.10;
10am-12.30am Sun-Thu, to 1am Fri & Sat;
Jaume I) Barcelona has plenty of Basque
and pseudo-Basque tapas bars, but this
is the real deal. It captures the feel of San
Sebastián better than many of its newer
competitors. Choose your *pintxos* (Basque
tapas piled on slices of bread), sip *txacolí*
(Basque white wine) and keep the tooth-
picks so the staff can count them up and
work out your bill.

Bormuth — Tapas €

(Map p250; 93 310 21 86; Carrer del Rec 31;
tapas €4-10; noon-1.30am Sun-Thu, to 2.30am
Fri & Sat; Jaume I) Bormuth has tapped
into the vogue for old-school tapas with
modern-day service and decor, and serves
all the old favourites – *patatas bravas, en-
saladilla* (Russian salad) and tortilla – along
with some less predictable and superbly
prepared numbers (try the chargrilled red
pepper with black pudding).

En Aparté — French €

(93 269 13 35; www.enaparte.es; Carrer de
Lluís el Piadós 2; mains €8.50-13; 10am-1am
Mon-Thu, to 2am Fri & Sat, to 12.30am Sun;
Arc de Triomf) A great low-key place to eat
good-quality French food, just off the quiet
Plaça de Sant Pere. The restaurant is small
but spacious, with sewing-machine tables
and vintage details, and floor-to-ceiling
windows that bring in some wonderful
early-afternoon sunlight.

Paradiso/Pastrami Bar — Smokery €

(Map p250; 639 310671; www.rooftopsmoke
house.com; Carrer de Rera Palau 4; mains €7-9;
7pm-2am Mon-Thu, to 3am Fri & Sat;
Barceloneta) A kind of Narnia-in-reverse,
Paradiso is fronted with a snowy-white
space, not much bigger than a wardrobe,
with pastrami sandwiches, pulled pork and
other home-cured delights. But this is only
the portal – pull open the huge wooden

fridge door, and step through into a glam,
sexy speakeasy of a cocktail bar guaranteed
to raise the most world-weary of eyebrows.

Nakashita — Japanese €€

(93 295 53 78; www.nakashitabcn.com; Carrer
del Rec Comtal 15; mains €12-22; 1.30-4pm &
8.30pm-midnight Mon-Sun; Arc de Triomf)
Brazil's particular immigration story means
it has a tradition of superb Japanese food,
and the Brazilian chef at Nakashita is no
slouch, turning out excellent sashimi, maki
rolls, soft shell crab and kakiage (a mix of
tempura). One of the best Japanese restaurants in the city, with just a handful of tables.

Cal Pep — Tapas €€

(Map p250; 93 310 79 61; www.calpep.com;
Plaça de les Olles 8; mains €13-20; 7.30-
11.30pm Mon, 1-3.45pm & 7.30-11.30pm Tue-Sat,
closed last 3 weeks Aug; Barceloneta) It's
getting a foot in the door of this legendary
fish restaurant that's the problem – there
can be queues out into the square. And if
you want one of the five tables out the back,
you'll need to call ahead. Most people are
happy elbowing their way to the bar for
some of the tastiest seafood tapas in town.

El Atril — International €€

(93 310 12 20; www.elatrilbarcelona.es; Carrer
dels Carders 23; mains €11-18; 11am-11.30pm
Sun-Thu, to midnight Fri & Sat; Jaume I) El
Atril is influenced by culinary flavours from
all over the globe, so while you'll see plenty
of tapas (the *patatas bravas* are recommended), you'll also find kangaroo fillet,
moules frites, duck cannelloni and a good
selection of substantial salads. There's also
a mix of meats you can cook yourself on a
salt block (€19, minimum two people).

Casa Delfín — Catalan €€

(Map p250; 93 319 50 88; www.tallerdetapas.
com/eng/casa-delfin; Passeig del Born 36;
mains €10-17; 8am-midnight Sun-Thu, to 1am
Fri & Sat; Jaume I) One of Barcelona's
culinary delights, Casa Delfín is everything
you dream of when you think of Catalan
(and Mediterranean) cooking. Start with
the tangy and sweet *calçots* (February and
March only) or salt-strewn *Padrón* peppers,

Barcelona on a Plate

Typical accompaniment to *mar i muntanya* (meat and seafood combination) dishes.

Bread or toast is used as a thickener.

Traditionally made with dried *cuerno de cabra* ('goat horn') peppers.

The nuts can be almonds, hazelnuts, pine nuts or a combination.

Tastes great over grilled fish.

Salsa Romesco

NITO/SHUTTERSTOCK ©

A Catalan Classic

This classic Catalan sauce pervades the region's cuisine, popping up in numerous dishes as an accompaniment to roasted vegetables, grilled meats and fish. It's a rich, garlicky, nutty combination based on peppers and tomatoes. A thickened version, *salvitxada*, is the de rigueur dipping accompaniment for the late winter barbecues of *calçots*, the delicious leek-like onions beloved of Catalans.

Calçots with romesco sauce
ALEXANDRE AROCAS/SHUTTERSTOCK ©

☆ Top Five for Romesco Dishes

El 58 This French-Catalan place serves imaginative, beautifully prepared tapas dishes.

Vivanda Magnificent Catalan cooking with dishes showcasing seasonal fare.

Belmonte This tiny tapas joint in the southern reaches of Barri Gòtic whips up beautifully prepared small plates.

Casa Delfín A culinary delight, this place is everything you dream of when you think of Catalan (and Mediterranean) cooking.

El Glop The secret to this raucous restaurant is no-nonsense, slap-up meals.

moving on to grilled sardines speckled with parsley, then tackle the meaty monkfish roasted in white wine and garlic.

Bar del Pla   Tapas €€

(Map p250; ☎93 268 30 03; www.bardelpla.cat; Carrer de Montcada 2; mains €12-16; ☺noon-11pm Mon-Thu, to midnight Fri & Sat; ☎; MJaume I) A bright and occasionally rowdy place, with glorious Catalan tiling, a vaulted ceiling and bottles of wine lining the walls. At first glance, the tapas at informal Bar del Pla are traditionally Spanish, but the riffs on a theme display an assured touch. Try the ham croquettes, the wagyu burger, T-bone steak or the marinated salmon, yoghurt and mustard.

Bar del Convent   Cafe

(☎93 256 50 17; www.bardelconvent.com; Plaça de l'Acadèmia; ☺10am-9pm Tue-Sat; ﹢; MArc de Triomf) Alongside the Gothic arches of what remains of the Sant Agusti convent's cloister is this pleasant cafe-bar – particularly good for people with children. Kids often play football in the cloister grounds, and there are children's books and toys in the cafe itself. You can also enter at Carrer del Comerç 36 through James Turrell's light sculpture.

✪ La Sagrada Família & L'Eixample

Tapas 24   Tapas €

(Map p254; ☎93 488 09 77; www.carlesabellan. com; Carrer de la Diputació 269; tapas €2.20-12; ☺9am-midnight; ☎; MPasseig de Gràcia) Hotshot chef Carles Abellán runs this basement tapas haven known for its gourmet versions of old faves. Highlights include the *bikini* (toasted ham and cheese sandwich – here the ham is cured and the truffle makes all the difference) and zesty *boquerones al limón* (lemon-marinated anchovies).

Copasetic   Cafe €

(Map p249; ☎93 532 76 66; www.copasetic barcelona.com; Carrer de la Diputació 55; mains €6-13.50; ☺10.30am-midnight Tue & Wed, to 1am Thu, to 2am Fri & Sat, to 5.30pm Sun; ☎☂; MRocafort) Decked out with retro furniture,

Copasetic has a fun, friendly vibe. The menu holds plenty for everyone, whether your thing is eggs Benedict, wild-berry tartlets or a juicy burger. There are lots of vegetarian, gluten-free and organic options, and superb weekend brunches. Lunch *menús* (Tuesday to Friday) cost between €9.50 and €12.

Cremeria Toscana   Gelato €

(☎93 539 38 25; www.cremeriatoscana.es; Carrer de Muntaner 161; ice cream €2.80-5.40; ☺1pm-midnight Mon-Thu, to 1am Fri & Sat, noon-midnight Sun Apr-Oct, 1-9pm Tue-Thu, to 11pm Fri & Sat, noon-11pm Sun Nov-Mar; MHospital Clínic) At the most authentic gelato outlet in town, all flavours are natural and most are gluten-free. Along with classic Italian choices such as creamy *stracciatella* and wavy hazelnut *nocciola* are more unusual offerings such as goats cheese and caramelised fig, pear and chocolate or plum and pink grapefruit. Buy a cone or a tub.

Cafè del Centre   Cafe €

(Map p254; ☎93 488 11 01; Carrer de Girona 69; ☺9am-11pm Mon-Fri, 11am-11pm Sat; ☎; MGirona) Step back into the 19th century in this cafe that's been in business since 1873. The mahogany bar extends down the right side as you enter, fronted by marble-topped tables and wooden chairs. It exudes an almost melancholy air by day but gets busy at night, when live jazz piano plays. It stocks 50 beers and 15 loose-leaf teas.

Cosmo   Cafe €

(Map p254; ☎93 105 79 92; www.galeriacosmo. com; Carrer d'Enric Granados 3; ☺10am-10pm; MUniversitat) Set on a pedestrian strip just behind the university, this groovy cafe-gallery has a bicycle hanging from the high, white walls, bright splashy murals and gaily painted ventilation pipes, and even makes a feature of its fire hose. Along with fresh juices, hot chocolate, teas, pastries and snacks, it serves beer and wine.

Auto Rosellon   International €€

(Map p254; ☎93 853 93 20; www.autorosellon. com; Carrer de Rosselló 182; mains €12-18; ☺8am-1am Mon-Wed, 8am-2am Thu & Fri, 9am-2am Sat, 9am-midnight Sun; ☎☂; ℝFGC

 Markets

Barcelona has some fantastic food markets. Foodies will enjoy the sounds, smells and, most importantly, tastes of the **Mercat de la Boqueria** (p48). This is probably Spain's biggest and best market, and it's conveniently located right off La Rambla. Here you can find temptations of all sorts – plump fruits and veggies, freshly squeezed juices, artisanal cheeses, smoked meats, seafood and pastries. The best feature: an array of tapas bars and food stalls where you can sample amazingly fresh ingredients cooked to perfection. Some other great market options:

Mercat de Sant Antoni (p169)
Mercat de Santa Caterina (p110)
Mercat del Ninot (p168)
Mercat de l'Abaceria Central (p162)
Mercat de la Llibertat (www.mercatsbcn. com; Plaça de la Llibertat 27; ⊗8am-8pm Mon-Fri, to 3pm Sat; ℝFGC Gràcia)

Tapas at the Mercat de la Boqueria
DEATONPHOTOS/SHUTTERSTOCK ©

Provença) ✓ With cornflower-blue paintwork and all its fresh produce on display, Auto Rosellon utilises mostly organic ingredients sourced from small producers and its own garden in dishes from eggs Benedict to salmon tartare with avocado, ricotta gnocchi with confit tomatoes and thyme, and slow-roasted pork tacos. Homemade juices and rose lemonade are exceptional; there are also great cocktails and craft beers.

Casa Amalia Catalan €€
(Map p254; ☑93 458 94 58; www.casamaliabcn. com; Passatge del Mercat 4-6; mains €9-20; ⊗1-3.30pm & 9-10.30pm Tue-Sat, 1-3.30pm Sun; MGirona) This very local split-level restaurant is popular for its hearty Catalan cooking that uses fresh produce from the busy market next door. On Thursdays during winter it offers the mountain classic, *escudella* (Catalan stew). Otherwise, try light variations on local cuisine like the *bacallà al allioli de poma* (cod in apple-based aioli sauce). The three-course *menú del día* is a bargain at €15.50.

Cerveseria Catalana Tapas €€
(Map p254; ☑93 216 03 68; Carrer de Mallorca 236; tapas €3-14; ⊗9am-1.30am; ℝFGC Provença) The 'Catalan Brewery' is perfect at all hours: for a morning coffee and croissant, or sangria, *montaditos* (canapés) and tapas at lunch or dinner. You can sit at the bar, on the pavement terrace or in the restaurant at the back. The variety of hot tapas, salads and other snacks draws a well-dressed crowd. No reservations.

Entrepanes Díaz Sandwiches €
(Map p254; ☑93 415 75 82; Carrer de Pau Claris 189; sandwiches €6-10, tapas €3-10; ⊗1pm-midnight; MDiagonal) Gourmet sandwiches, from roast beef to suckling pig or crispy squid with squid-ink aioli, are the highlight at this sparkling old-style bar, along with sharing plates of Spanish specialities such as sea urchins and prawn fritters or blood-sausage croquettes. The policy of only hiring experienced waiters over 50 lends a certain gravitas to the operation and some especially charming service.

Parking Pizza Pizza €€
(☑93 633 96 45; www.parkingpizza.com; Carrer de Londres 98; pizza €9.50-14.50; ⊗1-4pm & 8-11pm Mon-Sat, 1-4pm Sun; ℝFGC Provença) In this garage-style space, you might well have to share a long unvarnished wooden table, squeezed in on a cardboard box stool. The wood-fired pizzas more than make up for any forced intimacy, however, as do the

starters, which include a creamy *burrata 'stracciatella'* and a superb red quinoa salad with guacamole and a poached egg.

Chicha Limoná   Mediterranean €€

(Map p254; ☑93 277 64 03; www.chichalimona. com; Passeig de Sant Joan 80; mains €12-17; ☺9.30am-1am Tue-Thu, to 2am Fri & Sat, to 5pm Sun; ☎; ⓂTetuan) Passeig de Sant Joan is a hipster hot spot, and bright, bustling Chicha Limoná has provided them with somewhere great to eat. Steak tartare with yuzu dressing, rabbit tacos, yoghurt-marinated salmon, and tequila, mango and chilli sorbet are among the oft-changing dishes (set menu €13.90), along with steaming pizza.

Can Kenji   Japanese €€

(Map p254; ☑93 476 18 23; www.cankenji.com; Carrer del Rosselló 325; mains €10-14; ☺1-3.30pm & 8.30-11pm; ⓂVerdaguer) The chef of this understated little *izakaya* (the Japanese version of a tavern) gets his ingredients fresh from the city's markets, with traditional Japanese recipes receiving a Mediterranean touch. Choices include sardine tempura with an aubergine, miso and anchovy purée, or *tataki* (lightly grilled meat) of *bonito* (tuna) with *salmorejo* (a Cordoban cold tomato and bread soup).

Disfrutar   Modern European €€€

(☑93 348 68 96; http://en.disfrutarbarcelona. com; Carrer de Villarroel 163; tasting menus €120-185; ☺1-2.45pm & 8-9.45pm Tue-Sat; ⓂHospital Clínic) Disfrutar ('enjoy' in Catalan) is among the city's finest restaurants, with two Michelin stars. Run by alumni of Ferran Adrià's game-changing (now closed) El Bulli restaurant, nothing is as it seems, such as black and green olives that are actually chocolate ganache with orange blossom water.

Lasarte   Modern European €€€

(Map p254; ☑93 445 32 42; www.restaurant lasarte.com; Carrer de Mallorca 259; mains €52-58; ☺1.30-3.30pm & 8.30-10.30pm Tue-Sat, closed first 3 weeks Aug; ⓂDiagonal) One of the preeminent restaurants in Barcelona – and the city's first to gain three Michelin stars –

Lasarte is overseen by lauded chef Martín Berasategui. From Duroc pigs' trotters with quince to squid tartare with kaffir consommé, this is seriously sophisticated stuff, served in an ultra-contemporary dining room by waitstaff who could put the most overawed diners at ease.

Mont Bar   Bistro €€€

(☑93 323 95 90; www.montbar.com; Carrer de la Diputació 220; tapas €2-13, mains €12.50-26.50; ☺noon-3.30pm & 7pm-midnight; ⓂUniversitat) Named after the owner's Val d'Aran hometown, this stylish wine-bar-style space with black-and-white floors, forest-green banquette and bottle-lined walls offers next-level cooking. Exquisite tapas (pigs trotters with baby shrimp; plankton meringue with sea anemone and Mascarpone) precede 'small plate' mains (eg tuna belly with pine nut emulsion) and showstopping desserts (sheep's milk ice cream with blackcurrant liqueur sauce). Reservations essential.

Cinc Sentits   International €€€

(Map p254; ☑93 323 94 90; www.cincsentits. com; Carrer d'Aribau 58; tasting menus €100-120; ☺1.30-2.30pm & 8.30-9.30pm Tue-Sat; ⓂPasseig de Gràcia) Enter the realm of the 'Five Senses' to indulge in a jaw-dropping tasting menu consisting of a series of small, experimental dishes (there is no à la carte, although dishes can be tweaked to suit diners' requests). The use of fresh local produce, such as Costa Brava line-caught fish and top-quality Extremadura suckling pig, is key.

Casa Calvet   Catalan €€€

(Map p254; ☑93 412 40 12; www.casacalvet.es; Carrer de Casp 48; mains €27-35; ☺1-3.30pm & 8-10.30pm Mon-Sat; ⓂUrquinaona) An early Gaudí masterpiece loaded with his trademark curvy features houses a swish restaurant (just to the right of the building's main entrance). Dress up and ask for an intimate *taula cabina* (wooden booth). You could opt for scallop- and prawn-stuffed artichokes, partridge and chestnut casserole or veal with duck liver sauce.

Speakeasy International €€€

(☑93 217 50 80; www.drymartiniorg.com; Carrer d'Aribau 162; mains €18.50-28; ☺8-11pm Mon-Sat; ℝFGC Provença) This clandestine restaurant lurks behind the Dry Martini bar (p187). You will be shown a door through the open kitchen area to the 'storeroom', lined with hundreds of bottles of backlit, quality tipples. Tempting menu options might include prawn ravioli with parmesan crème or venison with braised celery.

Monvínic Spanish €€€

(Map p254; ☑93 272 61 87; www.monvinic. com; Carrer de la Diputació 249; mains €17-36; ☺1.30-3.30pm & 8-10.30pm Tue-Fri, 8-10.30pm Mon & Sat; ℳPasseig de Gracia) ✿ Opening to a leafy, table-filled garden, this is the 'espacio culinario' of world-famous wine emporium Monvínic (p186). The menu offers elaborate confections such as sea urchin and lobster consommé, char-grilled duck with red wine-poached pears or langoustine ravioli. Its ingredients, wine and building materials are all sourced from Catalonia.

✪ Montjuïc, Poble Sec & Sant Antoni

Federal Cafe €

(Map p256; ☑93 187 36 07; www.federalcafe.es; Carrer del Parlament 39; mains €9-12; ☺8am-11pm Mon-Thu, 8am-1am Fri, 9am-1am Sat, 9am-5.30pm Sun; 🛜🍴; ℳSant Antoni) On a stretch that now teems with cafes, Australian-run Federal was the trailblazer, with its good coffee (including a decent flat white) and superb brunches. Later in the day, healthy, tasty options span snacks (prawn toast, polenta chips with gorgonzola) to larger dishes like veggie burgers or grilled salmon with soba noodles.

Agust Gastrobar Bistro €€

(Map p249; ☑93 162 67 33; www.agustbarcelona. com; Carrer del Parlament 54; mains €12.50-24; ☺kitchen 7pm-midnight Mon-Thu, 2pm-midnight Fri-Sun, bar to 2am; ℳPoble Sec) Set up by two French chefs (one of whom trained under Gordon Ramsay), Agust occupies a fabulous mezzanine space with timber

beams, exposed brick and textured metro tiles. Baby scallops with seaweed butter and prawn-stuffed avocado cannelloni are savoury standouts; desserts include the extraordinary 'el cactus' (chocolate-crumble soil, mojito mousse and prickly pear sorbet) served in a terracotta flower pot.

Quimet i Quimet Tapas €

(Map p256; ☑93 442 31 42; Carrer del Poeta Cabanyes 25; tapas €4-10, montaditos €2.80-4; ☺noon-4pm & 7-10.30pm Mon-Fri, noon-4pm Sat, closed Aug; ℳParal·lel) Quimet i Quimet is a family-run business that has been passed down from generation to generation. There's barely space to swing a *calamar* (squid) in this bottle-lined, standing-room-only place, but it is a treat for the palate, with *montaditos* (tapas on a slice of bread) made to order.

Mano Rota Bistro €€

(Map p256; ☑93 164 80 41; www.manorota.com; Carrer de la Creu dels Molers 4; mains €15-22; ☺8-11.30pm Mon, 1-3.30pm & 8-11.30pm Tue-Sat, 1-3.30pm Sun; ℳPoble Sec) Exposed brick, aluminium pipes, industrial light fittings and recycled timbers create a hip, contemporary setting for inspired bistro cooking at Mano Rota (which literally translates as 'broken hand', but is actually a Spanish idiom for consummate skill). Asian, South American and Mediterranean flavours combine in dishes such as crispy squid with yuzu aioli or *dorade* (bream) with pak choy pesto.

Lascar 74 Peruvian €€

(Map p256; ☑93 017 98 72; www.lascar.es; Carrer del Roser 74; mains €12-15; ☺7-11.30pm Mon-Thu, 2-5pm & 7pm-11.30pm Fri-Sun; ℳParal·lel) At this self-styled 'ceviche and pisco bar', exquisite Peruvian ceviches are served alongside renditions from Thailand, Japan and Mexico, and oyster shooters with *leche de tigre* (the traditional ceviche marinade). Pisco sours are the real deal.

Malamén Catalan €€

(Map p256; ☑93 252 77 63; www.malamen.es; Carrer de Blai 53; mains €12-24; ☺8pm-midnight Tue-Sun; ℳPoble Sec) Carrer de Blai is lined with bars and restaurants, but Malamén

🍽️ Vegetarians & Vegans

Vegetarians, and especially vegans, can have a hard time in Spain, but in Barcelona a growing battery of vegetarian restaurants offers welcome relief. Be careful when ordering salads (such as the *amanida catalana*), which may contain popular 'vegetables' such as ham or tuna.

towers above most for its elegant art deco-inspired design, immaculate service and gourmet versions of Catalan classics. Its shortish menu spans confit tuna, dill and caper salad to a juicy steak with creamed mushrooms and blue cheese croquettes. The wine list is equally concise.

Palo Cortao   Tapas €€

(Map p256; ☎93 188 90 67; www.palocortao.es; Carrer de Nou de la Rambla 146; mains €10-15; ⏰8pm-1am Tue-Fri, 1-5pm & 8pm-1am Sat & Sun; Ⓜ Paral·lel) Contemporary Palo Cortao is renowned for its beautifully executed seafood and meat dishes, served at fair prices. Highlights include roast oxtail with vermouth jus, octopus with white bean hummus, smoked mackerel with pickled jalapeño and tuna tataki tempura.

Bodega 1900   Tapas €€

(Map p256; ☎93 325 26 59; www.bodega1900. com; Carrer de Tamarit 91; tapas €6-15; ⏰1-10.30pm Tue-Sat, closed Aug; Ⓜ Poble Sec) Bodega 1900 mimics an old-school tapas and vermouth bar, but don't be fooled: this venture from the world-famous Adrià brothers creates gastronomic tapas such as its *mollete de calamars*, probably the best squid sandwich in the world, hot from the pan and served with chipotle mayonnaise, kimchi and lemon zest; and 'spherified' reconstructed olives.

Oleum   Mediterranean €€

(Map p256; ☎93 289 06 79; www.oleum restaurant.com; 1st floor, Museu Nacional d'Art de Catalunya (MNAC), Mirador del Palau Nacional; mains €14-21; ⏰12.30-4pm Tue-Thu & Sun,

12.30-4pm & 8.30-11pm Fri & Sat; ☐55, Ⓜ Espanya) Situated in the former throne room of the Palau Nacional, Oleum has soaring ceilings and gorgeous city views. The regularly changing Mediterranean menu is small but well executed. A meal here combines perfectly with a visit to the Museu Nacional d'Art de Catalunya (MNAC; p56), where the restaurant resides (no museum ticket is required to dine here).

Enigma   Gastronomy €€€

(Map p256; ☎616 696322; www.enigmaconcept. es; Carrer de Sepúlveda 38-40; tasting menu €220; ⏰1-4pm & 4.30-10.30pm Tue-Fri, noon-5.30pm & 6-10.30pm Sat; Ⓜ Espanya) Resembling a 3D art installation, this conceptual offering from the famed Adrià brothers is a 40-course tour de force of cutting-edge gastronomy across six different dining spaces. A meal takes 3½ hours all-up and includes customised cocktail pairings (you can order additional drinks). There's a minimum of two diners; reserve months in advance. A €100 deposit is required upon booking.

Tickets   Tapas, Gastronomy €€€

(Map p256; ☎93 292 42 50; www.ticketsbar. es; Avinguda del Paral·lel 164; tapas €3-26; ⏰7-11.30pm Tue-Fri, 1-3.30pm & 7-11.30pm Sat, closed Aug; Ⓜ Paral·lel) A flamboyant affair playing with circus images and theatre lights, this is one of the sizzling tickets in the restaurant world, a Michelin-starred tapas bar opened by Ferran Adrià, of the legendary (since closed) El Bulli, and his brother Albert. Bookings are only taken online two months in advance, but you can try calling for last-minute cancellations.

Martínez   Spanish €€€

(Map p256; ☎93 106 60 52; www.martinez barcelona.com; Carretera de Miramar 38; mains €21.50-32; ⏰1-11pm; ☐21, ☐ Teleférico del Puerto) With a fabulous panorama over the city and port, Martínez is a standout among the lacklustre dining options atop Montjuïc. On warm days, head to the outdoor terrace for its signature rice and paella dishes (€38 to €62 for two). There are also oysters, calamari, fresh market fish and other seafood hits, plus *jamón* and grilled meat dishes.

TREASURE HUNT

Begin your shopping adventure

Treasure Hunt

If your doctor has prescribed an intense round of retail therapy to deal with the blues, then Barcelona is the place. Across Ciutat Vella (Barri Gòtic, El Raval and La Ribera), L'Eixample and Gràcia is spread a thick mantle of boutiques, historic shops, original one-off stores, gourmet corners, wine dens and designer labels. You name it, you'll find it here.

For high fashion, design, jewellery and department stores, the principal shopping axis starts on Plaça de Catalunya, proceeds up Passeig de Gràcia and turns left into Avinguda Diagonal, along which it extends as far as Plaça de la Reina Maria Cristina. The densely packed section between Plaça de Francesc Macià and Plaça de la Reina Maria Cristina is an especially good hunting ground.

In This Section

Useful Phrases

I'd like to buy... *Quería comprar...* ke·ria kom·prar...

I'm just looking *Sólo estoy mirando* so·lo es·toy mee·ran·do

Can I look at it? *¿Puedo verlo?* pwe·do ver·lo

Do you have other sizes? *¿Tienes más tallas?* tyen·es mas·tie·yas

How much is it? *¿Cuánto cuesta?* kwan·to kwes·ta

Gràcia & Park Güell
A bit of everything in this intriguing, locally focused district
(p159)

Camp Nou, Pedralbes & La Zona Alta
Large-scale shops and the FC Barcelona stadium store
(p157)

La Sagrada Família & L'Eixample
Big-name designers and upmarket boutiques
(p167)

La Ribera
Great market and numerous gourmet food outlets
(p165)

El Raval
Alternative, bohemian design, clothing and vintage stores
(p158)

La Rambla & Barri Gòtic
Intriguing quirky shops on narrow lanes among tourist traps
(p162)

Barceloneta & the Waterfront
Great flea market and craft market choices
(p156)

Montjuïc, Poble Sec & Sant Antoni
Small, quirky boutiques, pop-ups and cutting-edge streetwear
(p169)

Port Olímpic

Mediterranean Sea

Port Vell

Opening Hours

In general, shops are open between 9am or 10am and 1.30pm or 2pm, and then from around 4pm or 4.30pm to 8pm or 8.30pm Monday to Friday. Many shops keep the same hours on Saturday, although some don't bother with the evening session.

Large supermarkets, malls and department stores stay open all day Monday to Saturday, from about 10am to 10pm.

A few shops open on Sundays and holidays, and the number increases in the run-up to key consumer holiday periods.

Sales

The winter sales start after Reis (6 January) and, depending on the shop, can go on well into February. The summer sales start in July, with shops trying to entice locals to part with one last wad of euros before they flood out of the city on holiday in August.

The Best...

Experience Barcelona's best shopping

For Vintage

L'Arca (p163) Ethereal gowns, often used in films.

El Bulevard dels Antiquaris (p169) A quirky hotchpotch of antique shops.

Els Encants Vells (p156; pictured above) Stunningly remodelled flea market, where you can unearth retro homeware and kitschy bric-a-brac.

Port Antic (p157) A quirky street market with finds from vintage toys to tiny oil paintings.

For Design & Craft

Drap-Art (p164) Weird and wonderful recycled art and accessories.

Arlequí Màscares (p167) Handmade masks to rival any in Venice; the perfect souvenir.

Fantastik (p159) A temple to kitsch, with kooky wonders from all around the world.

Teranyina (p159) The 'Spider's Web', so called for its intricate designs in intricate textiles.

Markets

Mercat de la Boqueria (p48; pictured above) The quintessential Barcelona food market.

Mercat de Santa Caterina (p110) A colourful alternative to La Boqueria, with fewer crowds and lower prices.

Els Encants Vells (p156) A sprawling flea market in a spanking new building.

El Bulevard dels Antiquaris (p169) A labyrinth of tiny antique shops that merits a morning's browsing.

For Food & Wine

Casa Gispert (p111) The speciality is roast nuts of every type, but you'll also find chocolate, conserves and olive oils.

Vila Viniteca (p111) A jaw-dropping cathedral of wines from Catalonia and elsewhere in Spain.

Formatgeria La Seu (p162) Superb cheeses from small producers.

Caelum (p142; pictured above) Deliciously wicked sweet treats made by nuns, with a little tea room downstairs.

For Souvenirs & Gifts

Born Centre de Cultura i Memòria
(p85) The gift shop at this exhibition
space stocks tasteful, well-made souvenirs, and books about the city.

Les Topettes (p158) Creams, oils,
perfumes and soaps that look every bit
as tantalising as they smell.

Sabater Hermanos (p162) Divinely
fragranced shop selling handmade
soaps in pretty gift boxes.

MACBA (p94) The modern art museum's gift shop has some colourful and
covetable books and gifts.

For Fashion

Coquette (p167; pictured above)
Offbeat women's clothes that share an
ethereal elegance.

Holala! Plaza (p159) Today vintage is
the new designer, and nowhere has a
better selection than Holala!

Bagués-Masriera (p171) Exquisite
jewellery from a company with a long
tradition.

Custo Barcelona (p167) Quirky, colourful clothes that are not for the shy.

Loisaida (p167) Cute, smart and somewhat retro clothing for men and women.

☆ Lonely Planet's Top Choices

Mercat de la Boqueria (p48) Stock
up on budget delicacies amid one of
Europe's most vibrant food markets.

Vila Viniteca (p111) Oenophiles unite at
this wonderful wine shop.

Coquette (p167) Simple and beautiful
designer clothes for women.

Loisaida (p167) Men's and women's
fashion, antiques and retro vinyl.

⊕ Barceloneta & the Waterfront

Vernita Children's Clothing
(📞625 092341; www.facebook.com/Vernita StudioShop; Carrer del Joncar 27; ⊘10am-1.30pm & 5-8pm Tue-Fri, 10am-2pm & 5-8pm Sat; Ⓜ Poblenou) Three mothers, Neli, Laura and Nacha, design and hand-stitch children's clothing and accessories such as animal-print cushions, bags, kids' jewellery, bow ties, towels (including adorable dinosaur designs) and washable nappies, as well as soft cuddly toys at this light, bright studio/boutique. During the evenings, they also offer sewing lessons and origami workshops for kids (English available).

System Action Clothing
(📞93 463 85 82; www.systemaction.es; Carrer de Pere IV 122; ⊘10am-7pm Fri & Sat; Ⓜ Llacuna) If you like discovering local producers, track down this outlet store on. Though System Action has stores across Catalonia (and in Madrid), its design headquarters are a few blocks south of here in a former Poblenou ice factory. Fashions are feminine but rugged, and you'll find good basics including very wearable sweaters, skirts, scarves and shoes.

Ultra-Local Records Music
(📞661 017638; www.ultralocalrecords.com; Carrer de Pujades 113; ⊘4-8.30pm Mon-Fri, 11am-8.30pm Sat; Ⓜ Llacuna) Along a fairly empty stretch of El Poblenou, this small, well-curated shop sells mostly used records (plus some re-releases and albums by current indie rock darlings) from Catalan, Spanish, French, American and British artists. Vinyl aside, you'll find a smaller CD selection, plus zines and a few other curiosities. There's a €1 bargain bin in front of the store.

La Bazart Fashion & Accessories
(📞633 455378; www.labazart.com; Carrer de la Ciutat de Granada 44; ⊘10.30am-6pm Mon, Tue, Thu & Fri, to 2.30pm Sat; Ⓜ Llacuna) If you can't make it to a handicrafts market in South America, La Bazart may be your next best

bet. This colourfully decorated shop stocks handcrafted goods from across the Andes. There are lots of great gift ideas, including silver jewellery from Ecuador, woven pillowcases from Bolivia, and alpaca gloves, scarves and blankets from the owner's native Chile.

Bestiari Books, Handicrafts
(Plaça de Pau Vila 3; ⊘10am-7pm Tue & Thu-Sat, to 8pm Wed, to 2.30pm Sun; Ⓜ Barceloneta) On the ground floor of the Museu d'Història de Catalunya (p91), this well-stocked shop sells books in English, Catalan and Spanish for all ages, along with Catalan-themed gift ideas: CDs, T-shirts, umbrellas, messenger bags, chess sets, mugs and toys (along the lines of build-your-own Gothic or Gaudí structures).

Mercat de la Barceloneta Market
(📞93 221 64 71; www.mercatdelabarceloneta.com; Plaça de la Font 1; ⊘7am-2pm Mon-Thu & Sat, to 8pm Fri, to 3pm Sun; Ⓜ Barceloneta) Set in a modern glass and steel building fronting a long plaza in the heart of Barceloneta, this airy market has seasonal produce and seafood stalls, as well as several places where you can enjoy a sit-down meal. **El Guindilla** (Plaça del Poeta Boscà 2; tapas €5-11, mains €10-16) deserves special mention for its good-value lunch specials and outdoor seating on the plaza.

Els Encants Vells Market
(Fira de Bellcaire; 📞93 246 30 30; www.encantsbcn.com; Plaça de les Glòries Catalanes; ⊘9am-8pm Mon, Wed, Fri & Sat; Ⓜ Glòries) In a gleaming open-sided complex, the 'Old Charms' flea market is the biggest of its kind in Barcelona. Over 500 vendors ply their wares beneath massive mirror-like panels. It's all here, from antique furniture to secondhand clothes. There's a lot of junk, but you'll occasionally stumble across a *ganga* (bargain).

Feria d'Artesanía del Palau de Mar Market
(Map p250; www.portvellbcn.com; Moll del Dipòsit; ⊘11am-8.30pm Sat & Sun Sep-Jun, daily Jul & Aug; Ⓜ Barceloneta) Artisans sell a range of crafty items, including jewellery, graphic

T-shirts, handwoven hats, fragrant candles and soaps, scarves, decorative items and souvenirs at this port-side market.

Port Antic
Market

(www.portvellbcn.com; Plaça del Portal de la Pau; ◷10am-8pm Sat & Sun; MDrassanes) At the base of La Rambla, this small market is a requisite stop for antique hunters. Here you'll find old photographs, frames, oil paintings, records, shawls, cameras, vintage toys and other odds and ends. Arrive early to beat the crowds.

Maremàgnum
Mall

(☑93 225 81 00; www.maremagnum.es; Moll d'Espanya 5; ◷10am-10pm; MDrassanes) Created out of largely abandoned docks, this buzzing shopping centre, with 19 places to eat, bars and cinemas, is home to 59 shops including youthful Spanish chain Mango, and eye-catching fashions from Barcelona-based Desigual. Football fans will be drawn to the paraphernalia at FC Botiga. It's particularly popular on Sundays when most other stores in the city remain shuttered.

🔒 Camp Nou, Pedralbes & La Zona Alta

Catalina House
Homewares

(☑93 140 96 39; www.facebook.com/catalina. house; Carrer d'Amigó 47; ◷10.30am-2pm & 5-8pm Mon-Fri, 10.30am-2pm Sat; ⭐FGC Muntaner) 🌿 After its decade-long success on the Balearic island of Formentera, Catalina House opened its second shop in Barcelona in 2016. Sustainable materials such as linen, cotton, stone, glass, terracotta and oil-treated recycled timbers are used in stylish Mediterranean designs for the home, including cushions, tableware, vases, sculptures and furniture.

Normandie
Children's Clothing

(☑93 209 14 11; www.normandiebaby.com; Plaça de Sant Gregori Taumaturg; ◷10.30am-2.30pm & 4.30-8.30pm Mon-Sat; ⭐FGC La Bonanova) Set up by Barcelona-born, Paris-trained designer Graziella Antón de Vez in 2000, this fashion label for babies and children

🛍 Antique Shopping

Antique collectors should set aside a Sunday morning for a trip to **Mercantic** (☑93 674 49 50; www.mercantic.com; Avinguda de Rius i Taulet 120; ◷10am-8pm Tue-Sat, to 4pm Sun; 🍴; ⭐FGC line S2 to Volpelleres), a collection of gaily painted wooden huts occupied by antique and bric-a-brac dealers selling records, books, vintage clothes, jewellery, artwork, home furnishings and much more. Ample food and drink vendors on hand add to the good cheer, and there's even live music some days.

The first Sunday of the month is delivery day, when the stall-holders take delivery of a new wave of old stuff. The permanent market, with some 80 stall holders, is open during the week too. There's also an activities and play area for children.

Antique toy cars at Mercantic
PERE RUBI/SHUTTERSTOCK ©

up to six years utilises all-natural materials such as angora, cotton, cashmere and wool. Adorable outfits are inspired by France's Normandy region, with vintage- and retro-style lines.

Ukka
Fashion & Accessories

(☑661 919 710; Carrer de Laforja 122; ◷10.30am-2pm & 5-8.30pm Mon-Fri, 11am-2pm & 5.30-8.30pm Sat; ⭐FGC Muntaner) Ukka makes its bohemian-inspired women's fashion and accessories (including scarves, hats and some eye-catching jewellery) at its Barcelona factory and sells them exclusively in this chic little terracotta-floored boutique.

 Outlet Excursion

For the ultimate discount-fashion over-dose, head out of town for some outlet shopping at **La Roca Village** (📞93 842 39 39; www.larocavillage.com; Santa Agnès de Malayanes; ⏲10am-9pm Mon-Fri, to 10pm Sat & Sun). Here, a village has been given over to consumer madness. At a long line of Spanish and international fashion boutiques you'll find clothes, shoes, accessories and designer homewares at (they claim) up to 60% off normal retail prices.

To get here, follow the AP-7 tollway north from Barcelona, take exit 12 (marked Cardedeu) and follow the signs for 'Centre Comercial'. The Sagalés Bus Company organises the Shopping Express from Passeig de Gràcia and the World Trade Center – see www.sagales. com for details. Alternatively, take a slower bus from the same company from Fabra i Puig metro station (four de-partures a day Monday to Friday, three in August) or a local train to Granollers and pick up the shuttle (Monday to Friday only) or a taxi there.

La Roca Village
PERE RUBI/SHUTTERSTOCK ©

Labperfum   Cosmetics
(📞93 298 95 12; www.labperfum.com; Carrer de Santaló 45; ⏲10am-2.30pm & 5-8.30pm Mon-Sat; 🚉FGC Muntaner) This tiny shop looks like an old apothecary, with its shelves lined with pretty glass bottles of extraordinary fragrances (for men and women) made in-house and beautifully packaged. Scents diverge from run-of-the-mill Obsession,

with varieties like tobacco, black orchid and leather. You can also buy scented candles, soaps and creams.

Mercat de Galvany   Market
(www.mercatgalvany.es; Carrer de Santaló 65; ⏲7am-2.30pm Mon-Thu & Sat, 7am-2.30pm & 7-8pm Fri; 🚉FGC Muntaner) Opened in 1927, Galvany is one of the city's most beautiful markets, with a brick facade and glass and cast-iron interior. Over 80 different stalls sell an enticing variety of bakery items, fresh produce and deli goods.

Oriol Balaguer   Food
(📞93 201 18 46; www.oriolbalaguer.com; Plaça de Sant Gregori Taumaturg 2; ⏲9am-2.30pm & 4-9pm Mon-Fri, 8.30am-2.30pm & 4-9pm Sat, 8.30am-2.30pm Sun; 🚉FGC La Bonanova) Magnificent cakes, sweets, ice cream, choc-olates and other sweet creations tantalise in this museumlike shop.

**FC Botiga
Megastore**   Gifts & Souvenirs
(📞93 409 02 71; www.fcbmegastore.com; Gate 9, off Avinguda Joan de XXIII; ⏲10am-7pm Mon-Sat, 10.30am-3.30pm Sun, until kick-off match days; Ⓜ Palau Reial) This sprawling three-storey shop at Camp Nou (p72) has footballs, shirts, scarves, socks, wallets, bags, foot-wear, smartphone covers – pretty much anything you can think of – all featuring the team's famous red-and-blue insignia.

El Corte Inglés   Department Store
(📞93 493 48 00; www.elcorteingles.es; Avinguda Diagonal 617; ⏲9.30am-9pm Mon-Sat; Ⓜ Maria Cristina) This massive shopping complex has a supermarket and a handful of eateries.

🔒 **El Raval**

Les Topettes   Cosmetics
(Map p249; 📞93 500 55 64; www.lestopettes. com; Carrer de Joaquín Costa 33; ⏲11am-2pm & 4-9pm Tue-Sat, 4-9pm Mon; Ⓜ Universitat) It's a sign of the times that such a chic little temple to soap and perfume can exist in El Raval. The items in Les Topettes' collection

have been picked for their designs as much as the products themselves, and you'll find gorgeously packaged scents, candles and unguents from Diptyque, Cowshed and L'Artisan Parfumeur, among others.

Chök
Food

(Map p250; ☎93 304 23 60; www.chokbarcel ona.com; Carrer del Carme 3; ⏰9am-9pm; ⓂLiceu) Set inside an old chocolate-maker's, with original wooden shelving and stained glass, Chök now specialises in all things sweet, but especially doughnuts. These come in a huge array of colours and flavours, but there are also cookies, macarons, marshmallows and, of course, the ubiquitous cronut. There's a tiny space where you can order and drink coffee.

Joan La Llar del Pernil
Food

(Map p250; ☎93 317 95 29; www.joanlallardel pernil.com; Stalls 667-671, Mercat de la Boqueria; ⏰8am-3pm Mon-Thu, to 8pm Fri & Sat; ⓂLiceu) This stall in the Mercat de la Boqueria sells some of the best ham and charcuterie in the city, much of which is sliced and presented in little cones as a snack.

Fantastik
Arts & Crafts

(Map p249; ☎93 301 30 68; www.fantastik. es; Carrer de Joaquín Costa 62; ⏰11am-2pm & 4-8.30pm Mon-Fri, 11am-3pm & 4-9pm Sat; ⓂUniversitat) Over 400 products, including a Mexican skull rattle, a robot moon explorer from China and recycled plastic zebras from South Africa, are to be found in this colourful shop, which sources its items from Mexico, India, Bulgaria, Russia, Senegal and 20 other countries. It's a perfect place to buy all the things you don't need but can't live without.

Holala! Plaza
Fashion & Accessories

(Map p249; www.holala-ibiza.com; Plaça de Castella 2; ⏰11am-9pm Mon-Sat; ⓂUniversitat) Backing on to Carrer de Valldonzella, where it boasts an exhibition space (Gallery) for temporary art displays, this Ibiza import is inspired by that island's long-established (and somewhat commercialised) hippie tradition. Vintage clothes are the name of the game, along with an eclectic program of exhibitions and activities.

Teranyina
Arts & Crafts

(Map p249; ☎93 317 94 36; www.textilteranyina. com; Carrer del Notariat 10; ⏰11am-2pm & 5-8pm Mon-Fri; ⓂCatalunya) Artist Teresa Rosa Aguayo runs this textile workshop in the heart of the artsy bit of El Raval. You can join courses at the loom, admire some of the rugs and other works that Teresa has created and, of course, buy them.

La Portorriqueña
Coffee

(Map p249; ☎93 317 34 38; Carrer d'en Xuclà 25; ⏰9am-2pm & 5-8pm Mon-Fri, 9am-2pm Sat; ⓂCatalunya) Coffee beans from around the world, freshly ground before your eyes, have been the winning formula in this store since 1902. It also offers all sorts of chocolate goodies. The street it's on is good for little old-fashioned food boutiques.

🅖 Gràcia & Park Güell

Colmillo de Morsa
Fashion & Accessories

(☎645 206365; www.facebook.com/colmillo demorsa; Carrer de Vic 15-17; ⏰4.30-8.30pm Mon, 11am-2.30pm & 4.30-8.30pm Tue-Sat; ®FGC Gràcia) Design team Javier Blanco and Elisbet Vallecillo have made waves at Madrid's Cibeles Fashion Week and Paris' fashion fair Who's Next. They showcase their Barcelona-made women's fashion here at their flagship boutique. They've also opened the floor to promote other young, up-and-coming local labels. The light-filled space also hosts art, graphic design and photography exhibitions and fashion shows.

Family Beer
Drinks

(Map p254; ☎93 219 29 88; www.family-beer.com; Carrer de Joan Blanques 55; ⏰5-8.30pm Mon, 10am-2pm & 5-8.30pm Tue-Thu & Sat, 10am-2pm & 5-9pm Fri; ⓂJoanic) Over 130 varieties of local and international craft beers and ciders are stocked in the fridges here, so you can pick up a cold brew to go. It also has brewing kits and books, and runs regular brewing workshops (three hours €45). It hosts free demonstrations of cheese making and cookery using beer, as well as 'meet the brewer' tastings.

🛍️ Design Shops

The heart of L'Eixample, bisected by Passeig de Gràcia, is known as the Quadrat d'Or (Golden Square) and is jammed with all sorts of glittering shops. Passeig de Gràcia is a bit of a who's who of international shopping – you'll find Spain's own high-end designers like Loewe, along with Armani, Chanel, Gucci, Stella McCartney and the rest.

El Born, particularly Carrer del Rec, is big on cool designers like Isabel Marant, Marni, Chloé and Hoss Intropia, in small, clean-line boutiques. Some Barcelona-based designs are also sold here. This is a great area if you have money to spend and hours to browse.

Can Luc   Cheese
(📞93 007 47 83; www.canluc.es; Carrer de Berga 4; ⏰5-9pm Mon, 10am-2.30pm & 5-8.30pm Tue-Sat; 🚉FGC Gràcia) At any one time, this brightly lit shop has 150 different varieties of cheese. Catalan cheeses are the speciality, but you'll also find a selection from France, Italy, the Netherlands, Switzerland and Britain. Expert staff provide guidance. Wines, condiments, crackers and cheese knives are also available. For a gourmet picnic, pre-order a brimming hamper (€25 to €100).

Amalia Vermell   Jewellery
(Map p254; 📞655 754008; www.amaliavermell. com; Carrer de Francisco Giner 49; ⏰11am-2pm & 5-9pm Mon-Sat; Ⓜ️Diagonal) Striking geometric jewellery made from high quality materials such as sterling silver is handcrafted by Amalia Vermell here in her atelier. Browse for pendants and necklaces, bracelets and rings, or sign up for a jewellery-making course (from €65 for two hours; English available).

Vinil Vintage   Music
(Map p254; 📞93 192 39 99; Carrer de Ramón y Cajal 45-47; ⏰10.30am-2pm & 5-8.30pm Tue-Sat; Ⓜ️Joanic) Crate diggers will love rummaging through the vinyl collection here. There's a huge range of rock, pop and jazz, including plenty of Spanish music. It also sells turntables and speakers.

Rekup & Co   Homewares
(Map p254; 📞694 472297; www.rekupandco. com; Carrer de Verdi 61; ⏰11am-2.30pm & 5-9pm; Ⓜ️Fontana) Recycled timbers and metals are used by French native Emmanuel Wagnon to create individual works of art that are functional too: chairs, tables, shelves, mirrors, lamps and quirkier items like shutters made from wooden pallets.

Lady Loquita   Clothing
(Map p254; 📞93 217 82 92; www.ladyloquita. com; Travessera de Gràcia 126; ⏰11am-2pm & 5-8.30pm Mon-Sat; Ⓜ️Fontana) At this hip little shop you can browse through light, locally made summer dresses by Tiralahilacha, evening wear by Japamala and handmade jewellery by local design label Klimbim. There are also whimsical odds and ends: dinner plates with dog people portraits and digital prints on wood by About Paola.

Amapola Vegan Shop   Clothing
(Map p254; 📞93 010 62 73; www.amapolavegan shop.com; Travessera de Gràcia 129; ⏰11am-2pm & 5-8.30pm Mon-Sat; Ⓜ️Fontana) 🌱 A shop with a heart of gold, Amapola proves that you need not toss your ethics aside in the quest for stylish clothing and accessories. You'll find sleek leather-alternatives for wallets, handbags and messenger bags by Matt & Nat, belts by Nae Vic, and elegant scarves by Barts.

La Festival   Wine
(Map p254; 📞93 023 22 81; Carrer de Verdi 67; ⏰5-9pm Mon, 10.30am-2.30pm & 5-9pm Tue-Thu, 10.30am-2.30pm & 5-9.30pm Fri & Sat, 10.30am-2.30pm & 5-8pm Sun; Ⓜ️Fontana) Knowledgeable English-speaking staff can give you a wealth of information about the excellent wines for sale here. Most are from Spanish producers, though there are a few French labels, and some organic and biodynamic wines. You can refill your bottle with wine or vermouth from one of the casks at the front, starting at €3 a bottle.

Picnic
Clothing

(Map p254; ☑93 016 69 53; www.picnicstore.es; Carrer de Verdi 17; ⊙11am-9pm Mon-Fri, 11am-3pm & 4-9pm Sat; MFontana) This tiny, beautifully curated boutique has many temptations: stylish sneakers by Meyba (a Barcelona brand), striped jerseys from Basque label Loreak Mendian and boldly patterned Mödernaked backpacks. Other finds include animal print ceramics for the home, small-scale art prints and fashion mags.

Surco
Music

(Map p254; ☑93 218 34 39; www.facebook.com/surcobcn; Travessera de Gràcia 144; ⊙10.30am-2pm & 5.30-9pm Mon-Sat; MFontana) Surco is an obligatory stop for music lovers, especially fans of vinyl. You'll find loads of new and used records and CDs here, with a mix of Tom Waits, Mishima (a Catalan indie pop band), Calexico and more.

Be
Gifts & Souvenirs

(Map p254; ☑93 218 89 49; www.bethestore.com; Carrer de Bonavista 7; ⊙10.30am-9pm Mon-Sat; MDiagonal) Be is a fun place to browse for accessories and gift ideas. You'll find rugged vintage-looking satchels, leather handbags, stylish (and reflective) Happy Socks, portable record players, sneakers (Vans, Pumas, old school Nikes) and gadgets (including richly hued Pantone micro speakers and Polaroid digital cameras).

Cabinet BCN
Homewares

(Map p254; ☑93 368 43 82; www.cabinetbcn.com; Travessera de Gràcia 133; ⊙5-8.30pm Mon, 11am-2.30pm & 5-8.30pm Tue-Sat; MFontana) Charming interiors shop Cabinet BCN stocks a tasteful selection of homewares – including throws, cushions, bowls, candles and lamps, as well as quirky little ornaments – that make excellent presents. It also has a small range of clothing, and custom designs furniture made out of iron, wood and other recycled materials. Shipping is available.

Bodega Bonavista
Wine

(Map p254; ☑93 218 81 99; Carrer de Bonavista 10; ⊙10am-2.30pm & 5-9pm Mon-Fri, noon-3pm & 6-9pm Sat, noon-3pm Sun; MFontana) An excellent little neighbourhood bodega,

🛍 Shopping Malls

Barcelona has no shortage of shopping malls. One of the first to arrive was **L'Illa Diagonal** (☑93 444 00 00; www.lilla.com; Avinguda Diagonal 557; ⊙9.30am-9pm Mon-Sat; MMaria Cristina), designed by star Spanish architect Rafael Moneo. The **Centre Comercial Diagonal Mar** (p121), by the sea, is one of the latest additions.

The city's other emporia include **Centre Comercial de les Glòries** (www.lesglories.com; Avinguda Diagonal 208; ⊙9am-9pm Mon, Tue, Thu & Fri, to 10pm Wed, to 9.30pm Sat; MGlòries), in the former Olivetti factory; **Heron City** (☑93 276 50 70; www.heroncitybarcelona.com; Avinguda de Rio de Janeiro 42; ⊙stores 9.30am-10pm Mon-Sat, cinema & restaurants 7am-1am; MFabra i Puig), just off Avinguda Meridiana, about 4km north of Plaça de les Glòries Catalanes; and the **Centre Comercial Gran Via 2** (☑902 30 14 44; www.granvia2.com; Gran Via de les Corts Catalanes 75; ⊙stores 9.30am-9pm Mon-Sat, restaurants & cinema 9am-1am; ℝFGC Ildefons Cerdà) in L'Hospitalet de Llobregat.

L'Illa Diagonal
XAVIER FORÉS/AGE FOTOSTOCK ©

Bonavista endeavours to seek out great wines at reasonable prices. The stock is mostly from Catalonia and elsewhere in Spain, but there's also a well-chosen selection from France. The Bonavista also acts as a deli, and there are some especially good cheeses. Tables in-store let you sample wines by the glass, along with cheeses and charcuterie.

Mushi Mushi Fashion & Accessories

(Map p254; [📞]93 292 29 74; www.mushimushi collection.com; Carrer de Bonavista 12; [🕙]11am-3pm & 4.30-8.30pm Mon-Sat; [Ⓜ]Diagonal) A gorgeous little fashion boutique in an area that's not short of them, Mushi Mushi specialises in quirky but elegant women's fashion and accessories. It stocks small labels such as Des Petits Hauts, Sessùn, Orion London, as well as jewellery by Adriana Llorens. The collection changes frequently, so a return visit can pay off.

Nostàlgic Photography

(Map p254; [📞]93 368 57 57; www.nostalgic.es; Carrer de Goya 18; [🕙]10.30am-2pm & 5-8pm Mon-Fri, 11am-2.30pm Sat; [Ⓜ]Fontana) In a beautiful space with exposed brick walls and wooden furniture, Nostàlgic specialises in all kinds of modern and vintage photography equipment. You'll find camera bags and tripods for the digital snappers, rolls of film, and quirky Lomo cameras. There is also a decent collection of photography books to buy or browse.

Hibernian Books

([📞]93 217 47 96; www.hibernian-books.com; Carrer de Montseny 17; [🕙]4-8.30pm Mon, 11am-8.30pm Tue-Sat; [Ⓜ]Fontana) Barcelona's biggest secondhand English bookshop stocks thousands of titles covering all sorts of subjects, from cookery to children's classics. There's a smaller collection of new books in English too.

Mercat de l'Abaceria Central Market

(Map p254; www.mercatabaceria.com; Travessera de Gràcia 186; [🕙]7am-2.30pm & 5.30-8pm Mon-Sat; [Ⓜ]Fontana, [Ⓡ]FGC Gràcia) Dating from 1892, this sprawling iron and brick market is an atmospheric place to browse for fresh produce, cheeses, bakery items and more. There are also several food stalls where you can grab a quick bite on the cheap.

Érase una Vez Fashion & Accessories

(Map p254; [📞]697 805409; www.eraseunavez. info; Carrer de Bonavista 13; [🕙]11am-2pm & 5-8.30pm Tue-Sat; [Ⓜ]Diagonal) 'Once Upon a Time' is the name of this fanciful boutique, which brings out the princess in you. It offers ethereal, delicate women's clothes as well as exquisite wedding dresses. You'll also find playful frocks for kids.

🅐 La Rambla & Barri Gòtic

Torrons Vicens Food

(Map p250; [📞]93 304 37 36; www.vicens.com; Carrer del Petritxol 15; [🕙]10am-8.30pm Mon-Sat, 11am-8pm Sun; [Ⓜ]Liceu) You can find the *turrón* (nougat) treat year-round at Torrons Vicens, which has been selling its signature sweets since 1775.

Sabater Hermanos Cosmetics

(Map p250; [📞]93 301 98 32; www.sabaterherm anos.es; Plaça de Sant Felip Neri 1; [🕙]10.30am-9pm; [Ⓜ]Jaume I) This fragrant little shop sells handcrafted soaps of all sizes. Varieties such as fig, cinnamon, grapefruit and chocolate smell good enough to eat, while sandalwood, magnolia, mint, cedar and jasmine add spice to any sink or bathtub.

Formatgeria La Seu Food

(Map p250; [📞]93 412 65 48; www.formatgeria laseu.com; Carrer de la Dagueria 16; [🕙]10am-2pm & 5-8pm Tue-Sat Sep-Jul; [Ⓜ]Jaume I) Dedicated to artisan cheeses from all across Spain, this small shop is run by the oh-so-knowledgeable Katherine McLaughlin and is the antithesis of mass production – it sells only the best from small-scale farmers and the stock changes regularly. Wine and cheese tastings in the cosy room at the back are fun.

Escribà Food & Drinks

(Map p250; [📞]93 301 60 27; www.escriba.es; La Rambla 83; [🕙]9am-9.30pm; [📶]; [Ⓜ]Liceu) Chocolates, dainty pastries and mouth-watering cakes can be nibbled behind the Modernista mosaic facade here or taken away for private, guilt-ridden consumption. This Barcelona favourite is owned by the Escribà family, a name synonymous with sinfully good sweet things. More than that, it adds a touch of authenticity to La Rambla.

L'Arca Vintage, Clothing

(Map p250; ☏93 302 15 98; www.larca.es; Carrer dels Banys Nous 20; ⌚11am-2pm & 4.30-8.30pm Mon-Sat; Ⓜ Liceu) Step inside this enchanting shop for a glimpse of beautifully crafted apparel from the past, including 18th-century embroidered silk vests, elaborate silk kimonos, and wedding dresses and shawls from the 1920s. Thanks to its incredible collection, it has provided clothing for films including *Titanic, Talk to Her* and *Perfume: The Story of a Murderer*.

Herboristeria del Rei Cosmetics

(Map p250; ☏93 318 05 12; www.herboristeria delrei.com; Carrer del Vidre 1; ⌚2.30-8.30pm Tue-Thu, 10.30am-8.30pm Fri & Sat; Ⓜ Liceu) Once patronised by Queen Isabel II, this timeless corner store flogs all sorts of weird and wonderful herbs, spices and medicinal plants. It's been doing so since 1823 and the decor has barely changed since the 1860s – some of the products have, however, and you'll find anything from fragrant soaps to massage oil nowadays.

Cereria Subirà Homewares

(Map p250; ☏93 315 26 06; www.cereriasubira. cat; Calle de la Llibreteria 7; ⌚9.30am-1.30pm & 4-8pm Mon-Thu, 9.30am-8pm Fri, 10am-8pm Sat; Ⓜ Jaume I) Even if you're not interested in myriad mounds of colourful wax, pop in just so you've been to the oldest shop in Barcelona. Cereria Subirà has been churning out candles since 1761 and at this address since the 19th century; the interior has a beautifully baroque quality, with a picturesque *Gone with the Wind*–style staircase.

Artesania Catalunya Arts & Crafts

(Map p250; ☏93 467 46 60; www.bcncrafts. com; Carrer dels Banys Nous 11; ⌚10am-8pm Mon-Sat, to 2pm Sun; Ⓜ Liceu) A celebration of Catalan products, this nicely designed store is a great place to browse for unique gifts. You'll find jewellery with designs inspired by Roman iconography (as well as works that reference Gaudí and Barcelona's Gothic era), plus pottery, wooden toys, silk scarves, notebooks, housewares and more.

> You can find the turrón *(nougat)* treat year-round here

Torrons Vicens

IAKOV FILIMONOV/SHUTTERSTOCK ©

🛍 Shopping Strips

Avinguda del Portal de l'Àngel This broad pedestrian avenue is lined with high-street chains, shoe shops, book-shops and more. It feeds into Carrer dels Boters and Carrer de la Portafer-rissa, characterised by stores offering light-hearted costume jewellery and youth-oriented streetwear.

Avinguda Diagonal This boulevard is loaded with international fashion names and design boutiques, suitably interspersed with cafes to allow weary shoppers to take a load off.

Carrer d'Avinyó Once a fairly squalid old city street, Carrer d'Avinyó has morphed into a dynamic young fashion street.

Carrer de la Riera Baixa The place to look for a gaggle of shops flogging preloved threads.

Carrer del Consell de Cent The heart of the private art-gallery scene in Bar-celona, between Passeig de Gràcia and Carrer de Muntaner.

Carrer del Petritxol Best for chocolate shops and art.

Carrer del Rec Another threads street, this one-time stream is lined with bright and cool boutiques. Check out Carrer del Bonaire and Carrer de l'Esparteria too. You'll find discount outlets and original local designers.

Carrer dels Banys Nous Along with nearby Carrer de la Palla, this is the place to look for antiques.

Passeig de Gràcia This is the premier shopping boulevard – chic with a capital 'C', and mostly given over to big-name international brands.

Drap-Art   Arts & Crafts
(Map p250; ☑93 268 48 89; www.drapart.org; Carrer Groc 1; ⊙11am-2pm & 5-8pm Tue-Fri, 6-9pm Sat; MJaume I) A non-profit arts or-ganisation runs this small store and gallery space, which exhibits wild designs made from recycled products. Works change reg-ularly, but you might find sculptures, jewel-lery, handbags and other accessories from artists near and far, as well as mixed-media installations.

La Colmena   Food
(Map p250; ☑93 315 13 56; www.pastisseriala colmena.com; Plaça de l'Angel 12; ⊙9am-9pm; MJaume I) A pastry shop selling many delicacies including pine-nut-encrusted *panellets* (sweet almond cakes), flavoured meringues and feather-light *ensaïmadas* (soft, sweet buns topped with powdered sugar) from Mallorca.

Taller de Marionetas Travi   Marionettes
(Map p250; ☑93 412 66 92; www.marionetas travi.com; Carrer de n'Amargós 4; ⊙noon-9pm Mon-Sat; MUrquinaona) Opened in the 1970s, this atmospheric shop sells beautifully handcrafted marionettes. Don Quixote, San-cho Panza and other iconic Spanish figures are on hand, as well as unusual works from other parts of the world – including rare Sicilian puppets and pieces from Myanmar (Burma), Indonesia and elsewhere.

Cómplices   Books
(Map p250; ☑93 412 72 83; www.libreriacomp lices.com; Carrer de Cervantes 4; ⊙10.30am-8pm Mon-Fri, from noon Sat; MJaume I) One of the most extensive gay and lesbian bookstores in the city has a mix of erotica in the form of DVDs and comics as well as books. It's a wel-coming place for all ages and orientations.

La Manual Alpargatera   Shoes
(Map p250; ☑93 301 01 72; www.lamanualal pargatera.es; Carrer d'Avinyó 7; ⊙9.30am-1.30pm & 4.30-8pm Mon-Fri, from 10am Sat; MLiceu) Clients from Salvador Dalí to Jean Paul Gaultier have ordered a pair of *espadrilles* (rope-soled canvas shoes) from this famous store. The shop was founded just after the Spanish Civil War, though the roots of the simple shoe design date back hundreds of years and originated in the Catalan Pyrenees.

Sala Parés   Arts & Crafts

(Map p250; ✆93 318 70 20; www.salapares. com; Carrer del Petritxol 5; ⏰10.30am-2pm & 4-8pm Tue-Thu, to 8.30pm Fri & Sat Jun-Sep, plus 11.30am-2pm Sun Oct-May; MLiceu) In business since 1877, this gallery has maintained its position as one of the city's leading purveyors of Catalan art, with works from the 19th century to the present. Increasingly it stocks more work from elsewhere in Spain and Europe.

FC Botiga   Gifts & Souvenirs

(Map p250; ✆93 269 15 32; Carrer de Jaume I 18; ⏰10am-9pm; MJaume I) Need a Lionel Messi football jersey, a blue and burgundy ball, or any other football paraphernalia pertaining to what many locals consider the greatest team in the world? This is a convenient spot to load up without traipsing to the stadium.

Papabubble   Food

(Map p250; ✆93 268 86 25; www.papabubble. com; Carrer Ample 28; ⏰10am-2pm & 4-8.30pm Mon-Fri, 10am-8.30pm Sat; MJaume I) It feels like a step into another era in this sweet shop, which makes up pots of rainbow-coloured boiled lollies, just like some of us remember from corner-store days as kids. Watch the sticky sweets being made before your eyes.

Petritxol Xocoa   Food

(Map p250; ✆93 301 82 91; www.petritxol.com; Carrer del Petritxol 11-13; ⏰9.30am-9pm; MLiceu) Tucked along 'chocolate street' Carrer del Petritxol, this den of dental devilry displays ranks and ranks of original bars in stunning designs, chocolates stuffed with sweet stuff, gooey pastries and more. It has various other branches scattered about town.

Obach   Fashion & Accessories

(Map p250; ✆93 318 40 94; Carrer del Call 2; ⏰10am-2pm & 4-8pm Mon-Sat Oct-Jul, 10am-2pm Mon-Sat Aug-Sep; MJaume I) Since 1924 this store has been purveying all manner of headgear. You'll find Kangol mohair *barrets* (berets), hipsterish short-brimmed hats, fedoras, elegant straw sun hats and a full-colour spectrum of berets.

La Basilica Galeria   Jewellery

(Map p250; ✆93 304 20 47; www.labasilica galeria.com; Carrer Sant Sever 7; ⏰noon-9pm Mon-Sat; ☎; MJaume I) A pure wonderland for the senses, La Basilica Galeria is a whimsical jewellery store with artful displays set among crystal- and flower-covered mannequins. In addition to eye-catching necklaces, delicate rings and fairy-tale pendants, there are a few original paintings for sale, though there's more artwork a few doors down in Basilica's gallery and perfume shop.

🄮 La Ribera

See p143 for fabulous food shopping choices in La Ribera.

El Rei de la Màgia   Magic

(Map p250; ✆93 319 39 20; www.elreydela magia.com; Carrer de la Princesa 11; ⏰10.30am-2pm & 4-7.30pm Mon-Sat; MJaume I) For more than 100 years, the owners – who also run the **Museu del Rei de la Magia** (Map p254; Carrer de les Jonqueres 15; adult/under 14yr €5/3; ⏰4-7pm Wed-Fri, 11am-2pm & 4-8pm Sat & Sun; 🚻; MUrquinaona) – have been keeping locals both astounded and amused. Should you decide to stay in Barcelona and make a living as a magician, this is the place to buy levitation brooms, glasses of disappearing milk and decks of magic cards.

MI.vintage   Vintage

(Map p250; www.mivintagelabel.com; Carrer dels Consellers 2; ⏰10am-8pm Mon-Sat; MBarceloneta) Opened in 2017, this breathtakingly hip vintage store stocks a mix of second-hand and revamped clothes – treated, repaired, improved or, as the owner says, made 'street-ready'. Expect silk bomber jackets aplenty, colourful leather blazers, Hawaiian shirts and Emian sunglasses, along with Taschen books, Casio digital watches and funky PVC jewellery.

Oggetto   Design

(Map p250; ✆93 515 31 11; www.oggettobcn.com; Carrer dels Canvis Nous 4; ⏰4.30pm-8.30pm Mon, 12.30pm-8.30pm Tue-Sat, from 4.30pm Tue-Sat Jul; closed Aug; MBarceloneta) A gorgeous

Five Must-Buy Souvenirs

Cured Meats

Instead of *jamón*, go for local sausage such as *fuet* or *botifarra*. It's best bought in one of the market halls. They'll vacuum-pack it for you.

FC Barcelona Gear

Sure, you can buy a rip-off Messi shirt in any market in the world, but the real deal plus harder-to-come-by Barça mementoes are in their official shops.

Wine

Look for something you can't get back home – some small-producer Catalan red, or a hard-to-get *cava* (sparkling wine). Shops in La Ribera have ample supplies.

Build a Gaudí

We might not have the maestro's imagination, but by damn we can reconstruct his buildings in miniature. Available in most Gaudí buildings and museum shops.

Fashion

Quality threads can be had all over town, but best seek out a small local design boutique to ensure you head back wearing something unique.

little showcase for designer homeware. The cushions are made locally and based on the typical 'mosaic' Barcelona floor tiles, but look out too for the Scandi tea sets, stunning hand-blown glassware from France and colourful wire baskets made in Milan.

Marsalada Gifts & Souvenirs

(Map p250; 609 285953; www.marsalada design.com; Carrer de Sant Jacint 6; 10am-2pm, 4-8pm Mon-Sat; Jaume I) For souvenirs with a difference, Marsalada has hand-printed tote bags in unbleached cotton, engravings and T-shirts. Each of these is emblazoned with a well-known Barcelona attraction, sketched in pen and ink and adorned with abstract colour mosaics.

Loisaida Clothing, Antiques

(Map p250; 93 295 54 92; Carrer dels Flassaders 42; 11am-9pm Mon-Sat, 11am-2pm & 4-8pm Sun; Jaume I) Housed in the former coach house and stables for the Royal Mint, Loisaida (from the Spanglish for 'Lower East Side') is a sight in its own right. It is a deceptively large emporium of colourful, retro and somewhat preppy clothing for men and women, costume jewellery, music from the 1940s and '50s and some covetable antiques.

Arlequí Màscares Arts & Crafts

(Map p250; 93 268 27 52; www.arlequimask. com; Carrer de la Princesa 7; 11.30am-8pm Mon, 10.30am-8pm Tue-Fri, 11am-8pm Sat, 11.30am-7pm Sun; Jaume I) A little oasis of originality, this shop specialises in masks for costume and decoration. Some of the pieces are superb, while stock also includes a beautiful range of decorative boxes in Catalan themes, and some old-style marionettes.

Coquette Fashion & Accessories

(Map p250; 93 319 29 76; www.coquettebcn. com; Carrer del Rec 65; 11am-3pm & 5-9pm Mon-Fri, 11.30am-9pm Sat; Barceloneta) With its spare, cut-back and designer look, this friendly fashion store is attractive in its own right. Women can browse through casual, feminine wear by such designers as Humanoid, Vanessa Bruno, UKE and Hoss

Intropia, with a further collection nearby at **Carrer de Bonaire 5** (93 310 35 35; Barceloneta).

Nu Sabates Shoes

(Map p250; 93 268 03 83; www.nusabates.com; Carrer dels Cotoners 14; 11am-8pm Mon-Sat; Jaume I) A modern-day Catalan cobbler has put together some original handmade leather shoes for men and women (and a handful of bags and other leather items) in their friendly and stylish locale.

Custo Barcelona Fashion & Accessories

(Map p250; 93 268 78 93; www.custo.com; Plaça de les Olles 7; noon-8.30pm Mon-Sat; Barceloneta) The psychedelic decor and casual atmosphere lend this avant-garde Barcelona fashion store a youthful edge. Custo presents daring new women's and men's collections each year on the New York catwalks. The dazzling colours and cut of everything from dinner jackets to hot pants are for the uninhibited.

La Sagrada Família & L'Eixample

Joan Múrria Food & Drinks

(Map p254; 93 215 57 89; www.murria.cat; Carrer de Roger de Llúria 85; 10am-8.30pm Tue-Fri, 10am-2pm & 5-8.30pm Sat; Girona) Ramon Casas designed the 1898 Modernista shopfront advertisements featured at this culinary temple of speciality food goods from around Catalonia and beyond. Artisan cheeses, Iberian hams, caviar, canned delicacies, smoked fish, *cavas* and wines, coffee and loose-leaf teas are among the treats in store.

Flores Navarro Flowers

(Map p254; 93 457 40 99; www.floristerias navarro.com; Carrer de València 320; 24hr; Girona) You never know when you might need flowers, and this florist never closes. Established in 1960, it's a vast space (or a couple of spaces, in fact), and worth a visit just for the bank of colour and wonderful fragrance.

Cacao Sampaka
Food

(Map p254; ☑93 272 08 33; www.cacaosampaka. com; Carrer del Consell de Cent 292; ⊘9am-9pm Mon-Sat; ⓂPasseig de Gràcia) Chocoholics will be convinced they have died and passed on to a better place. Load up in the shop or head for the bar out the back where you can have a classic *xocolata* (hot chocolate) and munch on exquisite chocolate cakes, tarts, ice cream, sweets and sandwiches.

Altaïr
Books

(Map p254; ☑93 342 71 71; www.altair.es; Gran Via de les Corts Catalanes 616; ⊘10am-8.30pm Mon-Sat; 🛜; ⓂCatalunya) Enter a wonderland of travel in this extensive bookshop, which has enough guidebooks, maps, travel literature and other books to induce a severe case of itchy feet. It has a travellers' noticeboard and, downstairs, a cafe.

Dr Bloom
Fashion & Accessories

(Map p254; ☑93 292 23 27; www.drbloom.es; Rambla de Catalunya 30; ⊘10am-9pm Mon-Sat; ⓂPasseig de Gràcia) A new collection comes out every month at Dr Bloom, so the stock is constantly rotating. Designed and made in Barcelona, the label's dresses, tops, shawls and more have an emphasis on bright colours and bold prints no matter the season.

Sergio Aranda
Jewellery

(Map p254; ☑648 796029; www.sergioaranda. shop; Carrer Roger de Llúria 93; ⊘10am-2pm & 5-8pm Mon-Fri, noon-2.30pm Sat; ⓂPasseig de Gràcia) Swiss-born jeweller Sergio Aranda has worked throughout Europe for some of the world's most prestigious names, and now creates unique pieces incorporating materials such as coins and cultured pearls. Exquisite items in his collections span all budgets.

Lurdes Bergada
Fashion & Accessories

(Map p254; ☑93 218 48 51; www.lurdesbergada. es; Rambla de Catalunya 112; ⊘10.30am-8.30pm Mon-Sat; ⓂDiagonal) Mother-and-son design team Lurdes Bergada and Syngman Cucala's classy men's and women's fashions are made from natural fibres and have attracted a cult following.

El Corte Inglés
Department Store

(Map p254; ☑93 306 38 00; www.elcorteingles. es; Plaça de Catalunya 23; ⊘9.30am-9pm Mon-Sat; ⓂCatalunya) Spain's only remaining department store chain stocks everything you'd expect, from computers to cushions, and high fashion to homewares. Fabulous city views extend from the top-floor restaurant. Nearby branches include one at **Avinguda Diagonal 471-473** (☑93 493 48 00; ⊘9.30am-9pm Mon-Sat; ⓂHospital Clínic).

Purificación García
Fashion & Accessories

(Map p254; ☑93 496 13 36; www.purificacion garcia.com; Carrer de Provença 292; ⊘10am-8.30pm Mon-Sat; ⓂDiagonal) Spanish designer Purificación García's collections are breathtaking as much for their breadth as anything else. You'll find all kinds of clothing over this shop's two floors, from women's cardigans to men's ties, as well as light summer dresses and jeans.

Regia
Cosmetics

(Map p254; ☑93 216 01 21; www.regia.es; Passeig de Gràcia 39; ⊘9.30am-8.30pm Mon-Fri, 10.30am-8.30pm Sat; ⓂPasseig de Gràcia) In business since 1928, Regia stocks all the name brands and also has a private **perfume museum** (Map p254; www.museudel perfum.com; adult/child €5/free; ⊘10.30am-8pm Mon-Fri, 11am-2pm Sat) out the back. Fragrances aside, it carries a range of cosmetics and has its own line of bath products.

Mercat del Ninot
Market

(www.mercatdelninot.com; Carrer de Mallorca 133; ⊘9am-8pm Mon-Fri, to 2pm Sat; 🛜; ⓂHospital Clínic) A gleaming, modern neighbourhood food market, selling mostly meat and fish, Mercat del Ninot also has a couple of stalls where you can grab a bite to eat.

Mercat de la Concepció
Market

(Map p254; www.laconcepcio.cat; Carrer d'Aragó 313-317; ⊘8am-8pm Tue-Fri, to 3pm Mon & Sat; ⓂGirona) Mercat de la Concepció has 54 stalls selling food, flowers, wine and more, and also has several on-site bars.

El Bulevard dels
Antiquaris   Antiques
(Map p254; 📞93 215 44 99; www.bulevarddel
santiquaris.com; Passeig de Gràcia 55-57;
🕐10.30am-8.30pm Mon-Sat; Ⓜ Passeig de
Gràcia) More than 70 stores are gathered
under one roof to offer the most varied
selection of collector's pieces. These range
from old porcelain dolls to fine crystal,
from Asian antique furniture to old French
goods, and from African and other ethnic
art to jewellery.

Cubiña   Homewares
(Map p254; 📞93 476 57 21; www.cubinya.es;
Casa Thomas, Carrer de Mallorca 291; 🕐10am-
2pm & 4.30-8.30pm Mon-Sat; Ⓜ Verdaguer)
Even if interior design doesn't ring your
bell, it's worth visiting this extensive temple
to furniture, lamps and just about any
home accessory imaginable, just to see
this Domènech i Montaner building. Admire
the enormous and whimsical wrought-iron
decoration at street level before heading
inside to marvel at the brick columns and
timber work.

Loewe   Fashion & Accessories
(Map p254; 📞93 216 04 00; www.loewe.com;
Passeig de Gràcia 35; 🕐10am-8.30pm Mon-Sat;
Ⓜ Passeig de Gràcia) Loewe is one of Spain's
leading and oldest fashion stores, founded
in 1846. It specialises in luxury leather
(shoes, accessories and travel bags) and
also has lines in perfume, sunglasses, cuff
links, silk scarves and jewellery. This branch
opened in 1943 in the Modernista Casa
Lleó Morera (p55).

Laie   Books
(Map p254; 📞93 318 17 39; www.laie.es; Carrer
de Pau Claris 85; 🕐9am-9pm Mon-Fri, 10am-9pm
Sat; Ⓜ Urquinaona) Laie has novels and books
on architecture, art and film in English,
French, Spanish and Catalan. It also has a
great upstairs cafe.

⊙ Montjuïc, Poble Sec
& Sant Antoni

Mercat de la Terra   Market
(Map p256; Jardins de les Tres Xemeneies,
Avinguda del Paral·lel; 🕐10am-4pm Sat May-Sep;
Ⓜ Paral·lel) On a summer Saturday, this
farmers market is the ultimate place to pick
up provisions for a picnic in the neighbourhood's parks and gardens it is laden with
artisan cheeses and breads, preserves,
wine, *cava* and homemade vermouth, and
bushels of fresh produce.

Popcorn
Store   Fashion & Accessories
(Map p256; Carrer Viladomat 30-32; 🕐11am-3pm
& 4.30-8.30pm Mon-Sat) Cutting-edge Barcelona labels for women at this 2017-opened
boutique include Sister Dew, with asym-
metrical tops, jackets, dresses and more,
and Ester Gueroa, with bold prints and
lace. Men will find stylish shirts, trousers
and belts from Italian and other European
designers.

10000 Records   Music
(Map p249; 📞93 292 77 76; www.10000records.
es; Carrer de Floridablanca 70; 🕐5-8pm Mon,
10am-2pm & 5-8pm Tue-Fri, 10am-2pm Sat; Ⓜ Poble Sec) As its name suggests, this record
shop overflows with vintage and new vinyl
in all genres but especially rock, pop, metal
and jazz. You'll also unearth retro radios,
cassettes and music books.

Mercat de Sant Antoni   Market
(Map p249; 📞93 426 35 21; www.mercat
desantantoni.com; Carrer de Comte d'Urgell 1;
🕐7am-2.30pm & 5-8.30pm Mon-Thu, 7am-
8.30pm Fri & Sat; Ⓜ Sant Antoni) Just beyond
the western edge of El Raval is Mercat de
Sant Antoni, a glorious old iron and brick
building constructed between 1872 and
1882. The secondhand book market takes
place alongside on Sunday mornings.

BAR OPEN

Cocktails, *cava* and clubs galore

Bar Open

Barcelona is a nightlife-lovers' town, with an enticing spread of candlelit wine bars, old-school taverns, stylish lounges and kaleidoscopic nightclubs where the party continues until daybreak.

The atmosphere varies tremendously – mural-covered chambers in the medieval quarter, antique-filled converted storefronts and buzzing Modernista spaces are all part of the scene. Of course, where to go depends as much on the crowd as it does on ambience – and whether you're in the mood for drinking with hipsters (try Sant Antoni), a bohemian crowd (El Raval) or young expats (Gràcia). You'll find a scene that suits in Barcelona. Wherever you end up, keep in mind that eating and drinking go hand in hand, and some of the liveliest bars serve tapas as well as alcohol.

In This Section

Opening Hours

Bars Typically open around 6pm and close at 2am (3am on weekends), though many are open all day.

Clubs Open from midnight until 6am, Thursday to Saturday.

Beach Bars 10am to around midnight (later on weekends) from April through October.

Gràcia & Park Güell
Young hipster crowd
(p181)

**Camp Nou, Pedralbes
& La Zona Alta**
High-end clubs
(p178)

**La Sagrada Família
& L'Eixample**
Student bars, tiny
lounges, LGBTIQ venues
(p186)

La Ribera
Cava and wine
bars, lounges
(p185)

El Raval
Bohemian bars,
small clubs
(p178)

**La Rambla &
Barri Gòtic**
Atmospheric bars, cafes,
outdoor spots, clubs
(p183)

**Barceloneta &
the Waterfront**
Neighbourhood taverns,
seaside bars,
touristy clubs
(p176)

*Port
Olímpic*

**Montjuïc, Poble Sec
& Sant Antoni**
Art-minded bars, trendy cafes,
open-air spots
(p189)

*Port
Vell*

*Mediterranean
Sea*

Costs & Tipping

A coffee costs €1.20 to €1.80, a glass of wine will run €2 to €3.50 in most places and mixed drinks and cocktails will set you back €6 to €10. Nightclubs charge anywhere from nothing to €20 for admission. Tipping is not customary or necessary.

Useful Phrases
Coffee
con leche – half coffee, half milk

solo – an espresso

cortado – an espresso with a dash of milk

Beer
cerveza – beer (bottle)

caña – small draught beer

tubo – large draught beer

quinto – a 200mL bottle

tercio – a 330mL bottle

clara – a shandy; a beer with a hefty dash of lemonade

The Best...

Experience Barcelona's best drinking & nightlife spots

For Cocktails

Paradiso (p143) Walk through a fridge to this glam speakeasy.

Balius (p177) Beautifully mixed elixirs in Poblenou.

Elephanta (p181) The place to linger over a creative concoction.

Dry Martini (p187) Expertly made cocktails in a classy setting.

Boadas (p185) An iconic drinking den that's been going strong since the 1930s.

For Beer

BlackLab (p176) Creative microbrewery near the waterfront.

La Cervecita Nuestra de Cada Día (p177) A Poblenou brew bar for beer nerds.

Napar BCN (p186) The glitzy space makes an upmarket setting for sipping beers made on site.

El Drapaire (p179) Atmospheric tapas and creative microbrew joint in El Raval.

Bohemian Hang-outs

Gran Bodega Saltó (p202) Poble Sec icon with psychedelic decor and an eclectic crowd.

Madame George (p177) Tiny, dramatically designed space with soulful DJs.

El Rouge (p189) Bordello-esque lounge with great people-watching.

Bar Marsella (p179; pictured above) Historic absinthe bar that's seen them all.

For Dancing

Marula Cafè (p183) Barri Gòtic favourite for its lively dance floor.

Sala Apolo (p202; pictured above) Gorgeous dancehall with varied program of electro, funk and more.

Moog (p180) A small Raval club that draws a fun, dance-loving crowd.

Antilla BCN (p187) The top name in town for salsa lovers.

City Hall (p187) A legendary Eixample dance club.

For Views

La Caseta del Migdia (p189) Great hillside spot for a sundowner.

Mirablau (p178) The whole city stretches out beneath you from the foot of Tibidabo.

La Terrrazza (p191) Party beneath palms in Poble Espanyol.

Martínez (p149; pictured above) Drinking and dining with views on Montjuïc.

For Old-World Ambience

Raïm (p183) Old-fashioned tavern with more than a hint of Havana.

Cafè de l'Ópera (p142; pictured above) Serving opera-goers and passers-by for decades.

Bar Marsella (p179) History lives on in this 1820 watering hole.

Bar Pastís (p179) Atmospheric little bar with the warble of French cabaret tunes playing overhead.

Casa Almirall (p179) Step back into the 1860s inside this atmospheric drinking den.

Drinking & Nightlife

Paradiso (p143) Glamorous, cavernous, speakeasy-style cocktail bar.

Guzzo (p185) Relaxed bar with great DJs, live music and tables outside.

La Caseta del Migdia (p189) An open-air charmer, hidden high among the trees on Montjuïc.

Sor Rita (p183) Join festive crowds in a whimsical Almodovar-esque world.

El Xampanyet (p185) Sip cheap pink *cava* and munch on a bacon butty in this convivial classic.

Dry Martini (p187; pictured above) This elegant drinking den serves perfect martinis and goldfish-bowl-sized gin and tonics.

☆ Top Choices for Wine

Viblioteca (p182) A small, modern space famed for its wine (and cheese) selections.

Perikete (p176) A large and lively new wine bar in Barceloneta.

Monvínic (p186) With a staggering 3000 varieties of wines, you won't lack for options.

La Vinya del Senyor (p185) Long wine list and tables in the shadow of Basílica de Santa Maria del Mar.

🕒 Barceloneta & the Waterfront

Perikete   Wine Bar
(Map p250; www.gruporeini.net/perikete; Carrer de Llauder 6; ⊙11am-1am; MBarceloneta) Since opening in 2017, this fabulous wine bar has been jam-packed with locals. Hams hang from the ceilings, barrels of vermouth sit above the bar and wine bottles cram every available shelf space – over 200 varieties are available by the glass or bottle, accompanied by 50-plus tapas dishes. In the evening, the action spills into the street.

Bodega Vidrios y Cristales   Wine Bar
(Map p250; www.gruposagardi.com/restaurante/bodega-vidrios-y-cristales; Passeig d'Isabel II 6; ⊙noon-midnight Sun-Thu, to 1am Fri & Sat; MBarceloneta) In a history-steeped, stone-floored building dating from 1840, this atmospheric little jewel recreates a neighbourhood bodega, with tins of sardines, anchovies and other delicacies (used in exquisite tapas dishes) lining the shelves, house-made vermouth, and a wonderful array of wines. Be prepared to stand as there are no seats (a handful of upturned wine barrels let you rest your glass).

BlackLab   Microbrewery
(Map p250; ☎93 221 83 60; www.blacklab.es; Plaça de Pau Vila 1; ⊙noon-1.30am; MBarceloneta) Barcelona's first brewhouse opened back in 2014 inside the historic Palau de Mar. Its taps feature 18 house-made brews, including saisons, double IPAs and dry stouts, and the brewmasters constantly experiment with new flavours, such as a sour Berliner Weisse with fiery jalapeño. One-hour tours (5pm Sunday; €12) offer a behind-the-scenes look at the brewers in action and includes four samples.

Absenta   Bar
(☎93 221 36 38; www.absenta.bar; Carrer de Sant Carles 36; ⊙6pm-2am Mon-Thu, 11am-3am Fri & Sat, 6pm-1am Sun; MBarceloneta) Decorated with old paintings, vintage lamps and curious sculptures (including a dangling

butterfly woman), this whimsical drinking den specialises in absinthe, with over 20 varieties available. (Go easy, though: an alcohol content of 50% to 90% provides a kick!) It also has a house-made vermouth, if you're not a fan of the green fairy.

Can Paixano   Wine Bar
(Map p250; ☎93 310 08 39; www.canpaixano.com; Carrer de la Reina Cristina 7; ⊙9am-10.30pm Mon-Sat; MBarceloneta) This lofty *cava* bar (also called La Xampanyeria) has long been run on a winning formula. The standard tipple is bubbly rosé in elegant little glasses, combined with bite-sized *bocadillos* (filled rolls) and tapas. Note that this place is usually packed to the rafters, and elbowing your way to the bar can be a titanic struggle.

Woki Playa   Cocktail Bar
(www.tribuwoki.com; Passeig Marítim de la Barceloneta 1; ⊙noon-9pm Sun-Thu, to midnight Fri & Sat; 🛜; MBarceloneta) 🍃 A corrugated-iron bar, recycled timbers and repurposed industrial lights give this neo-*chiringuito* (beach bar) a sharp, contemporary edge. Ingredients from its own organic market in L'Eixample are used in cocktails such as its signature Woki Mule (jasmine-infused vodka, honey, lime, cardamom and ginger beer).

La Deliciosa   Bar
(www.ladeliciosabeachbar.com; Passeig Marítim de la Barceloneta; ⊙10am-10pm Mar-Oct; 🛜; MBarceloneta) Surfboards frame this beach bar on the sand at Platja de la Barceloneta – an idyllic spot for fresh juices, regional wines and cocktails such as Basil Instinct (vodka, pineapple juice, lemon, ginger, raspberries and basil) or Passion Smash (Jack Daniels, passion fruit pulp and mint).

The Mint   Cocktail Bar
(Map p250; ☎647 737707; www.facebook.com/themintbarcelona; Passeig d'Isabel II 4; ⊙7.30pm-2.30am Sun-Thu, to 3am Fri & Sat; MBarceloneta) Named after the prized cocktail ingredient, this mojito-loving spot has an upstairs bar where you can peruse the first-rate house-infused gins (over 20 on hand, including creative blends like lemongrass

and Jamaican pepper). Downstairs in the brick-vaulted cellars, red lights and driving beats create a more celebratory vibe.

La Cervecita Nuestra de Cada Día
Bar

(Carrer de Llull 184; ⊙11.30am-2pm & 5.30-9.30pm Tue-Sat, 5.30-9.30pm Sun & Mon; MLlacuna) Equal parts beer shop and craft brew bar, La Cervecita has a changing selection of unique beers from around Europe and the USA. You might stumble across a Catalan sour fruit beer, a rare English stout, a potent Belgian triple ale or half a dozen other draughts on hand – plus many more varieties by the bottle.

Madame George
Lounge

(www.madamegeorgebar.com; Carrer de Pujades 179; ⊙6pm-2am Mon-Thu, to 3am Fri & Sat, to 12.30am Sun; MPoblenou) A theatrical elegance marks the interior of this small, chandelier-lit lounge just off the Rambla del Poblenou. Deft bartenders stir well-balanced cocktails like a Lychee-tini (vanilla-infused vodka, fresh lychees, lychee liqueur and lemon juice) in vintage glassware, while a DJ spins vinyl in the corner.

Balius
Cocktail Bar

(☎93 315 86 50; www.baliusbar.com; Carrer de Pujades 196; ⊙6pm-2am Tue & Wed, 5pm-3am Thu-Sat, to 1am Sun; MPoblenou) There's an old-fashioned jauntiness to this vintage cocktail den in El Poblenou. Staff pour a mix of classic libations as well as vermouths. Stop by on Sundays to catch live jazz.

Santa Marta
Bar

(www.santamartabarcelona.com; Carrer de Grau i Torras 59; ⊙10am-midnight; MBarceloneta) Just back from the beach, this laidback bar attracts a garrulous mix of locals and expats, who come for prime people-watching at one of the outdoor tables near the boardwalk. Alongside classic cocktails, craft creations include Santa Delicious (tequila, Campari, pink grapefruit and mint).

Shôko
Club

(☎93 225 92 00; www.shoko.biz; Passeig Marítim de la Barceloneta 36; ⊙club midnight-6am,

👍 **Streets & Plazas to Bar-Hop**

Plaça Reial Barri Gòtic
Carrer dels Escudellers Barri Gòtic
Carrer de Joaquín Costa El Raval
Carrer Nou de la Rambla El Raval
Rambla del Raval El Raval
Plaça del Sol Gràcia
Plaça de la Vila de Gràcia Gràcia
Platja de la Barceloneta La Barceloneta
Passeig del Born La Ribera
Carrer d'Aribau L'Eixample
Carrer Nou de la Rambla Poble Sec
Carrer de Blai Poble Sec
Carrer del Parlament Sant Antoni

Plaça Reial
MIHAI-BOGDAN LAZAR/SHUTTERSTOCK ©

restaurant noon-midnight; MCiutadella Vila Olímpica) This stylish restaurant, club and beachfront bar evokes the Far East via potted bamboo, Japanese electro and Asian-Med fusion cuisine. As the food is cleared away, Shôko transforms into a deep-grooving, neon-lit nightspot with DJs spinning for the beautiful crowd. The open-sided beachfront lounge is a popular spot for a sundowner.

Opium
Club

(☎93 225 91 00; www.opiumbarcelona.com; Passeig Marítim de la Barceloneta 34; €10-20; ⊙club 10pm-5am Sun-Thu, to 6am Fri & Sat, restaurant from noon; MCiutadella Vila Olímpica) This seaside dance place has a spacious dance floor that only begins to fill from about 3am and is best in summer, when you can spill onto a terrace overlooking the beach.

⊖ Camp Nou, Pedralbes & La Zona Alta

El Maravillas — Cocktail Bar

(📞93 360 73 78; www.elmaravillas.cat; Plaça de la Concòrdia 15; ⊙noon-midnight Mon & Tue, to 1am Wed, to 2am Thu, to 3am Fri-Sun; ⓂMaria Cristina, 🚇T1, T2, T3 Numància) Overlooking the peaceful Plaça de la Concòrdia, El Maravillas feels like a secret hideaway – especially if you've just arrived from the crowded lanes of the *ciutat vella* (old city). The glittering bar has just a few tables, plus outdoor seating on the square in warm weather. Creative cocktails, good Spanish red wines and easy-drinking vermouths are the drinks of choice.

Dō Bar — Bar

(📞93 209 18 88; www.do-bcn.com; Carrer de Santaló 30; ⊙7pm-midnight Tue-Thu, 8pm-1am Fri & Sat; 🛜; 🚇FGC Muntaner) This neigh-bourhood charmer has a warm and inviting interior, where locals gather at wooden tables to enjoy excellent gin and tonics, wines by the glass, craft beer and satisfying small plates (anchovies, mussels, tacos, charcuterie). On warm nights, arrive early for one of the terrace tables out the front. Enter via Carrer de l'Avenir.

Mirablau — Bar

(📞93 418 58 79; www.mirablaubcn.com; Plaça del Doctor Andreu; ⊙11am-3.30am Mon-Wed, 11am-4.30am Thu, 10am-5am Fri-Sat, 10am-2.30am Sun; 🚇196, 🚇FGC Avinguda Tibidabo) Gaze out over the entire city from this priv-ileged balcony restaurant at the base of the Funicular del Tibidabo. The bar is renowned for its gin selection, with 30 different varieties. Wander downstairs to join the folk in the tiny dance space, which opens at 11.30pm. In summer you can step out onto the even smaller terrace for a breather.

Marcel — Bar

(📞93 209 89 48; Carrer de Santaló 42; ⊙7.30am-1am Mon-Thu, 7.30am-3am Fri & Sat, 9.30am-midnight Sun; 🚇FGC Muntaner) A classic meet-ing place, Marcel has a homely, old-world feel, with a wood bar, black-and-white floor

tiles and high windows. It offers snacks and tapas as well. Space is somewhat limited and customers inevitably spill out onto the footpath, where there are also a few tables.

Bikini — Club

(📞93 322 08 00; www.bikinibcn.com; Avinguda Diagonal 547; from €12; ⊙midnight-6am Thu-Sat; 🚇6, 7, 33, 34, 63, 67, L51, L57, 🚇T1, T2, T3 L'Illa) This old star of the Barcelona nightlife scene has been keeping the beat since 1953. Every possible kind of music gets a run, from Latin and Brazilian beats to 1980s disco, depending on the night and the space you choose.

Sutton Club — Club

(📞667 432759; www.thesuttonclub.com; Carrer de Tuset 13; from €15; ⊙11.30pm-5.30am Wed & Thu, to 6am Fri & Sat; 🚇FGC Gràcia) With main-stream sounds on the dance floor and some hopping house in a side bar, this neon-lit disco inevitably attracts just about every-one pouring in and out of the nearby bars at some stage of the evening. The main dance floor gets packed with a beautiful crowd and, even with reservations, the bouncers can be tough.

Berlin — Bar

(📞93 200 65 42; www.cafeberlinbarcelona.com; Carrer de Muntaner 240; ⊙10am-2am Mon-Thu, to 3am Fri & Sat; ⓂHospital Clínic) This elegant corner bar offers views over Avinguda Diagonal. There is a cluster of tables outside on the ground floor and designer lounges downstairs. Service can be harried, but the location is excellent for starting an uptown night before kicking on to nearby clubs.

⊖ El Raval

La Confitería — Cocktail Bar

(Map p256; 📞93 140 54 35; Carrer de Sant Pau 128; ⊙7pm-2.30am Mon-Thu, 6pm-3am Fri & Sat, 5pm-2.30am Sun; 🛜; ⓂParal·lel) This is a trip into the 19th century. Until the 1980s it was a confectioner's shop, and although the original cabinets are now lined with booze, the look of the place barely changed with its conversion. A recent refurb of the back room is similarly sympathetic, and the vibe these days is lively cocktail bar.

Bar Pastís   Bar

(Map p250; www.barpastis.es; Carrer de Santa Mònica 4; ☺8pm-2am Tue-Thu & Sun, to 3am Fri & Sat; 🛜; MDrassanes) A French cabaret theme (with lots of Piaf on the stereo) pervades this tiny, cluttered classic, which has been going, on and off, since the end of WWII. You'll need to be in before 9pm to have any hope of sitting or getting near the bar. On some nights it features live acts, usually performing French *chanson*.

Bar Marsella   Bar

(Map p250; ☐93 442 72 63; Carrer de Sant Pau 65; ☺10pm-2.30am Mon-Thu, to 3am Fri & Sat; MLiceu) Bar Marsella has been in business since 1820, and has served the likes of Hemingway, who was known to slump here over an *absenta* (absinthe). The bar still specialises in this drink, which is to be treated with respect.

Casa Almirall   Bar

(Map p249; ☐93 318 95 92; www.casaalmirall. com; Carrer de Joaquín Costa 33; ☺5.30pm-2am Mon-Wed, noon-2.30am Thu-Sat, noon-12.30am Sun; 🛜; MUniversitat) In business since the 1860s, this unchanged corner bar is dark and intriguing, with Modernista decor and a mixed clientele. There are some great original pieces in here, such as the marble counter, and the cast-iron statue of the muse of the Universal Exposition, held in Barcelona in 1888.

El Drapaire   Bar

(Map p249; ☐607 466446; www.drapaire.com; Carrer de les Sitges 11; ☺6pm-2am Sun-Thu, 3pm-3am Fri & Sat; 🛜; MCatalunya) Part of the recent explosion in the craft-beer scene, this cosy, beamed tavern has been given a new lease on life and now has 13 taps, featuring Spanish and international beers of all styles. There are tapas and platters of cheese and charcuterie to share. Live music on Fridays.

🍷 Catalan Wine

The bulk of DO wines in Catalonia are made from grapes produced in the Penedès area, which pumps out almost two million hectolitres a year. The other DO winemaking zones (spread as far apart as the Empordà area around Figueres in the north and the Terra Alta around Gandesa in the southwest) have a combined output of about half that produced in Penedès. The wines of the El Priorat area, which tend to be dark, heavy reds, have been promoted to DOC status, an honour shared only with those of La Rioja (categorised as such since 1926). Drops from the neighbouring Montsant area are frequently as good (or close) and considerably cheaper.

Most of the grapes grown in Catalonia are native to Spain and include white macabeo, garnatxa and xarel·lo (for whites), and black garnatxa, monastrell and ull de llebre (tempranillo) red varieties. Foreign varieties (such as chardonnay, riesling, chenin blanc, cabernet sauvignon, merlot and pinot noir) are also common.

There is plenty to look out for beyond Penedès. Raïmat, in the Costers del Segre DO area of Lleida province, produces fine reds and a couple of notable whites. Good fortified wines come from around Tarragona and some nice fresh wines are also produced in the Empordà area in the north.

Vineyard in the Penedès wine region
JOAN_BAUTISTA/SHUTTERSTOCK

Chiringuitos

During summer small wooden beach bars, known as *chiringuitos,* open up along the strand from Barceloneta all the way up to Platja de la Nova Mar Bella. Here you can dip your toes in the sand and nurse a cocktail while watching the city at play against the backdrop of the deep-blue Mediterranean. Ambient grooves add to the laid-back environment. *Chiringuitos* are also great spots for a snack – particularly the **Guingueta de la Barceloneta** (www.carlesabellan. com; Platja de Sant Sebastià; dishes €6-16; ⏱9am-midnight Mar-Nov; MBarceloneta) and **Guingueta del Bogatell** (Platja del Bogatell; ⏱9am-10.30pm May-Sep; MLlacuna) run by Michelin-starred chef Carles Abellán. The drink of choice at either is a refreshing *cava sangría.*

One of the liveliest beachside bars lies northeast of the city on Cavaió beach in Arenys de Mar (accessible from Barcelona by train). **Lasal** (www.lasal.com) hosts top-notch DJs and has a tropical-themed party atmosphere. It opens daily from mid-May to September.

Chiringuito on Barceloneta Beach
PI03/SHUTTERSTOCK ©

33|45 — Bar

(Map p249; ☎93 187 41 38; www.3345.struments. com; Carrer de Joaquín Costa 4; ⏱1pm-2am Sun-Mon, to 3am Fri & Sat; 🛜; MUniversitat) A super-trendy bar, this place has excellent mojitos, a fashionable crowd and a frequently changing exhibition of art on the walls. There are DJs most nights.

Moog — Club

(Map p250; ☎93 319 17 89; www.masimas. com/moog; Carrer de l'Arc del Teatre 3; €5-10; ⏱midnight-5am Sun-Thu, to 6am Fri & Sat; MDrassanes) This fun and minuscule club is a standing favourite with the downtown crowd. In the main dance area, DJs dish out house, techno and electro, while upstairs you can groove to a nice blend of indie and occasional classic-pop throwbacks.

Negroni — Cocktail Bar

(Map p249; www.negronicocktailbar.com; Carrer de Joaquín Costa 46; ⏱7pm-2.30am Sun-Thu, to 3am Fri & Sat; MUniversitat) Good things come in small packages and this dark, teeny cocktail bar confirms the rule. The mostly black decor lures in a largely student set to try out the cocktails, among them, of course, the celebrated Negroni: a Florentine invention with one part Campari, one part gin and one part sweet vermouth.

Marmalade — Bar

(Map p249; ☎93 442 39 66; www.marmalade barcelona.com; Carrer de la Riera Alta 4-6; ⏱6.30pm-2am Mon-Thu, 10am-3am Fri-Sun; 🛜; MSant Antoni) The golden hues of this backlit bar and restaurant beckon seductively through the glass facade. There are various distinct spaces, decorated in different but equally sumptuous styles, and a pool table next to the bar. Cocktails are big business here, and a selection of them are €5 all night.

Bar La Concha — Bar, Gay

(Map p250; www.laconchadelraval.com; Carrer de la Guàrdia 14; ⏱5pm-2.30am Sun-Thu, to 3am Fri & Sat; 🛜; MDrassanes) This place is dedicated to the actress Sara Montiel: the walls groan with more than 250 photos of the sultry star, now surrounding an incongruous large-screen TV. La Concha used to be a largely gay and transvestite haunt, but anyone is welcome and bound to have fun – especially when the drag queens come out to play.

Betty Ford's — Bar

(Map p249; ☎93 304 13 68; Carrer de Joaquín Costa 56; ⏱1pm-2.30am Tue-Sat, from 5pm Sun & Mon; 🛜; MUniversitat) This enticing corner bar is one of several good stops along the student-jammed run of Carrer de Joaquín Costa. It puts together some nice cocktails and the place fills with an even mix of locals and foreigners, generally aged not much over 30. There's a decent line in burgers and soups, too.

Kentucky
Bar

(Map p250; Carrer de l'Arc del Teatre 11; ⊙10pm-4am Wed-Sat; ⓂDrassanes) Once a haunt of visiting US Navy boys, this exercise in Americana kitsch is the perfect way to finish an evening – if you can squeeze in. All sorts of odd bods from the *barri* and beyond gather here. An institution in the wee hours, Kentucky often stays open (unofficially) until dawn.

❂ Gràcia & Park Güell

Bobby Gin
Cocktail Bar

(Map p254; ✆93 368 18 92; www.bobbygin.com; Carrer de Francisco Giner 47; ⊙4pm-2am Sun-Wed, to 2.30am Thu, to 3am Fri & Sat; ⓂDiagonal) With over 60 varieties, this whitewashed stone-walled bar is a haven for gin lovers. Try an infusion-based concoction (rose-tea-infused Hendrick's with strawberries and lime; tangerine-infused Tanqueray 10 with Agave nectar and bitter chamomile) or a cocktail like the Santa Maria (chardonnay, milk thistle syrup, thyme, sage and lemon). Fusion tapas choices include G&T-cured salmon.

Rabipelao
Cocktail Bar

(Map p254; ✆93 182 50 35; www.elrabipelao. com; Carrer del Torrent d'En Vidalet 22; ⊙7pm-1.30am Sun-Thu, to 3am Fri & Sat, 1-4.30pm Sun; ⓂJoanic) An anchor of Gràcia's nightlife, Rabipelao is a celebratory space with a shiny disco ball and DJs spinning salsa beats. A silent film plays in one corner beyond the red velvety wallpapered walls and there's a richly hued mural above the bar. Tropical cocktails like mojitos and caipirinhas pair with South American snacks such as *arepas* (meat-filled cornbread patties) and ceviche.

Elephanta
Bar

(Map p254; ✆93 237 69 06; www.elephanta.cat; Carrer del Torrent d'en Vidalet 37; ⊙6pm-1.30am Mon-Wed, to 2.30am Thu, to 3am Fri & Sat, to 10pm Sun; ⓢ; ⓂJoanic) Off the main drag, this petite cocktail bar has an old-fashioned vibe, with long, plush green banquettes, art-lined walls and a five-seat bar with vintage wood stools. Gin is the drink of choice, with more than 40 varieties on hand, and the cocktails are expertly mixed.

La Vermu
Bar

(Map p254; ✆93 171 80 87; Carrer de Sant Domènec 15; ⊙6.30pm-midnight Mon-Thu, 12.30-4.30pm & 7.30pm-12.30am Fri-Sun; ⓇFGC Gràcia) House-made *negre* (black) and *blanc* (white) vermouth, served with a slice of orange and an olive, is the speciality of this hip neighbourhood hang-out. The airy space with exposed timber beams and industrial lighting centres on a marble bar with seating and surrounding marble-topped tables. Vermouth aside, it also has a small but stellar wine list and stylishly presented tapas.

Sol de NIT
Bar

(Map p254; ✆93 237 39 37; http://sol-de-nit. eltenedor.rest; Plaça del Sol 9; ⊙1-3.30pm & 9-11pm; ⓂFontana) Happening little hang-out Sol de NIT has a small, cosy interior decorated with mosaics, old lamps and a soundtrack of jazz. It has a large terrace on Plaça del Sol that's heated in winter. Sangria is a speciality; there are great cocktails, too.

El Rincón Cubano
Bar

(Map p254; ✆93 143 77 01; Carrer de l'Or 19; ⊙7pm-1am Tue-Thu, 7pm-2am Fri, 6pm-2am Sat, 1pm-midnight Sun; ⓢ; ⓂFontana) Cuban cocktails (including Cuba libres and *el presidentes*) and beers (Mayabe, Tinima and Cacique) are served alongside authentic snacks such as *pasteles* (puff pastry with savoury fillings), Cuban sandwiches and *ropa vieja* (shredded steak in tomato sauce) at this bar with arched brickwork and terracotta-tiled floors. It's in its element on Sundays from 4pm when live acoustic Cuban music plays.

👍 Nightlife Guides

Clubbingspain.com (www.clubbing spain.com)
Barcelona Connect (www.barcelona connect.com)
Miniguide (www.miniguide.es)
Metropolitan (www.barcelona-metropolitan.com)
enBarcelona (www.enbarcelona.com)

La Vermuteria del Tano   Bar

(Map p254; ☎93 213 10 58; Carrer Joan Blanques 17; ☺9am-9pm Mon-Fri, noon-4pm Sat & Sun; Ⓜ Joanic) Scarcely changed in decades, with barrels on the walls, old fridges with wooden doors, vintage clocks and marble-topped tables, this vermouth bar is a local gathering point. Its house-speciality Peruchi is served traditionally with a glass of carbonated water. Tapas is also traditional, with most dishes utilising ingredients from tins (anchovies, smoked clams, cockles and pickled octopus).

Chatelet   Cocktail Bar

(Map p254; ☎93 284 95 90; Carrer de Torrijos 54; ☺6pm-2.30am Mon-Thu, 6pm-3am Fri, noon-3am Sat, noon-2.30am Sun; Ⓜ Joanic) A popular meeting point in the hood, Chatelet has big windows for watching the passing people parade, and a buzzing art-filled interior that sees a wide cross-section of Gràcia society. Blues and old-school American soul plays in the background. The cocktails are excellent, and the drink prices fair (with discounts before 10pm).

Viblioteca   Wine Bar

(Map p254; ☎93 284 42 02; www.viblioteca. com; Carrer de Vallfogona 12; ☺7pm-midnight; Ⓜ Fontana) A glass cabinet piled high with ripe cheese (over 50 varieties) entices you into this small, white, cleverly designed contemporary space. The real speciality at Viblioteca, however, is wine, and you can choose from 150 mostly local labels, many of them available by the glass.

La Cigale   Cocktail Bar

(Map p254; ☎93 457 58 23; www.facebook. com/La-Cigale-Barcelona; Carrer de Tordera 50; ☺6pm-2am Sun-Thu, to 3am Fri & Sat; Ⓜ Joanic) La Cigale is a very civilised place for a cocktail, with oil paintings on the walls, gilded mirrors and leatherbound volumes scattered about. Prop up the zinc bar, sink into a secondhand lounge chair around a teeny table or head upstairs.

El Sabor   Bar

(Map p254; ☎674 993075; Carrer de Francisco Giner 32; ☺9pm-2.30am Sun-Thu, to 3am Fri & Sat; Ⓜ Diagonal) Ruled since 1992 by the charismatic Havana-born Angelito is this home of *ron y son* (rum and sound). A mixed crowd of Cubans and fans of the Caribbean island come to drink mojitos and shake their stuff in this diminutive, good-humoured hang-out. Stop by on Mondays, Tuesdays and Wednesdays for a free two-hour salsa or bachata lesson (starting at 9.30pm).

Bar Canigó   Bar

(Map p254; ☎93 213 30 49; www.barcanigo.com; Carrer de Verdi 2; ☺10am-2am Mon-Thu, 10am-3am Fri, 8pm-3am Sat; Ⓜ Fontana) Now run by the third generation of owners, this corner bar overlooking Plaça de la Revolució de Setembre de 1868 is an animated spot. Sip on a house vermouth or an Estrella beer around rickety old marble-top tables, as people have done here since 1922.

Le Journal   Bar

(Map p254; ☎93 368 41 37; Carrer de Francisco Giner 36; ☺6pm-2am; Ⓜ Fontana) Newspapers plaster the wood-panelled walls and ceilings of this split-level bar (hence the name). Read the headlines of yesteryear while reclining in an old lounge. For a slightly more intimate feel, head upstairs to the rear gallery overlooking the bar. Try one of the gin infusions or house-speciality Hurricane (with dark rum and passionfruit juice).

Musical Maria   Bar

(Map p254; ☎93 501 04 60; Carrer de Maria 5; ☺9pm-2.30am Sun-Thu, to 3am Fri & Sat; 📶; Ⓜ Diagonal) Even the music hasn't changed since this place got going in the late 1970s.

Those longing for rock 'n' roll crowd into this animated bar, listen to old hits and knock back beers. Out the back there's a pool table and the bar serves pretty much all the variants of the local Estrella Damm brew.

La Fourmi
Bar

(Map p254; ☎93 213 30 52; Carrer de Milà i Fontanals 58; ☺9am-1.30am Mon-Thu, 9am-3am Fri, 10am-3am Sat, 10am-1.30am Sun; ⓂJoanic) La Fourmi is a small, cosy spot for a cocktail or a bite no matter the time of day. It draws a mix of students, old-timers and hipsters to its weekday breakfast and weekend brunch.

Raïm
Bar

(Map p254; Carrer del Progrés 48; ☺8pm-2am Tue-Thu, to 3am Fri & Sat; ⓂDiagonal) The walls in Raïm are alive with black-and-white photos of Cubans and Cuba. Weathered old wooden chairs of another epoch huddle around marble tables, while grand old wood-framed mirrors hang from the walls. It draws a friendly, garrulous crowd who pile in for first-rate mojitos and an excellent selection of rum.

⊖ La Rambla & Barri Gòtic

Marula Café
Bar

(Map p250; ☎93 318 76 90; www.marulacafe.com; Carrer dels Escudellers 49; up to €10; ☺11pm-5am Mon-Thu & Sun, 11.30pm-6am Fri, 9.30pm-6am Sat; ⓂLiceu) A fantastic find in the heart of the Barri Gòtic, Marula will transport you to the 1970s and the best in funk and soul. James Brown fans will think they've died and gone to heaven. It's not, however, a mono-thematic place and DJs slip in other tunes, from breakbeat to house. Samba and other Brazilian dance sounds also penetrate here.

L'Ascensor
Cocktail Bar

(Map p250; ☎93 318 53 47; Carrer de la Bellafila 3; ☺6pm-2.30am Mon-Thu, to 3am Fri-Sun; 🛜; ⓂJaume I) Named after the lift (elevator) doors that serve as the front door, this elegant drinking den with its vaulted brick ceilings, vintage mirrors and marble-topped bar gathers a faithful crowd that comes for

🍷🍸 Wine & Cava Bars

A growing number of wine bars scattered around the city provide a showcase for the great produce from Spain and beyond. Vine-minded spots such as **Monvínic** (p186) serve a huge selection of wines by the glass, with a particular focus on stellar new vintages. A big part of the experience is having a few bites while you drink. Expect sharing plates, platters of cheese and charcuterie, and plenty of tapas.

Cava bars tend to be more about the festive ambience than the actual drinking of *cava*, a sparkling white or rosé, most of which is produced in Catalonia's Penedès region. At the more famous *cava* bars you'll have to nudge your way through the garrulous crowds and enjoy your bubbly standing up. Two of the most famous *cava* bars are **El Xampanyet** (p185) in La Ribera and **Can Paixano** (p176) in Barceloneta.

A glass of *cava*
MANU SAENZ/SHUTTERSTOCK ©

old-fashioned cocktails and lively conversation against a soundtrack of up-tempo jazz and funk.

Sor Rita
Bar

(Map p250; ☎93 176 62 66; www.sorritabar.es; Carrer de la Mercè 27; ☺7pm-2.30am Sun-Thu, to 3am Fri & Sat; 🛜; ⓂJaume I) A lover of all things kitsch, Sor Rita is pure eye candy, from its leopard-print wallpaper to its high-heel-festooned ceiling and deliciously irreverent decorations inspired by the films of Almodóvar. It's a fun and festive scene, with special-event nights including tarot readings on Mondays, all-you-can-eat snack buffets (€7) on Tuesdays and karaoke on Thursdays.

Polaroid   Bar

(Map p250; ☑93 186 66 69; www.polaroidbar. es; Carrer dels Còdols 29; ⊙7.30pm-2.30am Sun-Thu, to 3am Fri & Sat; ☎; MDrassanes) For a dash of 1980s nostalgia, Polaroid is a blast from the past, with its wall-mounted VHS tapes, old film posters, comic-book-covered tables, action-figure displays and other kitschy decor. Not surprisingly, it draws a fun, unpretentious crowd who come for cheap *cañas* (draught beer), mojitos and free popcorn.

Bosc de les Fades   Lounge

(☑93 317 26 49; Passatge de la Banca 5; ⊙10am-1am Mon-Fri, from 11am Sat & Sun; MDrassanes) The 'Forest of the Fairies' is touristy but offers a whimsical retreat from the busy Rambla nearby, and has a wonderfully kitsch charm. Lounge chairs and lamplit tables are scattered beneath an indoor forest complete with trickling fountain and grotto. *Bocadillos* and snacks are available.

Manchester   Bar

(Map p250; ☑627 733081; Carrer de Milans 5; ⊙6.30pm-2.30am Sun-Thu, to 3am Fri & Sat; ☎; MLiceu) ✔ A drinking den that has undergone several transformations over the years now treats you to the sounds of great Manchester bands, from Joy Division to Oasis, but probably not the Hollies. It has a pleasing rough-and-tumble feel, with tables jammed in every which way. There are DJs on Thursdays.

Karma   Club

(Map p250; ☑93 302 56 80; www.karmadisco. com; Plaça Reial 10; ⊙noon-5am Tue-Thu, to 6am Fri & Sat; MLiceu) During the week Karma plays good, mainstream indie music, while on weekends the DJs spin anything from rock to disco. A golden oldie in Barcelona, tunnel-shaped Karma is small and becomes quite tightly packed (claustrophobic for some) with a good-natured crowd of locals and out-of-towners. The bar and terrace on Plaça Reial open at noon, but the club opens at midnight.

...this unchanged corner bar is dark and intriguing...

Casa Almirall (p179)

STEFANO POLITI MARKOVINA/ALAMY STOCK PHOTO ©

La Macarena   Club

(Map p250; ☑93 301 30 64; www.macarenaclub. com; Carrer Nou de Sant Francesc 5; €5-10; ☺midnight-5am Sun-Thu, to 6am Fri & Sat; ⓂDrassanes) You won't believe this was once a tile-lined Andalucian flamenco musos' bar. Now it is a dark dance space, of the kind where it is possible to sit at the bar, meet people around you and then stand up for a bit of a shake to the DJ's electro and house offerings, all within about five square metres.

Boadas   Cocktail Bar

(Map p250; ☑93 318 95 92; www.boadas cocktails.com; Carrer dels Tallers 1; ☺noon-2am Mon-Thu, to 3am Fri & Sat; ⓂCatalunya) One of the city's oldest cocktail bars, Boadas is famed for its daiquiris. Bow-tied waiters have been serving up unique, drinkable creations since Miguel Boadas opened it in 1933 – in fact Miró and Hemingway both drank here. Miguel was born in Havana, where he was the first barman at the immortal La Floridita.

❷ La Ribera

Guzzo   Cocktail Bar

(Map p250; ☑93 667 00 36; www.guzzoclub. es; Plaça Comercial 10; ☺6pm-2.30am Mon-Thu, to 3am Fri & Sat, noon-3am Sun; ☎; ⓂJaume I) This swish but relaxed cocktail bar is run by much-loved Barcelona DJ Fred Guzzo, who is often to be found at the decks, spinning his delicious selection of funk, soul and rare groove. You'll also find frequent live-music acts of consistently decent quality, and a funky atmosphere at almost any time of day.

La Vinya del Senyor   Wine Bar

(Map p250; ☑93 310 33 79; Plaça de Santa Maria del Mar 5; ☺noon-1am Mon-Thu, to 2am Fri & Sat, to midnight Sun; ☎; ⓂJaume I) Relax on the *terraza,* which lies in the shadow of the Basílica de Santa Maria del Mar, or crowd inside at the tiny bar. The wine list is as long as *War and Peace* and there's a table upstairs for those who opt to sample the wine away from the madding crowd.

Rubí   Bar

(Map p250; ☑647 737707; Carrer dels Banys Vells 6; ☺7.30pm-2.30am Sun-Thu, to 3am Fri & Sat; ☎; ⓂJaume I) With its boudoir lighting and cheap mojitos, Rubí is where the Born's *cognoscenti* head for a nightcap – or several – and superior bar food. It's a narrow, cosy space – push through to the back where you might just get one of the coveted tables.

El Born Bar   Bar

(Map p250; ☑93 319 53 33; www.elbornbar.com; Passeig del Born 26; ☺10am-2am Mon-Thu, 10am-3am Fri & Sat, noon-2.30am Sun; ☎; ⓂJaume I) Moss-green paintwork, marble tables and a chequered black-and-white tiled floor create a timeless look for this popular little cafe/bar. A spiral wrought-iron staircase leads to a quieter room upstairs. The twisting steps mean that there is no table service and hot drinks can't be carried upstairs.

El Xampanyet   Wine Bar

(Map p250; ☑93 319 70 03; Carrer de Montcada 22; ☺noon-3.30pm & 7-11.15pm Tue-Sat, noon-3.30pm Sun; ☎; ⓂJaume I) Nothing has changed for decades in this, one of the city's best-known *cava* bars. Plant yourself at the bar or seek out a table against the decoratively tiled walls for a glass or three of the cheap house *cava* and an assortment of tapas.

Miramelindo   Bar

(Map p250; ☑93 310 37 27; www.barmiramelindo bcn.com; Passeig del Born 15; ☺8pm-2.30am Mon-Thu, 8pm-3.30am Fri & Sat, 7pm-2.30am Sun; ☎; ⓂJaume I) A spacious tavern in a Gothic building, this remains a classic on Passeig del Born for mixed drinks, while soft jazz and soul sounds float overhead. Try for a comfy seat at a table towards the back before it fills to bursting. A couple of similarly barn-sized places sit on this side of the *passeig*.

Mudanzas   Bar

(Map p250; ☑93 319 11 37; Carrer de la Vidrieria 15; ☺8am-2.30am Mon-Fri, 10am-2.30am Sat & Sun; ☎; ⓂJaume I) This was one of the first bars to get things into gear in El Born and it still attracts a faithful crowd. With its chequered floor and marble-topped tables, it's an attractive, lively place for a beer and perhaps a sandwich or a tapa. It also has a nice line in rum and malt whisky.

Magic   Club

(Map p250; ☑93 310 72 67; www.magic-club. net; Passeig de Picasso 40; ⏰11pm-6am Thu-Sat; ⓂBarceloneta) Although it sometimes hosts live acts in its basement, Magic is basically a straightforward subterranean nightclub offering rock, mainstream dance faves and Spanish pop. It's an established favourite on the scene, and queues can be long.

🅾 La Sagrada Família & L'Eixample

Napar BCN   Brewery

(Map p254; ☑93 408 91 62; www.naparbcn.com; Carrer de la Diputació 223; ⏰5pm-midnight Tue & Wed, to 1am Thu, to 2am Fri & Sat; 🛜; ⓂUniversitat) A standout on Barcelona's burgeoning craft-beer scene, Napar has 14 beers on tap, six of which are brewed on site, including IPA, pale ale and stout. There's also an accomplished list of bottled beers. It's a stunning space, with a gleaming steampunk aesthetic and a great rock and indie soundtrack.

Monvínic   Wine Bar

(Map p254; ☑93 272 61 87; www.monvinic.com; Carrer de la Diputació 249; ⏰1-11pm Tue-Fri, 7-11pm Mon & Sat; ⓂPasseig de Gràcia) 🌊 At this rhapsody to wine, the digital wine list details more than 3000 international varieties searchable by origin, year or grape. Some 50 selections are available by the glass. You can, of course, order by the bottle too.

Feel free to talk to one of the six sommeliers who work on the list. At the back is the restaurant (p148), which specialises in Mediterranean cuisine. Both the wine bar and restaurant are a study in locavore practices and sustainability.

Milano   Cocktail Bar

(Map p254; ☑93 112 71 50; www.camparimilano. com; Ronda de la Universitat 35; ⏰noon-3am; ⓂCatalunya) Completely invisible from street

level, this gem of hidden Barcelona nightlife is a subterranean old-school cocktail bar with velvet banquettes and glass-fronted cabinets, presided over by white-jacketed waiters. Live music (Cuban, jazz, blues, flamenco and swing) plays nightly; a DJ takes over after 11pm. Fantastic cocktails include the Picasso (tequila, honey, absinthe and lemon) and six different bloody Marys.

Les Gens Que J'Aime   Bar

(Map p254; ☑93 215 68 79; www.lesgensque jaime.com; Carrer de València 286; ⏰6pm-2.30am Sun-Thu, 7pm-3am Fri & Sat; ⓂPasseig de Gràcia) Atmospheric and intimate, this basement relic of the 1960s follows a deceptively simple formula: chilled jazz music in the background, minimal lighting from an assortment of flea market lamps and a cosy, cramped scattering of red-velvet-backed lounges around tiny dark tables.

BierCaB   Craft Beer

(☑644 689045; www.biercab.com; Carrer de Muntaner 55; ⏰bar noon-midnight Mon-Thu, noon-2am Fri & Sat, 5pm-midnight Sun, shop 3.30pm-10pm Mon-Sat; 🛜; ⓂUniversitat) Beneath an artistic ceiling installation resembling a forest of giant matchsticks, this brilliant craft beer bar has 30 brews from around the world rotating on its taps. Burgers to accompany them are made from Wagyu beef and named after Barcelona neighbourhoods. Pop into its adjacent shop for another 500 bottled varieties kept cold in fridges.

Monkey Factory   Cocktail Bar

(☑93 681 78 93; Carrer de Còsega 234; ⏰6.30pm-2am Tue & Wed, to 3am Thu-Sat; 🚆FGC Provença) DJs spin on weekends at this high-spirited venue but it's positively hopping from early on most nights. Funky monkey (triple sec, gin, lime and egg white), chimpa sour (cardamom-infused pisco sour) and chita (passionfruit purée, vodka, cinnamon syrup and ginger) are among the inventive cocktails mixed up behind the neon-green-lit bar.

Garage Beer Co   Craft Beer

(Map p254; ☑93 528 59 89; www.garagebeer.co; Carrer del Consell de Cent 261; ⏰5pm-midnight

Mon-Thu, 5pm-2.30am Fri, noon-3am Sat, 2pm-midnight Sun; MUniversitat) One of the first of the slew of craft beer bars to pop up in Barcelona, Garage brews its own in a space at the bar, and offers around 10 different styles at a time. The eponymous Garage (a delicate session IPA) and Slinger (a more robust IPA) are always present on the board.

Dry Martini   Bar
(℡93 217 50 80; www.drymartiniorg.com; Carrer d'Aribau 162-166; ☉1pm-2.30am Mon-Thu, 1pm-3am Fri, 6.30pm-3am Sat, 6.30pm-2.30am Sun; ℝFGC Provença) Waiters make expert cocktail suggestions, but the house drink, taken at the bar or on one of the plush green banquettes, is always a good bet. The gin and tonic comes in an enormous mug-sized glass – one will take you most of the night. Out the back hides a superb restaurant, Speakeasy (p148).

El Viti   Bar
(Map p254; ℡93 633 83 36; www.elviti.com; Passeig de Sant Joan 62; ☉noon-midnight Sun-Thu, to 1am Fri & Sat; 🛜; MTetuan) Along the hip Passeig de Sant Joan, El Viti checks all the boxes – high ceilings, brick walls both bare

and glazed, black-clad staff and a barrel of artisanal vermouth on the bar. It also serves a good line in tapas.

Antilla BCN   Club
(Map p249; ℡93 451 45 64; www.antillasalsa.com; Carrer d'Aragó 141; Wed & Thu free, Fri & Sat €10; ☉10pm-4am Wed, 11pm-4am Thu, 11pm-6am Fri & Sat, 7pm-2am Sun; MUrgell) *The* salsateca in town, this is the place to come for Cuban *son,* merengue, salsa and a whole lot more.

City Hall   Club
(Map p254; ℡93 238 07 22; www.cityhall barcelona.com; Rambla de Catalunya 2-4; from €10; ☉10pm-6am Mon, 12.30am-6am Tue-Sun; MCatalunya) A long corridor leads to the dance floor of this venerable and popular club, located in a former theatre. Music styles, from house and other electric sounds to funk, change nightly; check the agenda online. The cover charge includes a drink.

> *...the real speciality is wine, and you can choose from 150 mostly local labels...*

Viblioteca (p182)

 **Discotecas**

Barcelona's *discotecas* (clubs) are at their best from Thursday to Saturday. Indeed, many open only on these nights. A surprising variety of spots lurk in the old-town labyrinth, ranging from plush former dance halls to grungy subterranean venues that fill to capacity.

Along the waterfront it's another story. At Port Olímpic sun-scorched crowds of visiting yachties mix it up with tourists and a few locals at noisy, back-to-back dance bars right on the waterfront.

A sprinkling of well-known clubs is spread over the classy parts of town, in L'Eixample and La Zona Alta. They attract a beautiful crowd.

Moog (p180)

Átame   Gay
(Map p254; ☑93 421 41 33; Carrer del Consell de Cent 257; ☻7.30pm-2.30am Tue, 8.30pm-2.30am Wed, Thu & Sun, 8.30pm-3am Fri & Sat; MUniversitat) Cool for a coffee earlier on, Átame (Tie Me Up) heats up later in the night when the gay crowd comes out to play. There is usually a raunchy show on Friday nights.

Aire   Lesbian
(Sala Diana; Map p254; ☑93 487 83 42; www.grupoarena.com; Carrer de la Diputació 233; Fri/Sat/Thu €5/6/free; ☻11pm-2.30am Thu-Sat; MPasseig de Gràcia) At this popular lesbian hang-out, the dance floor is spacious and there's usually a DJ in command of the tunes, which veer from hits of the '80s and '90s to Latin and techno. As a rule, only male friends of the girls are allowed entry,

although in practice the crowd tends to be fairly mixed.

Plata Bar   Gay
(Map p249; ☑93 452 46 36; www.platabar.com; Carrer del Consell de Cent 233; ☻8pm-1.30am Wed & Thu, to 3am Fri & Sat; MUniversitat) Summer seats on the corner terrace of this wide-open bar attract a lot of lads hopping between the area's gay bars. Inside, metallic horse-saddle stools are lined up at the bar and high tables, the music is a mix of dance and trance, and bartenders whip up eye-popping cocktails.

Cafè del Centre   Cafe
(Map p254; ☑93 488 11 01; Carrer de Girona 69; ☻9am-11pm Mon-Fri, 11am-11pm Sat; ☎; MGirona) Step back into the 19th century in this cafe that's been in business since 1873. The mahogany bar extends down the right side as you enter, fronted by marble-topped tables and wooden chairs. It exudes an almost melancholy air by day but gets busy at night, when live jazz piano plays. It stocks 50 beers and 15 loose-leaf teas.

Quilombo   Bar
(☑606 144272; Carrer d'Aribau 149; ☻9pm-2.30am Mon-Thu, 8.30pm-3am Fri & Sat; ☒FGC Provença) Some formulas just work, and this place has been working since the 1970s. Set up some guitars in the table-packed back room, add some cheapish pre-prepared mojitos and plastic tubs of nuts, and let the punters do the rest. They pour in, creating plenty of *quilombo* (fuss). Live music plays most nights from 11pm and impromptu parties are common.

La Fira   Bar
(Map p254; ☑682 323714; Carrer de Provença 171; €14; ☻11pm-5am Thu, to 6am Fri & Sat; ☒FGC Provença) Wander in past crazy mirrors, penny slot machines and other ancient fairground attractions from Germany as well as futuristic furniture like glowing cuboid stools. The music swings wildly from house to '90s hits to Spanish pop classics. Admission includes two drinks. With 150 spirits on hand, it claims to have 500 varieties of shots.

Punto BCN · Gay

(Map p254; 📞93 451 91 52; www.grupoarena.
com; Carrer de Muntaner 65; ⏰6pm-2.30am
Sun-Thu, to 3am Fri & Sat; Ⓜ️Universitat) It's an
oldie but a goody. A big bar over two levels
with a slightly older crowd, this place fills to
bursting on Friday and Saturday nights with
its blend of Spanish pop and dance. It's a
friendly early stop on a gay night out, and
you can shoot a round of pool here.

La Chapelle · Gay

(Map p254; 📞93 453 30 76; Carrer de Muntaner
67; ⏰4pm-2am Sun-Thu, to 2.30am Fri & Sat;
Ⓜ️Universitat) A typical long, narrow Eixample bar with white-tiled walls, La Chapelle
houses a plethora of crucifixes and niches
that far outdo what you'd find in any other
'chapel'. No need for six-pack abs here:
this is a relaxed gay meeting place that
welcomes all types.

Bacon Bear · Gay

(Map p249; 📞93 431 00 00; Carrer de Casanova
64; ⏰6pm-2.30am Mon-Thu & Sun, to 3am Fri
& Sat; Ⓜ️Urgell) Every bear needs a cave to
go to, and this is a rather friendly one. It's
really just a big bar for burly gay folk. The
music cranks up on weekends.

Michael Collins Pub · Irish Pub

(Map p254; 📞93 459 19 64; www.michaelcollins
pubs.com; Plaça de la Sagrada Família 4; ⏰1pm-
2.30am Sun-Thu, to 3am Fri & Sat; 📶; Ⓜ️Sagrada
Família) To be sure of a little Catalan-Irish
craic, this barn-sized, storming pub beloved
by locals and expats is just the ticket.
Traditional Irish music sessions strike up
on Mondays; live music also plays most
weekends.

Arena Madre · Gay

(Map p254; 📞93 487 83 42; www.grupoarena.
com; Carrer de Balmes 32; Sun-Fri €6, Sat €12;
⏰12.30-5.45am Sun-Thu, to 6.45am Fri & Sat;
Ⓜ️Passeig de Gràcia) Popular with a hot young
crowd, Arena Madre is one of the top clubs
in town for boys seeking boys. Mainly electronic and house music, with a striptease
show on Monday, techno on Thursday and
live shows throughout the week. Heteros
are welcome but a minority.

New Chaps · Gay

(Map p254; 📞93 215 53 65; http://newchaps.com;
Avinguda Diagonal 365; ⏰9pm-3am Sun-Thu, to
3.30am Fri & Sat; Ⓜ️Diagonal) Leather lovers
get in some close-quarters inspection on
the dance floor and especially in the dark
room, downstairs past the fairly dark loos in
the vaulted cellars. It's a classic handle-
bar-moustache, gay porn kinda place that
attracts an older crowd.

Arena Classic · Gay

(Map p254; 📞93 487 83 42; www.grupoarena.
com; Carrer de la Diputació 233; Fri/Sat €6/12;
⏰2.30am-6am Fri & Sat; Ⓜ️Passeig de Gràcia)
Spinning mostly techno, Arena Classic attracts an upbeat, energetic gay crowd. Entry
includes a drink.

🍴 Montjuïc, Poble Sec & Sant Antoni

Abirradero · Craft Beer

(Map p256; 📞93 461 94 46; www.abirradero.
com; Carrer Vila i Vilà 77; ⏰5pm-1am Mon-Thu,
noon-2am Fri & Sat, noon-1am Sun; 📶; Ⓜ️Paral·lel)
Barcelona is spoilt for choice with craft brew-
eries, and this bright, buzzing space has 20
of its own beers rotating on the taps, including IPAral·lel (a double IPA), Excuse Me While
I Kiss My Stout, and Tripel du Poble Sec.

La Caseta del Migdia · Bar

(📞617 956572; www.lacaseta.org; Mirador del Migdia; ⏰8pm-1am Wed-Fri, noon-1am Sat & Sun Apr-
Sep, noon-sunset Sat & Sun Oct-Mar; 🚌150) The
effort of getting to what is, for all intents and
purposes, a simple *chiringuito* (makeshift
cafe-bar) is worth it. Gaze out to sea over a
beer or coffee by day. As sunset approaches
the atmosphere changes, as reggae, samba
and funk wafts out over the hillside.

El Rouge · Bar

(Map p256; 📞666 251556; Carrer del Poeta
Cabanyes 21; ⏰9pm-2am Thu, 10pm-3am Fri &
Sat, 11am-2am Sun; 📶; Ⓜ️Poble Sec) Decadence
is the word that springs to mind in this
bordello-red lounge-cocktail bar, with acid
jazz, drum and bass and other sounds
drifting along in the background. The walls

Barcelona in a Glass

Cava consumption rockets up at Christmas time

Brut Nature, Extra Brut and Brut are the driest styles

Normally made from Macabeu, Parellada and Xarel·lo grapes

Reserva and Gran Reserva wines have extra bottle age

Dulce and Semi Seco are the sweet styles

Cava also comes in rosé

Cava

ALEX STAROSELTSEV/SHUTTERSTOCK ©, URBANBUZZ/SHUTTERSTOCK ©

¡Salud!

Produced in the vineyards of the Penedès region, *cava* is Spain's most prominent sparkling wine. It undergoes a creation process similar to that of champagne and comes in varying grades of dryness or sweetness.

Sangria, the refreshing summery blend of wine, fruit, sugar and a dash of something harder, is given a twist in Catalonia by using *cava* instead of cheap red.

Sangría de Cava
PAGE LIGHT STUDIOS/SHUTTERSTOCK ©

☆ Best Places to Drink *Cava*

El Xampanyet Nothing has changed for decades in this, one of the city's best-known *cava* bars.

Can Paixano This lofty *cava* bar has long been run on a winning formula: the standard tipple is bubbly rosé in elegant little glasses.

Perikete Since opening in 2017, this fabulous wine bar has been jam-packed with locals.

Viblioteca The real speciality here is wine, and you can choose from 150 mostly local labels, many of them available by the glass.

are covered in heavy-framed paintings, dim lamps and mirrors, and no two chairs are alike. You can sometimes catch DJs, risqué poetry soirées, cabaret shows or even nights of tango dancing.

Pervert Club @ The One   Gay
(Map p256; ☎93 453 05 10; http://pervert-club. negocio.site; Avinguda Francesc Ferrer i Guàrdia 13; from €18; ⏲midnight-6am Sat; ☐13, 23, 150, ⓂEspanya) This weekly fest takes place at The One in Poble Espanyol (p59). Electronic music dominates, and, in spite of the 6am finish, for many this is only the start of the 'evening'. Expect tanned and buff gym bunnies, and plenty of topless eye candy.

La Cambicha   Bar
(Map p256; ☎93 187 25 13; Carrer del Poeta Cabanyes 43; ⏲6pm-2am Mon-Wed, 1pm-2am Thu-Sun; ⓂParal·lel) This shoebox-sized bar feels a bit like a lost cabin in the woods with its newspaper-covered walls, lanterns and old sporting photos. Once you've wedged yourself alongside a tiny table, you can join the young soul- and blues-loving crowd over inexpensive empanadas and vermouth.

Bar Olimpia   Bar
(Map p256; ☎676 828232; Carrer d'Aldana 11; ⏲5pm-1am Mon-Wed, 5pm-2am Thu, 5pm-3am Fri, 1pm-3am Sat, 1pm-1am Sun; ⓂParal·lel) This great little neighbourhood bar is a little slice of Barcelona history. It was here (and on the surrounding block), where the popular Olimpia Theatre Circus performed between 1924 and 1947. Today, the retro setting draws a diverse crowd, who come for house-made vermouth, and gin and tonics.

Redrum   Bar
(Map p256; ☎670 269126; Carrer de Margarit 36; ⏲6pm-1am Mon-Thu, 6pm-2am Fri, 2pm-2am Sat, 6pm-12.30am Sun; ⓂPoble Sec) Redrum's craft brews and cocktails are complemented by Mexican street food (including excellent tacos and ceviche). It has a brightly coloured interior, and the service is friendly.

Bar Calders   Bar
(Map p256; ☎93 329 93 49; Carrer del Parlament 25; ⏲5pm-2am Mon-Fri, 11am-2.30am Sat, 11am-12.30am Sun; ⓂSant Antoni) It bills itself as a

wine bar, but actually the wine selection at Bar Calders is its weak point. As an all-day cafe and tapas bar, however, it's unbeatable, with outdoor tables on a tiny pedestrian lane. It has become the favoured meeting point for the neighbourhood's boho element.

Sala Plataforma   Club
(Map p256; ☎93 329 00 29; www.salaplataforma.com; Carrer Nou de la Rambla 145; from €6; ⏲10pm-6am Thu-Sat, 7pm-2am Sun; ⓂParal·lel) With two adjoining if smallish dance spaces, 'Platform' feels like a clandestine location in an otherwise quiet residential street. Inside this friendly, straightforward dance dive, you'll find popular '80s grooves, timeless rock and occasional live bands – plus drum and bass.

Tinta Roja   Bar
(Map p256; ☎93 443 32 43; www.tintaroja. cat; Carrer de la Creu dels Molers 17; ⏲8.30pm-12.30am Wed, to 2am Thu, to 3am Fri & Sat, closed Aug; ⓂPoble Sec) A succession of nooks and crannies – dotted with flea-market finds and dimly lit in violets, reds and yellows – makes Tinta Roja an intimate spot for a craft beer, cocktail or glass of Argentinean wine – and the occasional show in the back, featuring anything from actors to acrobats.

Metro   Gay
(Map p249; ☎93 323 52 27; www.metrodiscobcn. com; Carrer de Sepúlveda 185; before 2am from €8, after 2am from €20; ⏲12.15am-5.30am Sun-Thu, to 6.45am Fri & Sat; ⓂUniversitat) Metro attracts a fun-loving gay crowd with its two dance floors, three bars and very dark room. Keep an eye out for shows and parties, which can range from parades of models to bingo nights, plus the occasional striptease.

La Terrrazza   Club
(Map p256; ☎687 969825; www.laterrrazza.com; Avinguda de Francesc Ferrer i Guàrdia; from €15; ⏲midnight-6.30am Thu-Sat May-Sep; ☐13, 23, 150, ⓂEspanya) Come summer, La Terrrazza attracts squadrons of beautiful people, locals and foreigners alike, for a full-on night of music (mainly house, techno and electronica) and cocktails partly under the stars inside the Poble Espanyol complex.

SHOWTIME

Listen to live jazz, check out a gig
or dance the night away

Showtime

Barcelona teems with stages hosting all manner of entertainment from underground cabaret and comic opera to high drama. Dance companies are thick on the ground and popular local theatre companies, when not touring the rest of Spain, keep folks strapped to their seats.

Almost every big international rock and pop act has passed through Barcelona at some point, and the city is also blessed with a fine line-up of theatres for grand performances of classical music, opera and more.

In This Section

Tickets & Websites

The easiest way to get hold of tickets *(entradas)* for most venues throughout the city is through **Ticketea** (www.ticketea.com) or **Ticketmaster** (www.ticketmaster.es). Occasionally, there are discounted tickets to be had on www.atrapalo.com.

Luminescent stained glass at the Palau de la Música Catalana (p200)

The Best...

For Classical Music

Palau de la Música Catalana (p200) A Modernista fantasy, where the fabulous interior can distract from the finest musician.

Gran Teatre del Liceu (p199) One of Europe's most splendid opera houses, built to impress.

L'Auditori (p196) Fiercely modern concert venue, with a resident orchestra.

L'Ateneu (p199) This elegant old library is hard to enter if you're not a member – unless you catch one of its occasional concerts.

For Jazz

Harlem Jazz Club (p200) Not just jazz, but also funk, blues, bossa nova and plenty more.

Jazz Sí Club (p198) Small, lively, cramped and never less than fun.

Jamboree (p200) A basement bar that's seen them all under its vaulted ceiling.

✪ Barceloneta & the Waterfront

Sala Monasterio Live Music
(📞616 287197; www.facebook.com/sala.
monasterio; Moll de Mestral 30; tickets vary;
🕐10pm-5am Sun-Thu, to 6am Fri & Sat;
Ⓜ Ciutadella Vila Olímpica) Overlooking the
bobbing masts and slender palm trees of
Port Olímpic, this pocket-sized music spot
stages an eclectic line-up of live bands,
including jazz, *forró* (music from northeast-
ern Brazil), blues jams and rock.

Razzmatazz Live Music
(📞93 320 82 00; www.salarazzmatazz.com;
Carrer de Pamplona 88; tickets from €17; 🕐9pm-
4am; Ⓜ Bogatell) Bands from far and wide
occasionally create scenes of near hysteria
in this, one of the city's classic live-music
and clubbing venues. Bands can appear
throughout the week (check the website),
with different start times. On weekends live
music later gives way to club sounds.

Five different clubs in one huge post-
industrial space attract people of all dance
persuasions and ages. The main space, the
Razz Club, is a haven for the latest international rock and indie acts. **The Loft** does
house and electro, while the **Pop Bar** offers
anything from garage to soul. **The Lolita
Room** is the land of house, hip-hop and
dubstep, and upstairs in the **Rex Room** club-
goers sweat it out to experimental sounds.
You can save a few euros by purchasing
tickets to concerts in advance online.

L'Auditori Classical Music
(📞93 247 93 00; www.auditori.cat; Carrer de
Lepant 150; tickets free-€59; 🕐box office 5-9pm
Tue-Fri, 10am-1pm & 5-9pm Sat; Ⓜ Marina,
Monumental) Barcelona's modern home for
the Orquestra Simfònica de Barcelona i
Nacional de Catalunya, L'Auditori puts on
plenty of orchestral, chamber, religious and
other music. Designed by Rafael Moneo
and opened in 1999, the main auditorium
can accommodate over 2000 concertgo-
ers. The **Museu de la Música** (📞93 256
36 50; www.museumusica.bcn.cat; adult/child

 **La Fura dels Baus**

Keep your eyes peeled for any of the
eccentric (if not downright crazed) performances of Barcelona's **La Fura dels
Baus** (www.lafura.com) theatre group.
It has won worldwide acclaim for its
brand of startling, often acrobatic, theatre in which the audience is frequently
dragged into the chaos. The company
grew out of Barcelona's street-theatre
culture of the late 1970s and, although it
has grown in technical prowess and received great international acclaim, it has
not abandoned the rough-and-ready
edge of street performances.

La Fura dels Baus
SERGIO AZENHA/ALAMY STOCK PHOTO ©

€6/4.50, free from 3pm Sun; 🕐10am-6pm Tue,
Wed & Fri, to 9pm Thu, to 7pm Sat & Sun; Ⓜ Monumental) is located in the same building.

**Teatre Nacional
de Catalunya** Performing Arts
(📞93 306 57 00; www.tnc.cat; Plaça de les Arts 1;
tickets free-€28; 🕐box office 3-7pm Wed, 4-8pm
Thu-Sat, 4-6pm Sun; Ⓜ Glòries) The National
Theatre of Catalonia hosts a wide range of
performances, including dramas, come-
dies, musicals and dance in this ultra-
neoclassical theatre designed by Barcelona
architect Ricardo Bofill, which opened in
1996. Performances are in Catalan.

Sala Beckett Theatre
(📞93 284 53 12; www.salabeckett.cat; Carrer
de Pere IV 228-232; tickets from €3; Ⓜ Poblenou) One of the city's principal alternative
theatres, the Sala Beckett doesn't shy away

from challenging theatre, and stages an eclectic mix of productions. Performances are primarily in Catalan. Formerly based in Gràcia, the theatre moved in 2016 to this lovely space in a historic 1920s building.

Yelmo Cines Icària   Cinema

(📞902 220922; www.yelmocines.es; Carrer de Salvador Espriu 61; tickets adult/child €9.90/7.30; Ⓜ️Ciutadella Vila Olímpica) This vast cinema complex shows films in their original language on 15 screens, giving you plenty of choice. Aside from the screens, you'll find several cheerful places to eat, bars and the like to keep you occupied before and after the movies.

✪ Camp Nou, Pedralbes & La Zona Alta

Luz de Gas   Live Music

(📞93 209 77 11; www.luzdegas.com; Carrer de Muntaner 246; 🕐midnight-6am Thu-Sat; 🚌6, 7, 27, 32, 33, 34, H8, 🚋T1, T2, T3 Francesc Macià) Several nights a week this club, set in a grand former theatre, stages concerts ranging from rock, soul and salsa to jazz and pop. Concerts typically kick off around 1am; from about 2am, the place turns into a club that attracts a well-dressed crowd with varying musical tastes, depending on the night. Check the website for the latest schedule.

✪ El Raval

Filmoteca de Catalunya   Cinema

(Map p250; 📞93 567 10 70; www.filmoteca.cat; Plaça de Salvador Seguí 1-9; adult/concession €4/3; 🕐screenings 5-10pm, ticket office 10am-3pm & 4-9.30pm Tue-Sun; Ⓜ️Liceu) The Filmoteca de Catalunya – Catalonia's national cinema – sits in a modern 6000-sq-metre building, built in the midst of the most louche part of El Raval. The films shown are a mix of classics and more recent releases, with frequent themed cycles. A ten-session pass is an amazingly cheap €20.

In addition to two cinemas totalling 555 seats, the Filmoteca comprises a film library, a bookshop, a cafe, offices and a dedicated space for exhibitions.

L'Auditori

Chamber Music

Fundació Mas i Mas (☎93 319 17 89; www.masimas.com/fundacio; tickets €12-15) promotes chamber and classical music, offering concerts in a couple of locations. Classical concerts, usually involving Catalan performers, are held regularly in various venues around town. For intense 30-minute sessions of chamber music, see its program of performances at **L'Ateneu** (p199), a hallowed academic institution-cum-club.

L'Ateneu
DE ALAMBRE/SHUTTERSTOCK ©

23 Robadors Live Music
(Map p250; www.23robadors.wordpress.com; Carrer d'en Robador 23; ⏰8pm-2.30am; Ⓜ Liceu) On what remains a sleazy Raval street, where streetwalkers, junkies and other misfits hang out in spite of all the work being done to gentrify the area, this narrow little bar has made a name for itself with its shows and live music. Jazz is the name of the game, but you'll also find live poetry, flamenco and plenty more.

JazzSí Club Live Music
(Map p249; ☎93 329 00 20; www.tallerdemusics.com/en/jazzsi-club; Carrer de Requesens 2; incl drink €6-10; ⏰8.30-11pm Tue-Sat, 6.30-10pm Sun; Ⓜ Sant Antoni) A cramped little bar run by the Taller de Músics (Musicians' Workshop) serves as the stage for a varied program of jazz jams through to some good flamenco (Friday and Saturday nights). Thursday night is Cuban night, Tuesday and Sunday are rock, and the rest of the week is devoted to jazz and/or blues sessions. Concerts start around 9pm but the jam sessions can get going earlier.

Teatre Llantiol Theatre
(Map p249; ☎93 329 90 09; www.llantiol.com; Carrer de la Riereta 7; Ⓜ Sant Antoni) At this small, charming cafe-theatre, which has a certain scuffed elegance, all sorts of odd stuff, from concerts and theatre to magic shows, is staged. The speciality, though, is stand-up comedy, which is occasionally in English. (Eddie Izzard did his recent Barcelona gigs here.) Check the website for details.

Teatre Romea Theatre
(Map p250; ☎93 309 70 04; www.teatreromea.com; Carrer de l'Hospital 51; ⏰box office 5.30pm to start of show Tue-Fri, from 4.30pm Sat & Sun; Ⓜ Liceu) Just off La Rambla, this 19th-century theatre was resurrected at the end of the 1990s and is one of the city's key stages for quality drama. It usually fills up for a broad range of interesting plays, often classics with a contemporary flavour, in Catalan and Spanish.

El Cangrejo Live Performance
(Map p250; ☎93 301 29 78; Carrer de Montserrat 9; ⏰11pm-3am Fri & Sat; Ⓜ Drassanes) This altar to kitsch is a dingy dance hall that has transgressed since the 1920s, and for years starred the luminous underground cabaret figure of Carmen Mairena. It exudes a gorgeously tacky feel, especially with the midnight drag shows. Due to its popularity with tourists, getting in is all but impossible unless you turn up early.

✪ Gràcia & Park Güell

Cine Texas Cinema
(Map p254; ☎93 348 77 48; www.cinemestexas.cat; Carrer de Bailèn 205; Ⓜ Joanic) All films at this contemporary four-screen cinema are shown in their original languages (with subtitles in Catalan). Genres span art house through to Hollywood blockbusters. Catalan-language films are subtitled in English.

Soda Acústic — Live Music

(Map p254; ☑93 016 55 90; www.soda.cat; Carrer de les Guilleries 6; tickets from €2; ⊕8pm-2.30am Wed, Thu & Sun, to 3am Fri & Sat; MFontana) This low-lit modern space stages an eclectic line-up of bands and performing artists. Jazz, world music, Balkan swing, Latin rhythms and plenty of experimental, not easily classifiable musicians all receive their due. The acoustics are excellent. Check the website for upcoming shows.

Verdi Park — Cinema

(Map p254; ☑93 238 79 90; www.cines-verdi. com; Carrer de Torrijos 49; MFontana) Verdi Park is a perennially popular art-house cinema with four screens. Most films are shown in their original language.

Teatreneu — Theatre

(Map p254; ☑93 285 37 12; www.teatreneu.com; Carrer de Terol 26; MJoanic) This lively theatre experiments with all sorts of material, from monologues to social comedy, and also screens films. Aside from the main theatre, two cafe-style spaces serve as more intimate stage settings for small-scale productions. Most performances are in Catalan or Spanish. The box office opens one hour before performance times. The bustling, rambling downstairs bar faces the street.

Verdi — Cinema

(Map p254; ☑93 238 79 90; www.cines-verdi. com; Carrer de Verdi 32; MFontana) In the heart of Gràcia, this five-screen cinema shows art-house and blockbuster films in their original language as well as films in Catalan and Spanish. It's handy to lots of local eateries and bars for pre- and post-film enjoyment.

😣 La Rambla & Barri Gòtic

Gran Teatre del Liceu — Theatre, Live Music

(Map p250; ☑93 485 99 00; www.liceubarce lona.cat; La Rambla 51-59; ⊕box office 9.30am-7.30pm Mon-Fri, to 5.30pm Sat & Sun; MLiceu) Barcelona's grand old opera house, restored after a fire in 1994, is one of the

👍 Gigs

When major bands come to town, you'll more often than not find them playing at **Razzmatazz** (p196), **Bikini** (p178), **Sala Apolo** (p202) or **BARTS** (p202), although there are a number of other decent midsize venues. There are also abundant local gigs in institutions as diverse as **CaixaForum** (Map p256; ☑93 476 86 00; www.caixaforum.es; Avinguda de Francesc Ferrer i Guàrdia 6-8; adult/child €4/free, 1st Sun of month free; ⊕10am-8pm; MEspanya), **La Pedrera** (p76) and **L'Ateneu** (p199).

most technologically advanced theatres in the world. To take a seat in the grand auditorium, returned to all its 19th-century glory but with the very latest in acoustics, is to be transported to another age.

Tickets can cost anything from €10 for a cheap seat behind a pillar to €200 for a well-positioned night at the opera.

L'Ateneu — Classical Music

(Map p250; ☑93 343 61 21; www.ateneubcn. org; Carrer de la Canuda 6; tickets up to €10; MCatalunya) This historic private library and cultural centre (dating back 150 years) hosts a range of high-brow fare, from classical recitals to film screenings and literary readings.

El Paraigua — Live Music

(Map p250; ☑93 302 11 31; www.elparaigua.com; Carrer del Pas de l'Ensenyança 2; ⊕noon-2am Sun-Wed, to 1am Thu, to 3am Fri & Sat; MLiceu) **FREE** A tiny chocolate box of dark tinted Modernisme, the 'Umbrella' has been serving up drinks since the 1960s. The turn-of-the-20th-century decor was transferred here from a shop knocked down elsewhere in the district and cobbled back together to create this cosy locale.

Take a trip in time from Modernisme to medieval by heading downstairs to the brick and stone basement bar area. Amid 11th-century walls, live bands – funk, soul,

 Event Listings

For exhibitions and other forms of entertainment, see www.barcelona-metropolitan.com or www.timeout.cat, and for free activities, check out www.forfree.cat.

The **Palau de la Virreina** (p45) cultural information office has oodles of information on theatre, opera, classical music and more.

Good coverage of classical music is to be found on www.classictic.com (in English).

Palau de la Virreina
RADHARC IMAGES/ALAMY STOCK PHOTO ©

rock, blues – hold court on Fridays and Saturdays (from 11.30pm).

Sidecar Factory Club — Live Music

(Map p250; ☎93 302 15 86; www.sidecarfactoryclub.com; Plaça Reial 7; ⏰7pm-5am Mon-Thu, to 6am Fri & Sat; Ⓜ Liceu) Descend into the red-tinged, brick-vaulted bowels for live music most nights. Just about anything goes here, from UK indie to country punk, but rock and pop lead the way. Most shows start around 10pm and DJs take over at 12.30am. Upstairs at ground level you can get food (until midnight) or a few drinks (until 3am).

Jamboree — Live Music

(Map p250; ☎93 319 17 89; www.masimas.com/jamboree; Plaça Reial 17; tickets €5-20; ⏰8pm-6am; Ⓜ Liceu) For over half a century, Jamboree has been bringing joy to the jivers of Barcelona, with high-calibre acts featuring jazz trios, blues, Afrobeats, and Latin and big-band sounds. Two concerts are held

most nights (at 8pm and 10pm), after which Jamboree morphs into a DJ-spinning club at midnight. WTF jam sessions are held Mondays (entrance a mere €5).

Buy tickets online to save a few euros.

Harlem Jazz Club — Jazz

(Map p250; ☎93 310 07 55; www.harlemjazzclub.es; Carrer de la Comtessa de Sobradiel 8; tickets €7-10; ⏰8pm-3am Sun & Tue-Thu, to 5am Fri & Sat; Ⓜ Liceu) This narrow, old-city dive is one of the best spots in town for jazz, as well as funk, Latin, blues and gypsy jazz. It attracts a mixed crowd that maintains a respectful silence during the acts. Most concerts start around 10pm. Get in early if you want a seat in front of the stage.

Sala Tarantos — Flamenco

(Map p250; ☎93 304 12 10; www.masimas.com/tarantos; Plaça Reial 17; tickets €15; ⏰shows 7.30pm, 8.30pm & 9.30pm Oct-Jun, plus 10.30pm Jul-Sep; Ⓜ Liceu) Since 1963, this basement locale has been the stage for up-and-coming flamenco groups performing in Barcelona. These days Tarantos has become a mostly tourist-centric affair, with half-hour shows held three times a night. Still, it's a good introduction to flamenco, and not a bad setting for a drink.

❂ La Ribera

Palau de la Música Catalana — Classical Music

(Map p254; ☎93 295 72 00; www.palaumusica.cat; Carrer de Palau de la Música 4-6; tickets from €18; ⏰box office 9.30am-9pm Mon-Sat, 10am-3pm Sun; Ⓜ Urquinaona) A feast for the eyes, this Modernista confection is also the city's most traditional venue for classical and choral music, although it has a wide-ranging program, including flamenco, pop and – particularly – jazz. Just being here for a performance is an experience. Sip a pre-concert tipple in the foyer, its tiled pillars all a-glitter.

Head up the grand stairway to the main auditorium, a whirlpool of Modernista whimsy.

Tablao Nervión Dance

(Map p250; ☎93 315 21 03; www.restaurant
lenervion.com; Carrer de la Princesa 2; show
incl 1 drink €18, show & set dinner €30; ☺shows
8-10pm Wed-Sun; Ⓜ Jaume I) For admittedly
tourist-oriented flamenco, this unassuming
bar (shows take place in the basement) is
cheaper than most, and has good offerings.
Check the website for further details.

Palau Dalmases Live Performance

(Map p250; ☎93 310 06 73; www.palaudalmases.
com; Carrer de Montcada 20; ☺6pm-2am Tue-
Sat, to 10pm Sun; Ⓜ Jaume I) You can sip wine
or cocktails (both rather expensive) inside
the baroque courtyard and theatrical
interior of the originally medieval Palau
Dalmases. There are flamenco shows at
6pm, 7.30pm and 9.30pm (€25 including
one drink). On Wednesdays there is a free
jazz concert at 11pm, and on opera Thursdays (€20).

✪ La Sagrada Família & L'Eixample

City Hall Live Music

(Map p254; ☎93 238 07 22; www.cityhallbar
celona.com; Rambla de Catalunya 2-4; Ⓜ Catalunya) Also home to a nightclub (p187),
this former theatre is the perfect size and
shape for live music, holding a crowd of
around 500. The acoustics are great and
the layout means everyone gets a good
view of the stage.

👍 Flamenco

Seeing good performances of this
essentially Andalucian dance and music
is not easy. The few *tablaos* are touristy
and often tacky. You can catch flamenco
on Friday and Saturday nights at the
Jazz SíClub (p198); also watch out for
big-name performers at the **Palau de la
Música Catalana** (p200).

The **Festival de Flamenco de Ciutat
Vella** (www.ciutatflamenco.com) is held
in May. A series of concerts can be seen
from April to July as part of the **Barcelona Guitar Festival** (www.guitarbcn.
com).

Flamenco dancer
CORRADO BARATTA/SHUTTERSTOCK ©

Teatre Tívoli Theatre

(Map p254; ☎93 412 20 63; www.grupbalana.com;
Carrer de Casp 8; ticket prices vary; ☺box office
5-8pm & 90 minutes before shows; Ⓜ Catalunya)
Dating from 1919, this grand theatre has
three storeys of boxes and a generous stage.
There's a fairly rapid turnover of drama and
musicals, with pieces often not staying on
for more than a couple of weeks. Concerts
(such as Bruce Springsteen, Elvis Costello
and Radiohead) also take place here.

Mediterráneo Live Music

(Map p254; www.elmedi.net; Carrer de Balmes
129; ☺10.30pm-3am; ℝFGC Provença) Free live
music plays nightly at this student favourite. Order a beer and enjoy the free nuts at
one of the tiny tables while waiting for the
next act to tune up at the back. Often the
young performers are surprisingly good.

🎟 Alfresco Cinema

Outdoor cinema screens are set up in
summer in the moat of the **Castell de
Montjuïc** (www.salamontjuic.org), on
the beach and in El Fòrum. Foreign films
with subtitles and original soundtracks
are marked 'VO' *(versió original)* in
movie listings.

👍 Longing for Cuba

The oldest musical tradition to have survived to some degree in Catalonia is that of the *havaneres* – nostalgic songs and melancholy sea shanties brought back from Cuba by Catalans who lived, sailed and traded there in the 19th century. Even after Spain lost Cuba in 1898, the *havanera* tradition (a mix of European and Cuban rhythms) continued. A magical opportunity to enjoy these songs is the **Cantada d'Havaneres** (www.havanerescalella.cat), a one-day festival held on the Costa Brava (north of Barcelona) in early July. Otherwise you may stumble across performances elsewhere along the coast or even in Barcelona, but there is no set program.

Méliès Cinemes   Cinema
(Map p249; ☎93 451 00 51; www.meliescinemes. com; Carrer de Villarroel 102; tickets €4-7; ⓂUrgell) A cosy cinema with two screens, the Méliès specialises in the best of recent releases from Hollywood and Europe.

✪ Montjuïc, Poble Sec & Sant Antoni

Hiroshima   Live Performance
(Map p256; ☎93 315 54 58; www.hiroshima. cat; Carrer de Vilà i Vilà 67; Ⓞated 7-11pm Wed-Sun; ⓂParal·lel) Hiroshima is a creative lynchpin in Poble Sec. In a former elevator factory, it hosts emerging and avant-garde musicians, dancers and performing artists. There are two stages (seating 130 and 250 people, respectively) and a lively ground-floor bar where you can grab a drink after the show.

BARTS   Concert Venue
(Barcelona Arts on Stage; Map p256; ☎93 324 84 92; www.barts.cat; Avinguda del Paral·lel 62; ⓂParal·lel) BARTS has a solid reputation for its innovative line-up of urban dance troupes, electro swing, psychedelic pop and

other eclectic fare. Its smart design combines a comfortable mid-sized auditorium with excellent acoustics. Hours and ticket prices vary; check the agenda online.

Teatre Grec   Theatre
(Map p256; http://lameva.barcelona.cat/grec; Passeig de Santa Madrona; 🚌55, 150) Built in 1929 by Catalan architect Ramon Revento in ancient Greek style, this lovely stone amphitheatre on Montjuïc stages one of the city's best summer festivals, the Festival Grec de Barcelona, with theatre, dance and music events.

Gran Bodega Saltó   Live Music
(Map p256; ☎93 441 37 09; www.bodegasalto. net; Carrer de Blesa 36; Ⓞated 7pm-2am Mon-Thu, noon-3am Fri & Sat, noon-midnight Sun; ⓂParal·lel) The ranks of barrels give away the bar's history as a traditional bodega. Now, after a little homemade psychedelic redecoration with odd lamps, figurines and old Chinese beer ads, it's a magnet for an eclectic barfly crowd. The crowd is mixed and friendly, and gets pretty animated on nights when there's live music.

Sala Apolo   Live Music
(Map p256; ☎93 441 40 01; www.sala-apolo. com; Carrer Nou de la Rambla 113; club from €15, concerts vary; Ⓞated concerts from 8pm, club from midnight; ⓂParal·lel) This is a fine old theatre, where red velvet dominates and you feel as though you're in a movie-set dancehall scene. 'Nasty Mondays' and 'Crappy Tuesdays' are aimed at a diehard, never-stop-dancing crowd. Club entry includes a drink. Earlier in the evening, concerts generally take place, here and in 'La 2', a smaller auditorium downstairs.

Tastes are as eclectic as possible, from local bands and burlesque shows to big-name international acts.

Palau Sant Jordi   Stadium
(Map p256; ☎93 426 20 89; www.palausantjordi. cat; Passeig Olímpic 5-7; 🚌13, 150) Built for the 1992 Olympics, this huge indoor arena hosts big-name concerts (Adele, Metallica, Lady Gaga), as well as championship sports events.

Sardana Dancing

The Catalan dance *par excellence* is the *sardana*, whose roots lie in the far northern Empordà region of Catalonia. Compared with flamenco, it is sober indeed but not unlike a lot of other Mediterranean folk dances.

The dancers hold hands in a circle and wait for the 10 or so musicians to begin. The performance starts with the piping of the *flabiol*, a little wooden flute. When the other musicians join in, the dancers start – a series of steps to the right, one back and then the same to the left. As the music 'heats up' the steps become more complex, the leaps are higher and the dancers lift their arms. Then they return to the initial steps and continue. If newcomers wish to join in, space is made for them as the dance continues and the whole thing proceeds in a more or less seamless fashion.

In Barcelona the best chance you have of seeing people dancing the *sardana* is either at noon on Sunday or 6pm on Saturday in front of La Catedral. It is also performed sometimes in Plaça de Sant Jaume. For more information, contact the **Agrupació Cultural Folklòrica de Barcelona** (☎93 315 14 96; www.acfbarcelona.cat).

Sant Jordi Club   Live Music

(Map p256; ☎93 426 20 89; www.santjordiclub. cat; Passeig Olímpic 5-7; ☒55, 150) With capacity for more than 4500 people, this concert hall, annexed to the Olympic stadium Palau Sant Jordi, is used for big gigs that don't reach the epic proportions of headlining international acts.

Teatre Mercat De Les Flors   Dance

(Map p256; ☎93 256 26 00; www.mercatflors. cat; Carrer de Lleida 59; ☒box office 11am-2pm & 4-7pm Mon-Fri & 1hr before show; ☒55) Next door to the Teatre Lliure, and together with it known as the Ciutat de Teatre (Theatre City), this spacious modern stage is Barcelona's top venue for local and international contemporary dance acts.

Teatre Victòria   Theatre

(Map p256; ☎93 329 91 89; www.teatrevictoria. com; Avinguda del Paral·lel 67; ☒box office 2hr before show; MParal·lel) Rather nondescript looking from the street, this modern theatre stages musicals (usually in Catalan), flamenco and contemporary dance.

Teatre Lliure   Theatre

(Map p256; ☎93 289 27 70; www.teatrelliure.com; Plaça de Margarida Xirgu 1; ☒box office 9am-8pm & 2hr before performance; ☒55) Housed in the magnificent former Palau de l'Agricultura building on Montjuïc (opposite the Museu d'Arqueologia), the 'Free Theatre' consists of two modern theatre spaces (Espai Lliure and Sala Fabià Puigserver). It puts on a variety of quality drama (mostly in Catalan), contemporary dance and music.

Renoir Floridablanca   Cinema

(Map p249; ☎91 542 27 02; www.cinesrenoir. com; Carrer de Floridablanca 135; MSant Antoni) With seven screens, this cinema shows a mix of quality art-house flicks and blockbusters in their original language (with Spanish subtitles). It's handily located just beyond El Raval, so you'll find no shortage of post-film entertainment options nearby.

ACTIVE BARCELONA

Football, cycling and everything in between

Active Barcelona

Mediterranean oceanfront and a rambling hilly park overlooking the city make fine settings for a bit of outdoor activity beneath the (generally) sunny skies of Barcelona. For a break from museum-hopping and over-indulging at tapas bars, Barcelona has plenty of options– running, swimming, cycling or simply pumping fists in the air at a never-dull FC Barcelona match. Football here has the aura of religion and for much of the city's population, support of the city's principal team is an article of faith. There's also a variety of ways to get a more active look at the city, whether on a specialised walking tour through the Old City or on a bicycle excursion around the city centre.

In This Section

What to Watch

The football season runs from late August to May.

The basketball season runs from October to June.

Asobal, the handball league, runs from September to May or early June.

The professional tennis season is in spring; the big event here is the Barcelona Open in April.

Piscines Bernat Picornell (p208)

The Best...

Activities

Castell de Montjuïc (p63) Barcelona's easily accessible mountain offers a scenic setting for running and biking.

Parc de la Collserola (p98) The city's best mountain biking (and home to wild boar).

Camp Nou (p72) See FC Barcelona in action at their world-famous home stadium.

Piscines Bernat Picornell (p208) A truly Olympian setting for a swim.

Spas

Rituels d'Orient (p208) A beautiful spa in a historic setting of El Born.

Aqua Urban Spa (p208) Get the full range of relaxation treatments.

Flotarium (p209) Float weightlessly in a salt-filled chamber.

⊕ Activities

Base Nàutica
Municipal   Water Sports
(📞93 221 04 32; www.basenautica.org; Avinguda
de Litoral; 2hr lessons from €40, equipment hire
per hr from €20, wetsuit hire per day €10; ⊙10am-
7pm; MPoblenou) Just back from Platja de
la Mar Bella, at Base Nautica Municipal
you can learn the basics of kayaking,
windsurfing, catamaran sailing or stand
up paddleboarding (SUP). You can also
hire equipment here. Prices for lessons are
cheaper in groups of two or more. Longer
courses, running from eight to 12 hours over
several days, are also available.

Aire De Barcelona   Spa
(📞93 295 57 43; www.airedebarcelona.com; Passeig de Picasso 22; thermal baths & aromatherapy
Mon-Thu €36, Fri-Sun €39; ⊙9am-11pm Sun-Thu,
to midnight Fri & Sat; MArc de Triomf) With low
lighting and relaxing perfumes wafting
around you, this basement spa could be
the perfect way to end a day. Hot, warm
and cold baths, steam baths and options
for various massages, including on a slab of
hot marble, make for a delicious hour or so.
Book ahead and bring a swimming costume.

My Beautiful Parking   Cycling
(Map p250; 📞93 510 8724; www.mybeautiful
parking.com; Carrer de la Bòria 17; bike hire per
2hr/24hr €5/14; ⊙10.30am-8pm Mon-Sat, also
Sun Apr-Sep; MJaume I) Friendly shop with
three types of bikes – foldable, 'track' or
'city' – to rent.

Molokai SUP Center   Water Sports
(📞93 221 48 68; www.molokaisupcenter.com;
Carrer de Meer 39; 2hr private lesson €60, SUP
rental per hr €15; MBarceloneta) This respect-
ed outfit will give you a crash course in
stand-up paddleboarding. In addition to the
two-hour beginner's class, Molokai can help
you improve your technique (in intermedi-
ate and advanced lessons – all in two-hour
blocks); gear and wetsuits are included. If
you just want to hire a SUP board, staff can
get you out on the sea in no time.

Rituels d'Orient   Spa
(📞93 419 14 72; www.rituelsdorient.com; Carrer
de Loreto 50; baths per 45 min €29, treatments
from €21; ⊙11am-9pm Tue, Wed & Sun, to 10pm
Thu-Sat; MHospital Clínic) Rituels d'Orient
resembles a Moroccan fantasy, with dark
woods, window grills, candle lighting and
ancient-looking stone walls. It's a wonderfully relaxing setting for luxuriating in a
hammam and indulging in a massage, body
scrub, facial or hand and foot treatments.

Barcelona Biking   Cycling
(Map p250; 📞656 356300; www.barcelona
biking.com; Baixada de Sant Miquel 6; bike hire
per 1/24hr €5/15, tour €21; ⊙10am-8pm, tour
11am; MJaume I, Liceu) Hires city, road and
mountain bikes. Also offers a 3.5-hour tour.

Aqua Urban Spa   Spa
(Map p294; 📞93 238 41 60; www.aquaurbanspa.
es; Carrer Gran de Gràcia 7; 90-min baths
from €51; ⊙9am-9pm Mon-Sat; MDiagonal)
With treatments for everything from stress
to tired legs, this spa offers smallish pool
and shower areas, along with steam baths,
Roman-style baths and a series of massages and beauty treatment options such as
body scrubs.

Boardriders
Barceloneta   Water Sports
(📞93 221 44 91; Plaça del Mar 1; ⊙10am-10pm
Mon-Sat, 11am-9pm Sun; MBarceloneta)
Facing the seafront, Boardriders rents out
surfboards (per hour/half-day €12/25) and
SUPs (per hour/half-day €15/30), and also
sells surfwear, streetwear and skateboarding equipment.

Piscines Bernat
Picornell   Swimming
(Map p256; www.picornell.cat; Avinguda de
l'Estadi 30-38; adult/child €11.90/7.30, nudist
hours €6.55/4.70; ⊙6.45am-midnight Mon-Fri,
7am-9pm Sat, 7.30am-4pm Sun) Admission
to Barcelona's official Olympic pool on
Montjuïc also includes use of the complex's
fitness room, sauna, Jacuzzi, steam bath
and track. On Saturday nights, between
9pm and 11pm, the pool (with access to
sauna and steam bath) is open only to

👍 Urban Running

The waterfront esplanade and beaches are all perfect for an early-morning run, before the crowds come out. Locals who want to log some serious miles take to Parc de la Collserola, which is laced with trails. Among the best is the Carretera de les Aigües, a 9km-long track from Tibidabo to the suburb of Sant Just Desvern, with superb views over the city. More convenient are the gardens and parkland of Montjuïc or the smaller park of Ciutadella.

If you want to jog while you're in town, but don't want to go alone, you can join others in a casual running club. The Hotel Brummell Running Club has Tuesday-night runs (at 7.30pm) around Montjuïc, departing from the **hotel** (Carrer Nou de la Rambla 174). A Tuesday and Thursday night group meets outside Parc de la Ciutadella.

JOSEP LAGO/AFP/GETTY IMAGES ©

nudists. On Sundays between October and May the indoor pool also opens for nudists only from 4.15pm to 6pm.

Flotarium   Flotarium
(Map p254; ✏93 217 36 37; www.flotarium.com; Plaça de Narcís Oller 3; 50-minute session €40; ⏰3-9pm Mon, 10am-9pm Tue-Sat, 10am-3pm Sun; Ⓜ Diagonal) Be suspended in zero gravity and feel the stress ebb away. Each flotarium, like a little space capsule with water, is in a private room, with shower, towels and shampoo. Epsom salts allow you to float as if in the Dead Sea (using 300kg of salts to achieve the same density).

Club Natació Atlètic-Barcelona   Swimming
(✏93 221 00 10; www.cnab.cat; Plaça del Mar; day pass adult/child €12.55/7.15; ⏰7am-11pm Mon-Fri, to 10pm Sat, to 8pm Sun; 🚍V15, 39, 59, 64, Ⓜ Barceloneta) Operating since 1907, this athletic club has one indoor and two outdoor pools. One outdoor pool is heated for lap swimming in winter. Admission includes use of the gym, spa and private beach access.

⊙ Spectator Sports

Camp Nou   Football
(✏902 189900; www.fcbarcelona.com; Carrer d'Arístides Maillol; Ⓜ Palau Reial) The massive stadium of Camp Nou ('New Field' in Catalan) is home to the legendary Futbol Club Barcelona. Attending a game amid the roar of the crowds is an unforgettable experience; the season runs from late August to May. Alternatively, get a taste of all the excitement at the interactive Camp Nou Experience (p74), which includes a tour of the stadium.

Tickets to FC Barcelona matches are available at Camp Nou, online (through FC Barcelona's official website) and through various city locations. Tourist offices sell them – the branch (p239) at Plaça de Catalunya is a centrally located option – as do FC Botiga stores (p158 & p165). Tickets can cost anything from €39 to upwards of €250, depending on the seat and match.

Estadi RCD Espanyol   Football
(✏93 292 77 00; www.rcdespanyol.com; Avinguda del Baix Llobregat 100; tickets from €30; 🚉FGC Cornellà Riera) Espanyol, based at the 40,500-seat Estadi RCD Espanyol, plays second fiddle to Barça, but it does so with considerable passion.

⊙ Courses

Espai Boisà   Cooking
(✏93 192 60 21; www.espaiboisa.com; Passatge Lluís Pellicer 8; 2½-hr course from €45; Ⓜ Hospital Clínic) ✐ Run by a young, multilingual Venezuelan-Catalan couple, this first-rate outfit offers various themed

⬔ Where to Ride

Barcelona's long, enticing seafront makes a fine setting for a ride and the bike lane separate from traffic and pedestrians ensures you can get going a good clip (though you'll have to move slowly at peak times, like summer weekends). The city itself has over 180km of bike lanes, including along major streets like Passeig de Sant Joan, Consell de Cent, Avinguda Diagonal and Ronda de Sant Pau/Comte d'Urgell. Avid mountain bikers will want to make their way up to the vast Parc de Collserola with rambling trails on a wooded massif overlooking the city. There are also many options for bike tours and hire.

Cycling alongside Barceloneta Beach
MARGARET STEPIEN/LONELY PLANET ©

cooking courses. They emphasise organic, seasonal ingredients from local producers outside of Barcelona – put to good use in dishes including paella, a range of tapas and *crema catalana* (the Catalan version of crème brûlée).

Swing Maniacs   Dancing
(Map p254; ☏93 187 69 85; www.swingmaniacs. com; Carrer Roger de Flor 293; group/private 55min class from €14/40; ☺5pm-midnight Mon-Fri; Ⓜ Joanic) Swing dancing is increasingly popular in the Catalan capital, with old-fashioned dance parties happening in far-flung corners of the city every night. To learn the moves, sign up for a class here. You can join a drop-in class, and if you don't have a partner, one can be arranged for you.

🄯 Tours

There are many ways to get a more in-depth look at the city, whether on a specialised walking tour through the Ciutat Vella (Old City), on a bicycle excursion around the city centre or on a hop-on, hop-off bus tour all across town.

Barcelona Guide Bureau   Tours
(☏93 315 22 61; www.barcelonaguidebureau. com; Via Laietana 50) Barcelona Guide Bureau places professional guides at the disposal of groups for tailor-made tours of the city. Several languages are catered for. It also offers a series of daily tours, from a five-hour highlights tour (adult/child €68/34, departing at 10am) to a trip to Montserrat, leaving Barcelona at 3pm and lasting about four hours (adult/child €49/25).

Bus Turístic   Bus
(☏93 298 70 00; www.barcelonabusturistic.cat; 1 day adult/child €29/16, 2 days €39/16; ☺9am-8pm) This hop-on, hop-off service covers three circuits (44 stops) linking virtually all the major tourist sights. Tourist offices, TMB transport authority offices and many hotels have leaflets explaining the system. Each of the two main circuits takes approximately two hours.

Devour Barcelona   Tours
(☏695 111832; www.devourbarcelonafoodtours. com; €49-99) Knowledgeable guides lead food tours around Gràcia, the Old City and Barceloneta, mixing gastronomy with history. The various tastings and spots visited are especially focused on small, local producers and family-run joints. Most tours last three to four hours.

My Favourite Things   Tours
(☏637 265405; www.myft.net; from €26) Offers tours (with no more than 10 participants) based on numerous themes: street art, shopping, culinary tours, movies, musical journeys and forgotten neighbourhoods are among the offerings. Other activities include flamenco and salsa classes, cooking workshops and bicycle rides.

Runner Bean Tours Walking

(Map p249; ☑636 108776; www.runnerbean
tours.com; Carrer del Carme 44; ☺tours 11am &
4.30pm Apr-Sep, 11am & 3pm Oct-Mar; ⓂLiceu)
Runner Bean Tours offers several daily
thematic tours. It's a pay-what-you-wish
tour, with a collection for the guide taken at
the end. The Gothic Quarter tour explores
the Roman and medieval history of Barcelona, visiting highlights in the Ciutat Vella.
The Gaudí tour takes in the great works
of Modernista Barcelona. All tours depart
from Plaça Reial.

Barcelona By Bike Cycling

(☑671 307325; www.barcelonabybike.com;
Carrer de la Marina 13; from €24; ⓂCiutadella Vila
Olímpica) This outfit offers various tours by
bicycle, including 'The Original', a three-
hour pedal that takes in a bit of Gothic
Barcelona, L'Eixample (including Sagrada
Família) and the Barceloneta beachfront.

BCN Skytour Scenic Flights

(☑93 224 07 10; www.cathelicopters.com;
Heliport, Passeig de l'Escullera; tour 5/12/35min
per person €71.40/117.40/318.40; ☺by reservation; ⓂDrassanes, Paral·lel) A 12-minute
thrill 800m up in a helicopter will give a
real bird's-eye view of the city; there are
also five-minute tasters. A 35-minute trip
also takes in Montserrat. All prices include
taxes. Take a taxi to get to the heliport.

Orsom Cruise

(☑93 441 05 37; www.barcelona-orsom.com;
Moll de les Drassanes; adult/child €15.50/13.50;
☺May-early Oct; ⓂDrassanes) Orsom's large
sailing catamaran makes the 90-minute
journey to Port Olímpic and back. There are
up to four departures per day; the last of
the day is a jazz cruise.

CicloTour Cycling

(Map p249; ☑93 317 19 70; www.barcelonaciclo
tour.com; Carrer dels Tallers 45; €22; ☺11am,
2pm & 4.30pm May-Oct, 11am Mon-Fri, 11am &
4.30pm Sat & Sun Nov, plus 7.30pm Thu-Sun Jun-
Sep; ⓂUniversitat) Daily bike tours around
the city's main sights. The evening tour also
includes a visit to the Font Màgica.

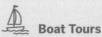

Boat Tours

Several companies take passengers
on short jaunts out on the water. These
depart several times daily (with many
departures in summer) from Moll de
las Drassanes near the southern end
of La Rambla. **Las Golondrinas** (www.
lasgolondrinas.com), **BC Naval Tours** (www.
barcelonanavaltours.com) and other companies offer scenic catamaran trips around
the harbour and beyond. Avoid going on
a windy day, when the seas can be rough.

Terra BikeTours Cycling

(Map p254; ☑93 416 08 05; www.terrabiketours.
com; Carrer de València 337; self-guided tour from
€29, 1-day guided tour from €57; ⓂVerdaguer)
This outfit offers a wide range of cycling
tours from one day to one week. Options
include mountain biking in the Parc de la
Collserola or outside of Barcelona in the
Pyrenees, and a road-biking tour on Barcelona's north coast and beyond. Self-guided
trips (which include preloaded GPS routes
and gear) are also available.

Barcelona Walking Tours Walking

(Map p254; ☑93 285 38 34; www.barcelona
turisme.com; Plaça de Catalunya 17; ⓂCatalunya)
The **Oficina d'Informació de Turisme
de Barcelona** (☺8.30am-9pm) organises
several one-hour guided walking tours
(available in English) exploring the Barri
Gòtic, Picasso's footsteps and Modernisme.
A two-hour gourmet food tour includes
tastings. Various street-art walking and
cycling tours also take place. There is a 10%
discount on all tours if you book online.

Bike Tours Barcelona Cycling

(Map p250; ☑93 268 21 05; www.biketours
barcelona.com; Carrer de l'Esparteria 3; €25;
☺10am-7pm; ⓂJaume I) One of numerous
operators offering daily three-hour tours
of the Barri Gòtic, waterfront, La Sagrada
Família and other Gaudí landmarks. Tours
depart from the tourist office on Plaça de
Sant Jaume.

REST YOUR HEAD

Top tips for the best accommodation

Rest Your Head

Barcelona has an excellent range of accommodation, with high-end luxury hotels, sharp boutique lodgings and a varied spread of midrange and budget selections. There are also small-scale B&B-style apartment rentals scattered around the city, which are a good-value choice. Wherever you stay it's wise to book well ahead. If you plan to travel around holidays such as Easter, Christmas or New Year's Eve, or in summer, reserve a room three or four months ahead of time.

In This Section

Prices

The following price ranges refer to a double room per night during high season, including tax. Prices include private bathroom unless otherwise stated.

€ less than €75

€€ €75–€200

€€€ more than €200

Accommodation near La Rambla (p42)

Reservations

○ Booking ahead is all but essential, especially during peak periods such as Easter, Christmas/New Year, trade fairs and throughout much of summer (although August can be quite a slack month owing to the heat and lack of business visitors).

○ If you arrive without prebooked lodging, the Plaça de Catalunya **tourist office** (p239) can help.

Useful Websites

Lonely Planet (www.lonelyplanet.com/barcelona) Neighbourhood profiles, plus extensive listings of hotels, hostels, guesthouses and apartments.

Oh Barcelona (www.oh-barcelona.com) Hotel and apartment listings, plus tips on deciding where to stay.

Barcelona Bed and Breakfasts (www.barcelonabedandbreakfasts.com) Listings of low-key, oft-overlooked lodging options.

🖴 Accommodation Types

Hotels

Hotels cover a broad range. At the bottom end there is often little to distinguish them from better *pensiones,* and from there they run up the scale to five-star luxury. Some of the better features to look out for include rooftop pools and lounges; views (either of the sea or city); and of course proximity to the important sights.

For around €100 to €160 there are extensive options for good doubles across a wide range of hotels and areas. Luxury hotels generally start at €250 for a double room and can easily rise to €500 (and beyond for suites).

Hostales, Pensiones & Hostels

Depending on the season you can pay as little as €15 to €25 for a dorm bed in a youth hostel. If dorm living is not your thing, but you are still looking for a budget deal, check around the many *pensiones* (also known as *hostales*) – family-run, small-scale hotels, often housed in sprawling apartments.

Some are fleapits, others immaculately maintained gems.

You're looking at a minimum of around €35/55 for basic *individual/doble* (single/double) rooms, mostly with shared bathrooms. It is occasionally possible to find cheaper rooms, but they may be unappealing.

Some places, especially at the lower end, offer triples and quads, which can be good value for groups. If you want a double bed (as opposed to two singles), ask for a *llit/cama matrimonial* (Catalan/Spanish). If your budget is especially tight, look at options outside the centre.

Apartment & Room Rentals

A cosier (and sometimes more cost-effective) alternative to hotels is a short-term apartment rental. A plethora of firms organise short lets across town. Typical prices are around €80 to €100 for two people per night. For four people you might be looking at an average of €160 a night.

Apartment-rental services:

Oh-Barcelona (www.oh-barcelona.com)
Aparteasy (www.aparteasy.com)
Rent the Sun (www.rentthesun.com)
Barcelona On Line (www.barcelona-on-line.es)
Friendly Rentals (www.friendlyrentals.com)
Rent a Flat in Barcelona (www.renta flatinbarcelona.com)
MH Apartments (www.mhapartments.com)

🖴 Travellers with Disabilities

Many hotels claim to be equipped for guests with disabilities but the reality frequently disappoints, although the situation is improving, particularly at the midrange and high-end levels. Check out www.barcelona-access.cat for further information.

Modern hotel in Barceloneta

EQROY/SHUTTERSTOCK ©

Where to Stay

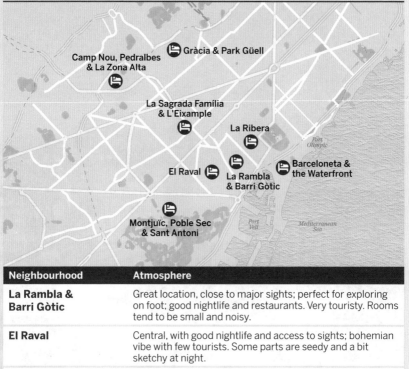

Neighbourhood	Atmosphere
La Rambla & Barri Gòtic	Great location, close to major sights; perfect for exploring on foot; good nightlife and restaurants. Very touristy. Rooms tend to be small and noisy.
El Raval	Central, with good nightlife and access to sights; bohemian vibe with few tourists. Some parts are seedy and a bit sketchy at night.
La Ribera	Central, with a great restaurant scene and neighbourhood exploring. Can be noisy and crowded, and is quite touristy.
Barceloneta & the Waterfront	Excellent seafood restaurants; handy for beaches. Not much accommodation. Barceloneta is central, the rest not very.
La Sagrada Família & L'Eixample	Wide range of options for all budgets; Modernista sights; good restaurants and nightlife; prime LGBTQI scene. Can be noisy with traffic. Not as strollable as the old city.
Montjuïc, Poble Sec & Sant Antoni	Near the museums, gardens and views of Montjuïc; great local exploring in Poble Sec. Area around Sants train station isn't great.
Gràcia & Park Güell	Youthful, local scene with lively restaurants and bars. It's quite far from the old town. Lots of rental rooms.
Camp Nou, Pedralbes & La Zona Alta	Good nightlife and restaurants in parts but very far from the action, requiring frequent metro travel. More geared for business travellers.

Plaça d'Espanya

In Focus

Catalan flags

Barcelona Today

Take a stroll through the streets of Barcelona, and you'll see more than a few estelades, the flag (with the lone star and red and yellow bars) that symbolises Catalonia's drive towards independence. Talk of separatism has reached fever pitch, and raised deep concerns across Europe. Of course, there's much more brewing than just self-rule. The city's deep commitment to innovation has led to improvements in transport, communications and urban design.

The State of Catalonia?

It's a historic moment in Barcelona. The drive towards independence is under way, with the idea that Catalonia could break away from Spain and become a sovereign republic gaining popularity. With its own language, unique traditions and proud history, Catalonia has always thought of itself as distinct from other parts of the country. But until recently, only a small fringe group sought a permanent and irrevocable break from Madrid.

In the last few years, however, the number of self-proclaimed separatists has skyrocketed. In 2015 regional elections, Catalan nationalists won a majority of the 135-seat regional assembly; soon afterwards legislation was under way to draft a Catalan constitution, create a new treasury and design a social security system.

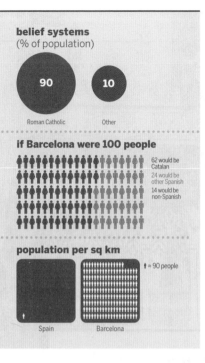

belief systems
(% of population)

90 — Roman Catholic
10 — Other

if Barcelona were 100 people

62 would be Catalan
24 would be other Spanish
14 would be non-Spanish

population per sq km

♦ ≈ 90 people

Spain   Barcelona

In September 2017 a referendum law was pushed through the Catalan parliament, and the vote (deemed illegal and unconstitutional by central government) went ahead on 1 October. There was a 42% turnout (few unionists – those against secession – took part in what they saw as an illegitimate referendum) and around 90% voted in favour of secession. The day was marked by violence doled out by the Guardia Civil (the Spanish police force, shipped in for the occasion) to those attempting to vote. A tense few days followed, in which a political stand-off saw Catalan leader Carles Puigdemont being vague about his intentions while insisting on dialogue with central government in Madrid. Spanish prime minister Mariano Rajoy refused to be drawn, while making obvious his intention to respond by triggering Article 155 of the constitution, thus imposing direct rule over the region.

Finally independence was declared and immediately quashed by Madrid (in the shape of Article 155), with several high-profile Catalan leaders arrested and charged with crimes including 'rebellion' and 'sedition'. Puigdemont, meanwhile, fled to Brussels and then to Germany (where he remains at the time of writing). Regional elections were held in December 2017, but the results simply shored up the status quo, with separatist parties losing the popular vote, but maintaining a parliamentary majority.

The repercussions of Catalan independence would be wide-reaching. It could undermine the financial stability of Spain – and cause economic shock waves across the eurozone. How it all shakes out is anybody's guess, but no one is expecting a smooth ride.

Land of Innovation

Barcelona has become a global model as a 'smart city' – a place where technology is harnessed to create a more sustainable, efficient, and interconnected environment. Some 120 projects comprise the Smart City initiative, including wide-reaching innovations affecting transport, communications, public and social services, and even tourism.

Making use of the 'internet of things', Barcelona now has sensors to detect parking spaces and pollution levels, and to manage traffic flow. Shrinking the city's carbon footprint is at the forefront of various new technologies. Self-powered lights installed along one stretch of beach use a combination of solar and wind energy. Barcelona has the cleanest fleet of buses in Europe, with a large share of hybrids and natural-gas-powered vehicles (plus antipollution filters on its remaining diesel motors). The city has launched new bus routes based on the flow of people using the system, creating a new, more intuitive grid that moves vertically, horizontally and diagonally across town. It has also been expanding its network for electric cars, with 300 existing charging stations and more in the works.

Barri Gòtic

DIMBAR76/SHUTTERSTOCK ©

History

The settlement of Barcelona has seen waves of immigrants and conquerors over its 2000-plus years, including Romans, Visigoths and Franks. Barcelona's fortunes have risen and fallen: from the golden era of princely power in the 14th century to the dark days of the Franco era. An independent streak has always run through Barcelona, which has often led to conflict with the Kingdom of Castilla – an antagonism that continues today, with a desire for more autonomy (or, increasingly, full independence) from Spain.

15 BC	AD 415	718
Caesar Augustus grants the town of Barcino the title of Colonia Iulia Augusta Faventia Paterna Barcino.	Visigoths under Ataülf, with captured Roman empress Galla Placidia as his wife, make Barcino their capital.	Barcelona falls to Tariq's mostly Arab and Berber troops on their march north into France.

Wilfred the Hairy & the Catalan Golden Age

It was the Romans who first etched Barcino onto Europe's map in the 3rd century BC, though the nascent settlement long played second fiddle to their provincial capital in Tarragona. The Visigoths came next, followed by the Moors, whose relatively brief occupation was usurped when the Franks put the city under the control of local counts in 801 as a buffer zone against the still Muslim-dominated caliphate to the south.

Eccentrically named Wilfred the Hairy (Count Guifré el Pelós) moulded the entity we now know as Catalonia in the 9th century by wresting control over several neighbouring territories and establishing Barcelona as its key city. The hirsute one founded a dynasty that lasted nearly five centuries and developed almost independently from the Reconquista wars that were playing out in the rest of Iberia. The counts of Barcelona gradually expanded their territory south and, in 1137, Ramon Berenguer IV, the Count of Barcelona, married Petronilla, heir to the throne of neighbouring Aragón. Thus, the combined Crown of Aragón was created.

801	**1137**	**1348**
Louis the Pious, Charlemagne's son and future Frankish king, takes control and establishes the Spanish March under local counts.	Count Ramon Berenguer IV is betrothed to one-year-old Petronila, the king of Aragón's daughter, creating a new state, Corona de Aragón.	Over 25% of Barcelona's population dies during the plague. A plague of locusts in 1358 and an earthquake in 1373 deal further blows.

Exterior of Reials Drassanes (Royal Shipyards; p90)

★ **Best Historical Reads**

Barcelona: The Great Enchantress (Robert Hughes)

Barcelona – A Thousand Years of the City's Past (Felipe Fernández Armesto)

Homage to Catalonia (George Orwell)

Homage to Barcelona (Colm Tóibín)

In the following centuries the kingdom became a flourishing merchant empire, seizing Valencia and the Balearic Islands from the Muslims and later taking territories as far flung as Sardinia, Sicily and parts of Greece. The 14th century marked the golden age of Barcelona. Its trading wealth paid for great Gothic buildings: La Catedral, the Capella Reial de Santa Àgata (inside the Museu d'Història de Barcelona) and the churches of Santa Maria del Pi and Santa Maria del Mar. King Pere III (1336–87) later created the breathtaking Reials Drassanes (Royal Shipyards) and extended the city walls yet again to include El Raval.

Marginalisation & Decline

Overstretched, racked by civil disobedience and decimated by the Black Death, Catalonia began to wobble. When the last count of Wilfred the Hairy's dynasty expired without leaving an heir, the Crown of Aragón was passed to a noble of Castilla. Soon these two Spanish kingdoms merged, with Catalonia left as a very junior partner. As business shifted from the Mediterranean to the Atlantic after the 'discovery' of the Americas in 1492, Catalans were increasingly marginalised from trade. The region, which had retained some autonomy in the running of its own affairs, was dealt a crushing blow when it supported the wrong side in the War of the Spanish Succession (1702–14). After a stubborn siege, Barcelona, under the auspices of British-backed archduke Charles of Austria, fell on 11 September 1714 (now celebrated as National Catalan Day) to the forces of Bourbon king Philip V, who established a unitary Castilian state. Barcelona faced a long backlash as the new king banned the writing and teaching of Catalan, swept away the remnants of local legal systems and tore down a whole district of medieval Barcelona in order to construct an immense fort (on the site of the present-day Parc de la Ciutadella), the sole purpose of which was to watch over Barcelona's troublemakers.

The Catalan Renaissance

Buoyed by the lifting of the ban on its trade with the Americas in 1778, Barcelona embarked on the road to industrial revolution, based initially on textiles but spreading to wine, cork and iron in the mid-19th century. It soon became Spain's leading city. As the economy

1469
Castilian heir to the throne Isabel marries Aragonese heir Fernando, uniting Spain's most powerful monarchies and subjugating Catalonia.

1640–52
Catalan peasants, after the Thirty Years' War, declare their independence under French protection, but are crushed by Spain.

1888
Showcasing its grand Modernista touches, Barcelona hosts Spain's first Universal Exposition in the Parc de la Ciutadella.

prospered, Barcelona outgrew its medieval walls, which were demolished in 1854–56. Work on the grid-plan L'Eixample (the Extension) district began soon after. The so-called Renaixença (Renaissance) brought a revival of Catalan culture, as well as political activism. It sowed the seeds of growing political tension in the early 20th century, as demands for autonomy from the central state became more insistent.

Masses & Classes

Adding to the fiery mix was growing discontent among the working class. The grand Catalan merchant-bourgeois families grew richer, displaying their wealth in a slew of whimsical private mansions built with verve and flair by Modernista architects such as Antoni Gaudí. At the same time, the industrial working class, housed in cramped quarters such as Barceloneta and El Raval, and oppressed by poverty and disease, became organised and, occasionally, violent. Spain's neutrality during WWI had boosted Barcelona's economy and from 1900 to 1930 the population doubled to one million, but the postwar global slump hit the city hard. Waves of strikes, organised principally by the anarchists' Confederación Nacional del Trabajo (CNT), brought tough responses. Left- and right-wing gangs took their ideological conflict to the streets. Tit-for-tat assassinations became common currency and the death toll mounted. When the Second Spanish Republic was created under a left-wing government in 1931, Catalonia declared independence. Later, under pressure, its leaders settled for devolution, which it then lost in 1934, when a right-wing government won power in Madrid. The election of a left-wing popular front in 1936 again sparked Catalan autonomy claims, but also led to the generals' rising that launched the Spanish Civil War (1936–39), from which Franco emerged the victor.

The War Years

The acting capital of Spain for much of the civil war, Barcelona was run by anarchists and the Partido Obrero de Unificación Marxista (Marxist Unification Workers' Party) Trotskyist militia until mid-1937. Unions took over factories and public services; hotels and mansions became hospitals and schools; everyone wore workers' clothes; bars and cafes were collectivised; trams and taxis were painted red and black (the colours of the anarchists); and one-way streets were ignored as they were seen to be part of the old system. The more radical anarchists were behind the burning of most of the city's churches and the shooting

Jewish Barcelona

The narrow Barri Gòtic lanes of El Call were once home to a thriving Jewish population. Catalan Jews worked as merchants, scholars, cartographers and teachers. By the 11th century, as many as 4000 Jews lived in El Call. As in much of Europe, during the 13th century a wave of anti-Semitism swept through Catalonia. Pogroms followed on from repressive laws; anti-Semitism peaked in 1391 when a frenzied mob tore through El Call, looting and destroying private homes and murdering hundreds of Jews. Most of the remaining Jews fled the city.

1909	1936–39	1992
After reserve troops are sent to fight a war in Morocco, *barcelonins* riot, and over 100 are killed in Setmana Tràgica (Tragic Week).	In the Spanish Civil War, nationalist forces are defeated by left-wing militia, workers and loyalist police but Franco's troops win.	Barcelona hosts the summer Olympic Games. The city undergoes a radical renovation program, which continues today.

Anarchists & the Tragic Week

When the political philosophy of anarchism began spreading through Europe, it was embraced by many industrial workers in Barcelona, who embarked on a road to social revolution through violent means. One anarchist bomb at the Liceu opera house on La Rambla in the 1890s killed 22 people. Anarchists were also blamed for the Setmana Tràgica (Tragic Week) in July 1909 when, following a military call-up for Spanish campaigns in Morocco, rampaging mobs wrecked 70 religious buildings, and workers were shot on the street in reprisal.

of hundreds of priests, monks and nuns. The anarchists in turn were shunted aside by the communists (directed by Stalin from Moscow) after a bloody internecine battle in Barcelona that left 1500 dead in May 1937. Later that year the Spanish Republican government fled Valencia and made Barcelona the official capital (the government had left besieged Madrid early in the war). The Republican defeat at the hands of the Nationalists in the Battle of the Ebro in southern Catalonia in the summer of 1938 left Barcelona undefended. It fell to the Nationalists on 25 January 1939, triggering a mass exodus of refugees to France, where most were long interned in makeshift camps. Purges and executions under Franco continued until well into the 1950s. Former Catalan president Lluís Companys was arrested in France by the Gestapo in August 1940, handed over to Franco, and shot on 15 October on Montjuïc, despite international outrage. He is reputed to have died with the words '*Visca Catalunya!*' ('Long live Catalonia!') on his lips.

Recent Times

When the death of Franco was announced in 1975, *barcelonins* took to the streets in celebration. The next five years saw the gradual return of democracy and in 1977 Catalonia was granted regional autonomy. Politics aside, the big event in post-Franco Barcelona was the successful 1992 Olympic Games, planned under the guidance of the popular Socialist mayor, Pasqual Maragall. The games spurred a burst of public works and brought new life to areas such as Montjuïc, where the major events were held. The once-shabby waterfront was transformed with promenades, beaches, marinas, restaurants, leisure attractions and new housing. After the turn of the millennium, Barcelona continued to invest in urban renewal. In recent years, soaring unemployment and painful austerity measures – not to mention Catalonia's heavy tax burden – have led to anger and resentment toward Madrid and fuelled the drive toward independence. Recent polls indicate about half of Catalans support the region becoming a new European state. Heavy-handed reaction from Madrid to the independence movement has increased support for it.

2015	**2017**	**2026**
In an election separatists take control of Catalonia's government, with an 18-month plan for full secession.	Catalonia's referendum is marked by police violence, but independence is declared. Direct Spanish rule is imposed.	Builders aim to finish La Sagrada Família by the centenary of Gaudí's death, over 140 years after construction began.

Enric Miralles' Edifici de Gas Natural in La Barceloneta

Architecture

Famed for its architectural treasures, Barcelona has striking Gothic cathedrals, fantastical Modernista creations and more-recent avant-garde works. The great building boom began in the late Middle Ages, when Barcelona was seat of the Catalan empire. In the late 19th century, the city expanded beyond its medieval confines and was transformed by bold new thinkers. The third notable era of design, from the late 1980s, continues today.

The Gothic Period

Barcelona had a major architectural flourish during the height of the Middle Ages, when its imposing Gothic churches, mansions and shipyards were raised, together creating what survives to this day as one of the most extensive Gothic quarters in Europe. Catalan Gothic did not follow the same course as the style typical of northern Europe. Decoration here tends to be more sparing and the most obvious defining characteristic is the triumph of breadth over height. While northern European cathedrals reach for the sky, Catalan Gothic has a tendency to push to the sides, stretching its vaulting design to the limit. Another notable departure from what you might have come to expect of Gothic north of the Pyrenees is the lack of spires and pinnacles.

Casa Batlló's Modernista roofline

★ **Best Modernista Creations**

La Pedrera (p76)
La Sagrada Família (p36)
Palau de la Música Catalana (p106)
Casa Batlló (p52)
Casa Amatller (p54)

Modernisme

The second wave of Catalan creativity, also carried on the wind of boom times, came around the turn of the 20th century. The urban expansion program known as L'Eixample (the Extension), designed to free the choking population from the city's bursting medieval confines, coincided with this blossoming of unfettered thinking in architecture that arrived in the back-draft of the 1888 Universal Exposition of Barcelona. A key uniting element of the Modernistas was the sensuous curve, implying movement, lightness and vitality. But as well as modernity, architects often looked to the past for inspiration. Gothic, Islamic and Renaissance design all had something to offer. At its most playful, Modernisme was able to intelligently flout the rule books of these styles and create exciting new cocktails.

Gaudí

Born in Reus to a long line of coppersmiths, Antoni Gaudí was initially trained in metalwork. In childhood he suffered from poor health, including rheumatism, and became an early adopter of a vegetarian diet. He was not a promising student. In 1878, when he obtained his architecture degree, the school's headmaster is reputed to have said: 'Who knows if we have given a diploma to a nutcase or a genius. Time will tell.'

As a young man, what most delighted Gaudí was being outdoors. Throughout his work, he sought to emulate the harmony he observed in the natural world, eschewing the straight line and favouring curvaceous forms and more organic shapes.

Gaudí's masterpiece was La Sagrada Família (begun in 1882); in it you can see the culminating vision of many ideas developed over the years. Its massive scale evokes the grandeur of Catalonia's Gothic cathedrals, while organic elements foreground its harmony with nature. The church is rife with symbols that tangibly express Gaudí's Catholic faith through architecture. As well as being a devout Catholic, he was a Catalan nationalist. He lived a simple life and was not averse to knocking on doors, literally begging for money to help fund construction on the basilica.

Gaudí died in 1926, struck down by a tram while taking his daily walk to the Sant Felip Neri church. Wearing ragged clothes, Gaudí was initially taken for a beggar and driven to a nearby hospital where he was left in a pauper's ward. He died two days later. Thousands attended his funeral procession to La Sagrada Família, where he was buried in the crypt.

Domènech i Montaner

Although overshadowed by Gaudí, Lluís Domènech i Montaner (1849–1923) was one of the great masters of Modernisme. He was a widely travelled man of prodigious intellect, with knowledge in everything from mineralogy to medieval heraldry; he was also an architectural professor, a prolific writer and a nationalist politician. The question of Catalan identity and how to create a national architecture consumed Domènech i Montaner, who designed more than a dozen large-scale works in his lifetime. The exuberant, steel-framed Palau de la Música Catalana is one of his masterpieces.

Gothic Masterpieces

La Catedral (p64)

Basílica de Santa Maria del Mar (p116)

Basílica de Santa Maria del Pi (p46)

Saló del Tinell in the **Museu d'Història de Barcelona** (p112)

The Drassanes, now the site of the **Museu Marítim** (p88)

The former monastery housing the **Museu-Monestir de Pedralbes** (p102)

Puig i Cadafalch

Like Domènech i Montaner, Josep Puig i Cadafalch (1867–1956) was a polymath; he was an archaeologist, an expert in Romanesque art and one of Catalonia's most prolific architects. As a politician – and later president of the Mancomunitat de Catalunya (Commonwealth of Catalonia) – he was instrumental in shaping the Catalan nationalist movement. One of his many Modernista gems is the Casa Amatller, a rather dramatic contrast to Gaudí's Casa Batlló next door; it is a house of startling beauty and invention blended with playful Gothic-style sculpture.

Modern Times

Barcelona's latest architectural revolution began in the 1980s when, in the run-up to the 1992 Olympics, the city set about its biggest phase of renewal since the heady days of L'Eixample.

In the new millennium, the Diagonal Mar district is characterised by striking modern architecture, including the hovering blue, triangular Edifici Fòrum by Swiss architects Herzog & de Meuron and a 24-storey whitewashed trapezoidal prism that serves as the headquarters for the national telephone company, Telefónica.

Another prominent addition to the city skyline came in 2005. The shimmering, cucumber-shaped Torre Agbar is a product of French architect Jean Nouvel.

Southwest, on the way to the airport, the new Fira M2 trade fair is now marked by red twisting twin landmark towers designed by Japanese star architect and confessed Gaudí fan Toyo Ito.

The heart of La Ribera got a fresh look with its brand-new Mercat de Santa Caterina. The market is quite a sight, with its wavy ceramic roof and tubular skeleton, designed by Enric Miralles, one of the most promising names in Catalan architecture until his premature death. Miralles' Edifici de Gas Natural, a 100m glass tower near the waterfront in La Barceloneta, is also extraordinary.

Detail of MACBA (Museu d'Art Contemporani de Barcelona; p94)

Modern Art

Three of Spain's greatest 20th-century artists have deep connections to Barcelona. Picasso spent his formative years in the city and maintained lifelong friendships with Catalans. It was Picasso's own idea to create a museum of his works here. Joan Miró is one of Barcelona's most famous native sons. His instantly recognisable style can be seen in public installations throughout the city. Although Salvador Dalí is more commonly associated with Figueres, Barcelona was a great source of inspiration for him, particularly the fantastical architectural works of Antoni Gaudí.

Pablo Picasso

It wasn't until the late 19th century that truly great artists began to emerge in Barcelona and its hinterland, led by dandy portraitist Ramón Casas (1866–1932). Casas, an early Modernista, founded a Barcelona bar known as Els Quatre Gats, which became the nucleus for the city's growing art movement, holding numerous shows and expositions. An early host was a young, then unknown, *malagueño* (man from Malaga) named Pablo Picasso (1881–1973).

Picasso lived sporadically in Barcelona between the innocence-losing ages of 16 and 24, and the city heavily influenced his early painting. This was the period in which he amassed the raw materials for his Blue Period. In 1904, the then-mature Picasso moved to Paris where he found fame, fortune and cubism, and went on to become one of the greatest artists of the 20th century.

Joan Miró

At the time the 13-year-old Picasso arrived in Barcelona, his near-contemporary Joan Miró (1893–1983) was still learning to crawl in the Barri Gòtic, where he was born. Miró spent a third of his life in Barcelona and later divided his time between France, the Tarragona countryside and the island of Mallorca, where he died.

★ **Best Places for Modern Art**

Museu Picasso (p80)

Fundació Joan Miró (p60)

Fundació Antoni Tàpies (p55)

MACBA (p94)

Museu Nacional d'Art de Catalunya (p56)

Like Picasso, Miró attended the Escola de Belles Artes de la Llotja. In Paris from 1920, he mixed with Picasso, Hemingway, Joyce and friends, and made his own mark, after several years of struggle, with an exhibition in 1925. The masterpiece from this, his so-called realist period, was La Masia (The Farmhouse). It was during WWII that Miró's definitive leitmotifs emerged – arrangements of lines and symbolic figures in primary colours, with shapes reduced to their essence. Declaring he was going to 'assassinate art', Miró wanted nothing to do with the constricting labels of the era, although he has often been called a pioneering surrealist, Dadaist and automatist.

Salvador Dalí

The great Catalan artist Salvador Dalí i Domènech (1904–89) was born and died in Figueres, where he left his single greatest artistic legacy, the Teatre-Museu Dalí. Although few of his famed works are in Barcelona, the city provided a stimulating atmosphere, and places like Park Güell, with its surrealist-like aspects, had a powerful effect on Dalí.

Prolific painter, showman, shameless self-promoter or just plain weirdo, Dalí was nothing if not a character – probably a little too much for the conservative small-town folk of Figueres. Every now and then a key moment arrives that can change the course of one's life. Dalí's came in 1929, when the French poet Paul Éluard visited Cadaqués with his Russian wife, Gala. The rest, as they say, is histrionics. Dalí shot off to Paris to be with Gala and plunged into the world of surrealism.

In the 1930s Salvador and Gala returned to live at Port Lligat on the north Catalan coast, where they played host to a long list of fashionable and art-world guests until the war years. The parties were by all accounts memorable and started again in Port Lligat in the 1950s. The stories of sexual romps and Gala's appetite for local young men are legendary. The 1960s saw Dalí painting pictures on a grand scale, including his 1962 reinterpretation of Marià Fortuny's Batalla de Tetuán. On his death in 1989, he was buried (according to his own wishes) in the Teatre-Museu he had created on the site of the old theatre in central Figueres, which also houses an awe-inspiring Dalí collection.

Antoni Tàpies

Picasso, Miró and Dalí were hard acts to follow. Few envied the task of Catalan Antoni Tàpies in reviving the red hot Modernista flame. An early admirer of Miró, Tàpies soon began pursuing his own esoteric path embracing 'art informal' (a Jackson Pollock–like use of spontaneity) and inventing painting that utilised clay, string and even bits of rubbish. He was arguably Spain's greatest living painter before his death in 2012.

Correfoc (fire run)

ANKY/SHUTTERSTOCK ©

Catalan Culture

The fortunes of Catalunya have risen and fallen over the years, as Barcelona has gone from wealthy mercantile capital to a city of repression under the Franco regime, followed by the boom and bust of more recent years. Despite today's economic challenges, Catalan culture continues to flourish, with a vigorous program of events, traditional music and dance, and abundant civic pride.

Language

In Barcelona, born-and-bred locals proudly speak Catalan, a Romance language related to French, Spanish (Castilian) and Italian. It was only relatively recently, however, that Catalan was deemed 'legitimate'. Since Barcelona was crushed in the War of the Spanish Succession in 1714, the use of Catalan was repeatedly banned or at least frowned upon. Franco was the last of Spain's rulers to clamp down on its public use. All that changed in 1980, when the first autonomous regional parliament was assembled and adopted new laws towards *normalització lingüística* (linguistic normalisation).

Today, Catalonia's state school system uses Catalan as the language of instruction, though most Catalan speakers end up bilingual, particularly in urban areas. Around town,

Catalan is the lingua franca: advertising and road signs are in Catalan, while newspapers, magazines and other publications can be found in both languages (though you'll find about twice as many options in Catalan as in Spanish). You'll also find a mix of Catalan and Spanish programming on radio and TV.

Festivals

Catalonia's best celebrations tend to revolve around religious holidays. *Festes* dedicated to Nostra Senyora de la Mercè (p14; Our Lady of Mercy) and Santa Eulàlia (p7) – Barcelona's two patron saints – are the city's biggest bashes. You'll see plenty of *sardana* dancing and *castell* building there. You'll also see *gegants* (huge papier-mâché giants: lords, princesses, sultans, fishers and historic and contemporary figures) and *capgrossos* (oversized heads worn by costumed actors).

Another feature of these Catalan fests is the *correfoc* (fire run): horned devils brandishing firework-spouting pitchforks wreak mayhem in the streets. They are sometimes accompanied by firework-spouting dragons, or even wooden carts that are set alight. Full coverings (hats, gloves, goggles) are highly recommended for anyone who wants to get near.

Best on Film

All About My Mother (1999) One of Almodóvar's best-loved films, complete with transsexual prostitutes and doe-eyed nuns.

Vicky Cristina Barcelona (2008) Woody Allen gives Barcelona the *Manhattan* treatment, showing a city of startling beauty and neuroticism.

L'Auberge espagnol (2002) A warmly told coming-of-age story about a mishmash of foreign-exchange students thrown together in Barcelona.

Barcelona (1994) A sharp and witty romantic comedy about two Americans living in Barcelona during the end of the Cold War.

Best Blogs

Driftwood Journals (www.driftwood journals.com) Beautifully photographed things to do and places to stay.

Foodie in Barcelona (www.foodiein barcelona.com) Entertaining descriptions of cafes, restaurants and food shops.

Homage to BCN (www.homagetobcn. com) Residents explain their 'perfect day' in Barcelona.

FC Barcelona

One of the city's best-loved names is FC Barça, which is deeply associated with Catalans and even Catalan nationalism. The team was long a rallying point for Catalans when other aspects of Catalan culture were suppressed. The club openly supported Catalonia's drive towards autonomy in 1918, and in 1921 the club's statutes were drafted in Catalan. The pro-Catalan leanings of the club and its siding with the republic during the Spanish Civil War earned reprisals from the government. Club president Josep Sunyol was murdered by Franco's soldiers in 1936, and the club building was bombed in 1938.

In 1968 club president Narcís de Carreras uttered the now famous words, *El Barça: més que un club* ('more than a club'), which became the team's motto – and emphasised its role as an anti-Franco symbol and catalyst for change in the province and beyond. Today FC Barça is one of the world's most admired teams, with membership at around 170,000 in recent years.

Music

Barcelona's vibrant music and dance scene has been shaped by artists both traditional and cutting edge. From Nova Cançó, composed during the dark years of the dictatorship, to the hybridised Catalan rumba to hands-in-the air rock ballads of the 1970s and '80s,

Pau Casals

Born in Catalonia, Pau Casals (1876–1973) was one of the greatest cellists of the 20th century. Living in exile in southern France, he declared he would not play in public as long as Western democracies continued to tolerate Franco's regime. In 1958 he was a candidate for the Nobel Peace Prize.

Barcelona's music evolves constantly. Today's groups continue to push musical boundaries, blending rhythms from all corners of the globe. In the realm of dance, flamenco has a small, loyal following, while the old-fashioned folk dance *sardana* continues to attract growing numbers.

Classical, Opera & Baroque

Spain's contribution to the world of classical music has been modest, but Catalonia has produced a few exceptional composers. Best known is Camprodon-born Isaac Albéniz (1860–1909), a gifted pianist who later turned his hand to composition. Among his best-remembered works is the *Iberia* cycle.

Montserrat Caballé is Barcelona's most successful voice. Born in Gràcia in 1933, the soprano made her debut in 1956 in Basel (Switzerland). Her home-town launch came four years later in the Gran Teatre del Liceu. In 1965 she performed to wild acclaim at New York's Carnegie Hall and went on to become one of the world's finest 20th-century sopranos. Her daughter, Montserrat Martí, is also a singer and they occasionally appear together. Another fine Catalan soprano was Victoria de los Ángeles (1923–2005), while Catalonia's other world-class opera star is the renowned tenor Josep (José) Carreras.

Jordi Savall has assumed the task of rediscovering a European heritage in music that predates the era of the classical greats. He and his late wife, soprano Montserrat Figueras, have, along with musicians from other countries, been largely responsible for resuscitating the beauties of medieval, Renaissance and baroque music. In 1987 Savall founded La Capella Reial de Catalunya and two years later he formed the baroque orchestra Le Concert des Nations. You can sometimes catch their recitals in locations such as the Gran Teatre del Liceu or the Basílica de Santa Maria del Mar.

Nova Cançó

Curiously, it was probably the Francoist repression that most helped foster a vigorous local music scene in Catalan. In the dark 1950s, the Nova Cançó (New Song) movement was born to resist linguistic oppression with music in Catalan (getting air time on the radio was long close to impossible), throwing up stars that in some cases won huge popularity throughout Spain, such as the Valencia-born Raimon.

More specifically loved in Catalonia as a Bob Dylan–style 1960s protest singer-songwriter was Lluís Llach, much of whose music was more or less antiregime. Joan Manuel Serrat is another legendary figure. His appeal stretches from Barcelona to Buenos Aires. Born in the Poble Sec district, this poet-singer is equally at ease in Catalan and in Spanish. He has repeatedly shown that record sales are not everything to him. In 1968 he refused to represent Spain at the Eurovision song contest if he was not allowed to sing in Catalan. Accused of being anti-Spanish, he was long banned from performing in Spain.

Born in Mallorca, the talented singer Maria del Mar Bonet arrived in Barcelona in 1967, and embarked on a long and celebrated singing career. She sang in Catalan, and many of her searing and powerful songs were banned by the dictatorship. On concert tours abroad, she attracted worldwide attention, and she has performed with distinguished groups and soloists across the globe.

Bicing (Barcelona's public bike borrowing service)

MIKHAIL GNATKOVSKIY/SHUTTERSTOCK ©

Survival Guide

Directory A–Z

Dangers & Annoyances

○ Violent crime is rare in Barcelona, but petty crime (bag-snatching, pickpocketing) is a major problem.

○ You're at your most vulnerable when dragging around luggage to or from your hotel; make sure you know your route before arriving.

○ Be mindful of your belongings, particularly in crowded areas.

○ Avoid walking around El Raval and the southern end of La Rambla late at night.

○ Don't wander down empty city streets at night. When in doubt, take a taxi.

○ Take nothing of value to the beach, and don't leave anything unattended.

Discount Cards

The **ISIC** (International Student Identity Card; www.isic.org) and the **European Youth Card** (www.euro26.org) are available from most national student organisations and

allow discounted access to some sights. Students generally pay just over half of adult admission prices, as do children aged under 12 and senior citizens (aged 65 and over) with appropriate ID.

Possession of a **Bus Turístic** (📞93 298 70 00; www.barcelonabusturistic.cat; 1 day adult/child €29/16, 2 days €39/16; ⏰9am-8pm) ticket entitles you to discounts at some museums.

Articket (www.articketbcn.org) gives admission to six sites for €30 and is valid for six months.

Barcelona Card (www.barcelonacard.com) is handy if you want to see lots in a limited time. It costs €20/45/55/60 for two/three/four/five days. You get free transport, discounted admission (up to 60% off) or free entry to many museums and other sights, and minor discounts on purchases at a small number of shops, restaurants and bars.

The **Ruta del Modernisme** (www.rutadelmodernisme.com) pack costs €12 and is well worth looking into for visiting Modernista sights at discounted rates.

Electricity

Spain uses 220V/50Hz, like the rest of continental Europe.

Type C 220V/230V/50Hz

Emergency & Important Numbers

Ambulance	📞061
EU standard emergency number	📞112
Country code	📞34
International access code	📞00
Tourist police	📞93 256 24 30

LGBTQI Travellers

Barcelona has a vibrant gay and lesbian scene, with a fine array of restaurants, bars and clubs in the district known as the 'Gaixample' (a portmanteau of gay and L'Eixample), an area about five to six blocks southwest of Passeig de Gràcia around Carrer del Consell de Cent.

Useful Websites

60by80 (www.60by80.com) An excellent website for gay travellers. Click on 'Barcelona' under 'City Guides' and take it from there.

Patroc (www.patroc.com) A European gay guide, the Barcelona section of which has a useful selection of hotels, clubs and so on. Particularly good on upcoming events.

Tillate (www.tillate.es) Discover upcoming parties in this nightlife guide to regions around Spain, including Catalonia.

GaySitges (www.gaysitges.com) A specific site dedicated to this LGBTQI-friendly coastal town.

Health

○ All foreigners have the same right as Spaniards to emergency medical treatment in public hospitals. EU citizens are entitled to the full range of health-care services in public hospitals, but must present a European Health Insurance Card (enquire at your national health service) and may have to pay upfront.

○ Non-EU citizens have to pay for anything other than emergency treatment. Most travel-insurance policies include medical cover.

○ For minor health problems you can try any *farmàcia* (pharmacy), where pharmaceuticals tend to be sold more freely without prescription than in places such as the USA, Australia or the UK.

○ If your country has a consulate in Barcelona, its staff should be able to refer you to doctors who speak your language.

Insurance

○ A travel-insurance policy to cover theft, loss, medical problems, and cancellation or delays of your travel arrangements is a good idea.

○ Paying for your ticket with a credit card can often provide limited travel-accident insurance, and you may be able to reclaim the payment if the operator doesn't deliver.

○ Worldwide travel insurance is available at lonelyplanet.com/travel-insurance. You can buy, extend and claim online any time – even if you're on the road.

Internet Access

In an increasingly wired city (where many folks have smartphones or web-enabled devices), internet cafes are a disappearing breed. Aside from an internet cafe, look also for *locutorios* (public phone centres), which often double as internet centres.

Places in our Barcelona listings that offer wi-fi have a wi-fi symbol.

Money

ATMs are widely available (La Rambla has many). Credit cards are accepted in most hotels, shops and restaurants.

Tipping

Restaurants Catalans typically leave 5% or less at restaurants. Leave more for exceptionally good service.

Taxis Optional, but most locals round up to the nearest euro.

Bars It's rare to leave a tip in bars, though a bit of small change is always appreciated.

Practicalities

○ **Currency** Euro (€)

○ **Smoking** Banned in restaurants and bars.

○ **Major Barcelona newspapers** *La Vanguardia* and *El Periódico* are available in Spanish and Catalan. *El País* publishes an online English supplement (www.elpais.com/elpais/inenglish.html).

Public Holidays

New Year's Day (Any Nou/Año Nuevo) 1 January

Epiphany/Three Kings' Day (Epifanía or El Dia dels Reis/Día de los Reyes Magos) 6 January

Good Friday (Divendres Sant/ Viernes Santo) March/April

Easter Monday (Dilluns de Pasqua Florida) March/April

Labour Day (Dia del Treball/ Fiesta del Trabajo) 1 May

Day after Pentecost Sunday (Dilluns de Pasqua Granda) May/June

Feast of St John the Baptist (Dia de Sant Joan/Día de San Juan Bautista) 24 June

Feast of the Assumption (L'Assumpció/La Asunción) 15 August

Catalonia's National Day (Diada Nacional de Catalunya) 11 September

Festes de la Mercè 24 September

Spanish National Day (Festa de la Hispanitat/Día de la Hispanidad) 12 October

All Saints Day (Dia de Tots Sants/Día de Todos los Santos) 1 November

Constitution Day (Día de la Constitución) 6 December

Feast of the Immaculate Conception (La Immaculada Concepció/La Inmaculada Concepción) 8 December

Christmas (Nadal/Navidad) 25 December

Boxing Day/St Stephen's Day (El Dia de Sant Esteve) 26 December

Taxes & Refunds

Value-added tax (VAT) is a 21% sales tax levied on most goods and services. For restaurants and hotels it's 10%. Most restaurants include VAT in their prices; it's usually included in hotel-room prices, too, but be sure to ask when booking.

Value-added tax (VAT) is also known as IVA (*impuesto sobre el valor añadido*; pronounced 'ee-ba'). IVA-free shopping is available in duty-free shops at all airports for people travelling between EU countries.

Non-EU residents are entitled to a refund of the 21% IVA on purchases costing more than €90 from any shop, if the goods are taken out of the EU within three months. Ask the shop for a Cashback (or similar) refund form showing the price and IVA paid for each item and identifying the vendor and purchaser. Then present the form at the customs booth for IVA refunds when you depart from Spain (or elsewhere in the EU). You will need your passport and a boarding card that shows you are leaving the EU, and your luggage (so do this before checking in bags). The officer will stamp the invoice and you hand it in at a bank at the departure point to receive a reimbursement.

Telephone

Public telephones Blue payphones are hard to find but easy to use for international and domestic calls. They accept coins, *tarjetas telefónicas* (phonecards) issued by the national phone company, Telefónica and, in some cases, credit cards. *Tarjetas telefónicas* are sold at post offices and tobacconists.

Mobile phones Local SIM cards can be used in unlocked

Climate Change & Travel

Every form of transport that relies on carbon-based fuel generates CO_2, the main cause of human-induced climate change. Modern travel is dependent on aeroplanes, which might use less fuel per kilometre per person than most cars but travel much greater distances. The altitude at which aircraft emit gases (including CO_2) and particles also contributes to their climate change impact. Many websites offer 'carbon calculators' that allow people to estimate the carbon emissions generated by their journey and, for those who wish to do so, to offset the impact of the greenhouse gases emitted with contributions to portfolios of climate-friendly initiatives throughout the world. Lonely Planet offsets the carbon footprint of all staff and author travel.

phones. Other phones must be set to roaming.

Call centres Various *locutorios*, which also double as internet centres, are scattered around the Old City, especially El Raval and Sant Pere. Check rates before making calls.

Making calls To call Barcelona from outside Spain, dial the international access code, followed by the code for Spain (34) and the full number (including Barcelona's area code, 93, which is an integral part of the number). To make an international call, dial the international access code (00), country code, area code and number.

Time

○ Spain is on CET, one hour ahead of GMT/UTC during winter, and two hours ahead during daylight saving (the last Sunday in March to the last Sunday in October).

○ Most other western European countries are on the same time as Spain year-round. The UK, Ireland and Portugal are one hour behind.

○ Spaniards use the 24-hour clock for official business (timetables etc) but generally switch to the 12-hour version in daily conversation.

Toilets

Public toilets aren't very common in Barcelona. Big shopping centres (or the El Corte Inglés department store) are an option, but ducking into a cafe or bar may be your best bet (it's polite to order something).

Tourist Information

Oficina d'Informació de Turisme de Barcelona (93 285 38 34; www.barcelona turisme.com; Plaça de Catalunya 17-S, underground; 8.30am-9pm; Catalunya) Provides maps, sights information, tours, concert and events tickets, and last-minute accommodation.

Travellers with Disabilities

○ Most hotels and public institutions have wheelchair access. All buses in Barcelona are wheelchair accessible and a growing number of metro stations are theoretically wheelchair accessible (generally by lift, although there have been complaints that they are only good for people with prams). Of 156 stations, all but 15 are completely adapted (you can check which ones by looking at a network

map at: www.tmb.cat/en/transport-accessible). Ticket vending machines in metro stations are adapted for disabled travellers, and have Braille options for those with a visual impairment.

○ Several taxi companies have adapted vehicles, including **Taxi Amic** (93 420 80 88; www.taxi-amic-adaptat.com) and **Green Taxi** (900 827900; www.greentaxi.es).

○ Most street crossings in central Barcelona are wheelchair-friendly.

Transport

Getting There & Away

Air

○ After Madrid, Barcelona is Spain's busiest international transport hub. A host of airlines, including many budget carriers, fly directly to Barcelona from around Europe. Ryanair also uses Girona and Reus airports (buses link Barcelona to both).

○ Most intercontinental flights require passengers to change flights in Madrid or another major European hub.

○ Iberia, Air Europa, Spanair and Vueling all have dense networks across the country.

o Barcelona's main airport is El Prat, with the majority of international flights arriving here. In addition, there are two other airports in nearby cities, which are used by some budget airlines.

Getting To/From El Prat Airport

Bus

The **A1 Aerobús** (☑902 100104; www.aerobusbcn.com; Plaça d'Espanya; one way/return €5.90/10.20; ⊙5am-1.05am) runs from Terminal 1 to Plaça de Catalunya (30 to 40 minutes depending on traffic) via Plaça d'Espanya, Gran Via de les Corts Catalanes (corner of Carrer del Comte d'Urgell) and Plaça de la Universitat every five to 10 minutes from 5.35am to 1.05am. Departures from Plaça de Catalunya are from 5am to 12.30am and stop at the corner of Carrer de Sepúlveda and Carrer del Comte d'Urgell, and at Plaça d'Espanya.

The **A2 Aerobús** from Terminal 2 (stops outside terminal areas A, B and C) runs every 10 minutes from 5am to 1am and follows the same route as the A1 Aerobús.

Buy tickets on the bus or from agents at the bus stop. Slower local buses (such as the No 46 to/from Plaça d'Espanya and two night buses, the N17 and N18, to/from Plaça de Catalunya) also serve Terminals 1 and 2.

Train

Train operator Renfe runs the R2 Nord line every half-hour from the airport (from 5.42am to 11.38pm) via several stops to Barcelona's main train station, **Estació Sants** (www.adif.es; Plaça dels Països Catalans; Ⓜ Sants Estació), and Passeig de Gràcia in central Barcelona, after which it heads north-west out of the city. The first service from Passeig de Gràcia leaves at 5.08am and the last at 11.07pm, and about five minutes later from Estació Sants. The trip between the airport and Passeig de Gràcia takes 25 minutes. A one-way ticket costs €2.50.

The airport train station is about a five-minute walk from Terminal 2. Regular shuttle buses run from the station and Terminal 2 to Terminal 1 – allow an extra 15 to 20 minutes.

Taxi

A taxi between either terminal and the city centre – about a half-hour ride depending on traffic – costs around €25. Fares and charges are posted inside the passenger side of the taxi; make sure the meter is used.

Train

o Train is the most convenient overland option for reaching Barcelona from major Spanish centres like Madrid and Valencia. It can be a long haul from other parts of Europe – budget

flights frequently offer a saving in time and money.

o A network of *rodalies/ cercanías* (Renfe-run local trains) serves towns around Barcelona (and the airport). Contact **Renfe** (☑91 232 03 20; www.renfe.es).

o Frequent high-speed Tren de Alta Velocidad Española (AVE) trains between Madrid and Barcelona run daily in both directions, several of them in under three hours.

Getting Around

Bicycle

Bike paths Over 180km of bike lanes have been laid out across the city. You can transport your bicycle on the metro on weekdays (except between 7am and 9.30am or 5pm and 8.30pm). At weekends and during holidays and July and August, there are no restrictions.

Bus

Transports Metropolitans de Barcelona (TMB; ☑93 298 70 00; www.tmb.net) buses run along most city routes every few minutes from between 5am and 6.30am to between 10pm and 11pm. Many routes pass through Plaça de Catalunya and/or Plaça de la Universitat. After 11pm a reduced network of yellow *nitbusos* (night buses) runs until 3am or 5am. All *nitbus* routes pass through Plaça de Catalunya and most run every 30 to 45 minutes.

Car & Motorcycle

With the convenience of public transport and the high price of parking in the city, it's unwise to drive in Barcelona. However, if you're planning a trip outside the city, a car is handy. Avis, Europcar, National/Atesa and Hertz have desks at El Prat airport, Estació Sants and Estació del Nord.

Cooltra (☑93 221 40 70; www.cooltra.com; Via Laietana 6; per day €28-35; ⊙10am-8pm; ⓂBarceloneta) rents scooters, as does **MondoRent** (☑93 295 32 68; http://mondo rent.com; Passeig de Joan de Borbó 80-84; per day from €35; ⊙10am-8pm; ⓂBarceloneta).

Local Transport

The metro, FGC trains, rodalies/cercanías (Renfe-run local trains) and buses come under a combined system. Single-ride tickets on all standard transport within Zone 1 cost €2.15.

Targetes are multitrip transport tickets. They are sold at all city-centre metro stations. The prices given here are for travel in Zone 1. Children under four years of age travel free. Options include the following:

Targeta T-10 (€10.20) 10 rides (each valid for 1¼ hours) on the metro, buses, FGC trains and rodalies. You can change between metro, FGC, rodalies and buses.

Targeta T-DIA (€8.60) Unlimited travel on all transport for one day.

Two-/three-/four-/five-day tickets (€15/22/28.50/35)
Unlimited travel on all transport except the Aerobús; buy them at metro stations and tourist offices.

Train

The easy-to-use **TMB metro** (TMB; ☑93 298 70 00; www.tmb.net) system has 11 numbered and colour-coded lines. It runs from 5am to midnight Sunday to Thursday and holidays, from 5am to 2am on Friday and days immediately preceding holidays, and 24 hours on Saturday.

Ongoing work to expand the metro continues on several lines. Línea 9 connects with the airport.

Suburban trains run by the **Ferrocarrils de la Generalitat de Catalunya** (FGC; ☑012; www.fgc.net) include a couple of useful city lines. All lines heading north from Plaça de Catalunya stop at Carrer de Provença and Gràcia. One of these lines (L7) goes to Tibidabo and another (L6 to Reina Elisenda) has a stop near the Monestir de Pedralbes. Most trains from Plaça de Catalunya continue beyond Barcelona to Sant Cugat, Sabadell and Terrassa. Other FGC lines head west from Plaça d'Espanya, including one for Manresa that is handy for the trip to Montserrat.

Depending on the line, these trains run from about 5am (with only one or two services before 6am) to 11pm or midnight Sunday to Thursday, and from 5am to about 1am on Friday and Saturday.

Taxi

Taxis charge €2.10 flag fall plus meter charges of €1.10 per kilometre (€1.30 from 8pm to 8am and all day on weekends). A further €3.10 is added for all trips to/from the airport, and €1 for luggage bigger than 55cm x 35cm x 35cm. The trip from Estació Sants to Plaça de Catalunya, about 3km, costs about €11. You can flag a taxi down in the streets or call one:

Fonotaxi (☑93 300 11 00; www.fonotaxi.net)

Radio Taxi 033 (☑93 303 30 33; www.radiotaxi033.com).

The call-out charge is €3.40 (€4.20 at night and on weekends). In many taxis it is possible to pay with a credit card and, if you have a local telephone number, you can join the T033 Ràdio taxi service for booking taxis online (www.radiotaxi033.com, in Spanish). You can also book online at https://catalunyataxi.com.

Taxi Amic (☑93 420 80 88; www.taxi-amic-adaptat.com) is a special taxi service for people with disabilities or difficult situations (such as transport of big objects). Book at least 24 hours in advance if possible.

Tram

There is a handful of **tram lines** (☑900 701181; www.tram.cat) in the city. All standard transport passes are valid. A scenic option is the tramvia blau (blue tram), which runs up to the foot of Tibidabo.

Language

Catalan and Spanish both have official-language status in Catalonia. In Barcelona, you'll hear as much Spanish as Catalan, so we've provided some Spanish to get you started. Spanish pronunciation is not difficult as most of its sounds are also found in English. You can read our pronunciation guides below as if they were English and you'll be understood just fine. And if you pronounce 'th' in our guides with a lisp and 'kh' as a throaty sound, you'll even sound like a real Spanish person.

To enhance your trip with a phrasebook, visit **lonelyplanet.com**. Lonely Planet iPhone phrasebooks are available through the Apple App store.

Basics

Hello.
Hola. · *o·*la

How are you?
¿Qué tal? · ke tal

I'm fine, thanks.
Bien, gracias. · byen *gra·*thyas

Excuse me. (to get attention)
Disculpe. · dees·*kool·*pe

Yes./No.
Sí./No. · see/no

Thank you.
Gracias. · *gra·*thyas

You're welcome./That's fine.
De nada. · de *na·*da

Goodbye. /See you later.
Adiós./Hasta luego. · a·*dyos/as·*ta *lwe·*go

Do you speak English?
¿Habla inglés? · a·bla een·*gles*

I don't understand.
No entiendo. · no en·*tyen·*do

How much is this?
¿Cuánto cuesta? · kwan·to *kwes·*ta

Can you reduce the price a little?
¿Podría bajar un · po·*dree·*a ba·*khar* oon
poco el precio? · *po·*ko el *pre·*thyo

Accommodation

I'd like to make a booking.
Quisiera reservar · kee·*sye·*ra re·ser·*var*
una habitación. · *oo·*na a·bee·ta·*thyon*

How much is it per night?
¿Cuánto cuesta por noche? · kwan·to *kwes·*ta por *no·*che

Eating & Drinking

I'd like ..., please.
Quisiera ..., por favor. · kee·*sye·*ra ... por fa·*vor*

That was delicious!
¡Estaba buenísimo! · es·*ta·*ba bwe·*nee·*see·mo

Bring the bill/check, please.
La cuenta, por favor. · la *kwen·*ta por fa·*vor*

I'm allergic to ...
Soy alérgico/a al ... (m/f) · soy a·*ler·*khee·ko/a al ...

I don't eat ...
No como ... · no *ko·*mo ...

chicken	*pollo*	*po·*lyo
fish	*pescado*	pes·*ka·*do
meat	*carne*	*kar·*ne

Emergencies

I'm ill.
Estoy enfermo/a. (m/f) · es·*toy* en·*fer·*mo/a

Help!
¡Socorro! · so·*ko·*ro

Call a doctor!
¡Llame a un médico! · *lya·*me a oon *me·*dee·ko

Call the police!
¡Llame a la policía! · *lya·*me a la po·lee·*thee·*a

Directions

I'm looking for a/an/the ...
Estoy buscando ... · es·*toy* boos·*kan·*do ...

ATM
un cajero · oon ka·*khe·*ro
automático · ow·to·*ma·*tee·ko

bank
el banco · el *ban·*ko

... embassy
la embajada de ... · la em·ba·*kha·*da de ...

market
el mercado · el mer·*ka·*do

museum
el museo · el moo·*se·*o

restaurant
un restaurante · oon res·tow·*ran·*te

toilet
los servicios · los ser·*vee·*thyos

tourist office
la oficina de · la o·fee·*thee·*na de
turismo · too·*rees·*mo

Behind The Scenes

Acknowledgements

Climate map data adapted from Peel MC, Finlayson BL & McMahon TA (2007) 'Updated World Map of the Köppen-Geiger Climate Classification', Hydrology and Earth System Sciences, 11, 163344.

This Book

This guidebook was curated by Andy Symington and researched and written by Sally Davies and Catherine Le Nevez. The previous edition was also curated by Andy Symington, who researched and wrote it along with Josephine Quintero. This guidebook was produced by the following:

Destination Editor Tom Stainer

Product Editors Jenna Myers, Genna Patterson

Senior Cartographer Anthony Phelan

Book Designers Katherine Marsh, Wendy Wright

Assisting Cartograhers Laura Bailey, Mark Griffiths

Assisting Editors Barbara Delissen, Samantha Forge, Emma Gibbs, Jodie Martire, Sarah Reid, Gabbi Stefanos

Cover Researcher Brendan Demspey-Spencer

Thanks to Andi Jones, Elizabeth Jones, Anne Mason, Saralinda Turner

Send Us Your Feedback

We love to hear from travellers – your comments keep us on our toes and help make our books better. Our well-travelled team reads every word on what you loved or loathed about this book. Although we cannot reply individually to postal submissions, we always guarantee that your feedback goes straight to the appropriate authors, in time for the next edition. Each person who sends us information is thanked in the next edition, the most useful submissions are rewarded with a selection of digital PDF chapters.

Visit lonelyplanet.com/contact to submit your updates and suggestions or to ask for help. Our award-winning website also features inspirational travel stories, news and discussions.

Note: We may edit, reproduce and incorporate your comments in Lonely Planet products such as guidebooks, websites and digital products, so let us know if you don't want your comments reproduced or your name acknowledged. For a copy of our privacy policy visit lonelyplanet.com/privacy.

Index

Barcelona Maps

El Raval & Sant Antoni

◎ Sights
1 Antic Hospital de la Santa Creu	D2
2 Centre de Cultura Contemporània de Barcelona	D1
3 MACBA	D2

⊕ Activities, Courses & Tours
4 CicloTour	D1
5 Runner Bean Tours	D2

🛍 Shopping
6 10000 Records	B3
7 Fantastik	C2
8 Holala! Plaza	D1
9 La Portorriqueña	D2
10 Les Topettes	C2
11 Mercat de Sant Antoni	C3
12 Teranyina	D2

⊗ Eating
13 Agust Gastrobar	C3
14 Can Lluís	C3
15 Copasetic	A2
16 Flax & Kale	C1
17 Sésamo	C3

⊙ Drinking & Nightlife
18 33|45	D2
19 Antilla BCN	A1
20 Bacon Bear	B1
21 Betty Ford's	C2
Casa Almirall	(see 10)
22 El Drapaire	D1
23 Marmalade	D2
24 Metro	C1
25 Negroni	C2
26 Plata Bar	B1

⊕ Entertainment
27 Jazz Sí Club	C3
28 Méliès Cinemes	A1
29 Renoir Floridablanca	C2
30 Teatre Llantiol	D3

Barri Gòtic, Ciutat Vella & La Ribera

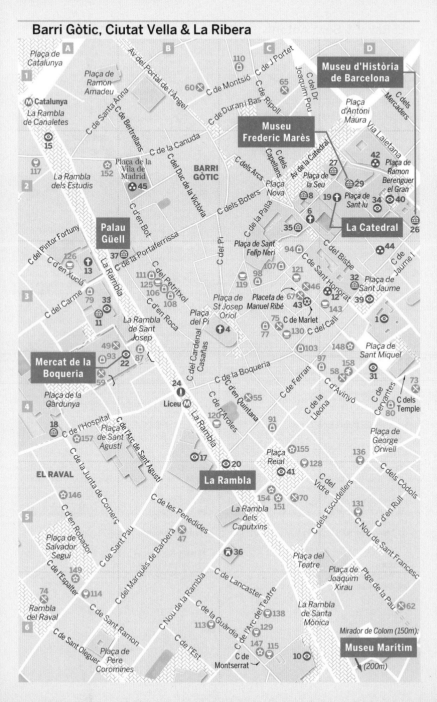

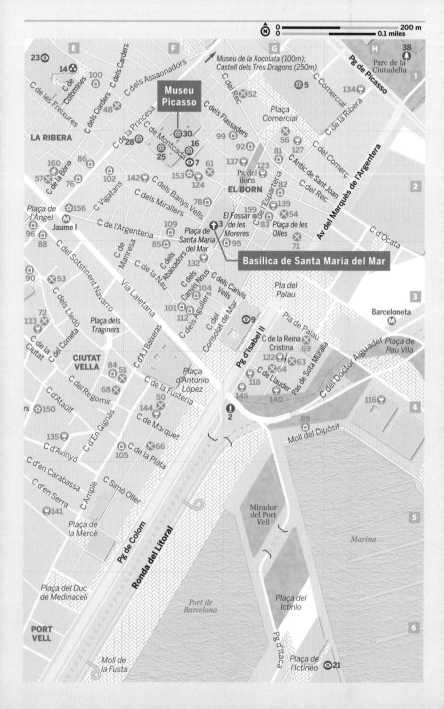

Barri Gòtic, Ciutat Vella & La Ribera

◉ Sights

1 Ajuntament...D3
2 Barcelona Head..G4
3 Basílica de Santa Maria del Mar..............F2
4 Basílica de Santa Maria del Pi..................C3
5 Born Centre de Cultura i Memòria..........G1
6 Capella de Santa Llúcia.............................C2
7 Carrer de Montcada.....................................F2
8 Casa de l'Ardiaca..C2
9 Casa Llotja de Mar......................................G3
10 Centre d'Art Santa Mònica.......................C6
11 Centre de la Imatge....................................A3
12 Domus de Sant Honorat............................D3
13 Església de Betlem......................................A3
14 Espai Santa Caterina..................................E1
15 Font de Canaletes.......................................A2
16 Fundació Gaspar..F2
17 Gran Teatre del Liceu.................................B4
18 La Capella...A4
19 La Catedral...D2
20 La Rambla...C5
21 L'Aquàrium...H6
22 Mercat de la Boqueria................................B4
23 Mercat de Santa Caterina.........................E1
24 Mosaïc de Miró..B4
25 Museu de Cultures del Món.......................F2
26 Museu d'Història de Barcelona................D2
27 Museu Diocesà/Gaudí Exhibition
    Center..D2
28 Museu Europeu d'Art Modern...................F2
29 Museu Frederic Marès...............................D2
30 Museu Picasso...F2
31 Palau Centelles...D4
32 Palau de la Generalitat..............................D3
33 Palau de la Virreina....................................A3
34 Palau del Lloctinent...................................D2
35 Palau Episcopal...C2
36 Palau Güell...C5
37 Palau Moja..B3
38 Parc de la Ciutadella..................................H1
39 Plaça de Sant Jaume..................................D3
40 Plaça del Rei...D2
41 Plaça Reial..C5
42 Roman Walls...D2

43 Sinagoga Major..C3
44 Temple d'August..D3
45 Via Sepulcral Romana................................B2

◈ Eating

46 Alcoba Azul...C3
47 Bar Cañete..B5
48 Bar del Pla..E1
49 Bar Pinotxo...A3
50 Belmonte...F4
51 Benedict..E4
52 Bormuth..G1
53 Cafè de l'Acadèmia.....................................E3
54 Cal Pep..G2
55 Can Culleretes...C4
56 Casa Delfín...G2
57 Cat Bar...E2
58 Cerería..D4
59 El Quim..A4
60 Els Quatre Gats..B1
61 Euskal Etxea...F2
62 Federal..D6
63 Green Spot..G4
64 Isla Tortuga..G4
65 Koy Shunka...C1
66 La Plata..F4
67 La Vinateria del Call...................................C3
68 Milk...E4
69 Oaxaca...G3
70 Ocaña...C5
   Opera Samfaina...............................(see 17)
71 Paradiso/Pastrami Bar...............................G2
72 Pla...E3
73 Rasoterra..D4
74 Suculent..A6
75 Xurreria...C3

◉ Shopping

76 Arlequí Màscares...E2
77 Artesania Catalunya...................................C3
78 Casa Gispert...F2
   Cereria Subirà..................................(see 26)
79 Chök...A3
80 Cómplices...D4

L'Eixample & Gràcia

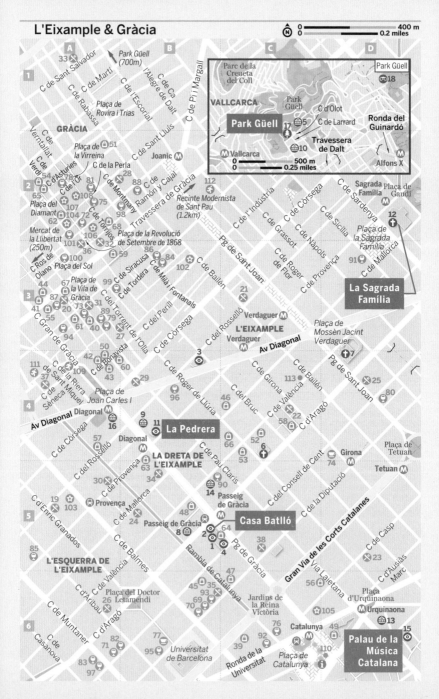

0 ——— 400 m
0 ——— 0.2 miles

Park Güell
(700m)

C de Sant Salvador
C de Martí
C de Ca l'Alegre de Dalt
C de l'Escorial
C de Pi i Margall

Plaça de Rovira i Trias

GRÀCIA

C de Verntallat
C de Verdi
C d'Astúries

Plaça de la Virreina
C de la Perla
C de Sant Lluís

Joanic

Plaça del Diamant
C del Or
C de Montmany
C de Ramón y Cajal
Travessera de Gràcia

Recinte Modernista de Sant Pau (1.2km)

Mercat de la Llibertat (250m)

Plaça de la Revolució de Setembre de 1868

C Ros de Olano
Plaça del Sol

Plaça de la Vila de Gràcia
C del Torrent de l'Olla
C de Siracusa
C de Tordera
C de Mila i Fontanals
C de Bailèn

C de Gran de Gràcia
C de Sant Miquel
C de la Riera
C de Sèneca

Plaça de Joan Carles I

Av Diagonal   Diagonal

Av Diagonal
C de Còrsega

Diagonal

La Pedrera

LA DRETA DE L'EIXAMPLE

C del Rosselló
C de Provença
C de Pau Claris

C d'Enric Granados

Provença

C de Mallorca

C de Balmes
Passeig de Gràcia

Passeig de Gràcia

Casa Batlló

L'ESQUERRA DE L'EIXAMPLE

C de València
C d'Aribau
Plaça del Doctor Letamendi
Rambla de Catalunya

C de Muntaner
C d'Aragó
C de Casanova

Jardins de la Reina Victòria

Universitat de Barcelona

Ronda de la Universitat

Plaça de Catalunya

C de l'Indústria
C de Còrsega
C de Sicília
C de Sardenya

Sagrada Família   Plaça de Gaudí

C de Grassot
C de Nàpols
C de Roger de Flor
Pg de Sant Joan

Plaça de la Sagrada Família

C de Mallorca

La Sagrada Família

C de Provença

L'EIXAMPLE

Verdaguer

Verdaguer

Plaça de Mossèn Jacint Verdaguer

C de Rosselló
C de Girona
C de Bailèn
Pg de Sant Joan

C de València

C d'Aragó

Plaça de Tetuan

Girona

Tetuan

Gran Via de les Corts Catalanes

C de Consell de Cent
C de la Diputació
Via Laietana

Plaça d'Urquinaona

Urquinaona

Catalunya

C de Casp
C d'Ausiàs Marc

Plaça de la Música Catalana

Palau de la Música Catalana

INSET: Park Güell

Parc de la Creueta del Coll

Park Güell

VALLCARCA

Park Güell

C d'Olot
C de Larrard

Ronda del Guinardó

Vallcarca

Travessera de Dalt

Alfons X

0 ——— 500 m
0 ——— 0.25 miles

L'Eixample & Gràcia

◎ Sights

◎ Eating

◎ Shopping

◎ Drinking & Nightlife

◎ Entertainment

◎ Activities, Courses & Tours

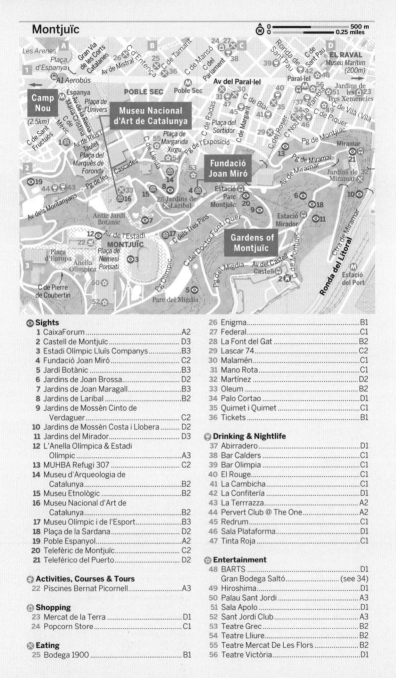

Montjuïc

Symbols & Map Key

Look for these symbols to quickly identify listings:

- ⊙ Sights
- ✪ Activities
- ✪ Courses
- ✪ Tours
- ✪ Festivals & Events
- ✪ Eating
- ✪ Drinking
- ✪ Entertainment
- ✪ Shopping
- ✪ Information & Transport

These symbols and abbreviations give vital information for each listing:

- 🌿 Sustainable or green recommendation
- **FREE** No payment required

- ☎ Telephone number
- ☺ Opening hours
- Ⓟ Parking
- ☺ Nonsmoking
- ❄ Air-conditioning
- @ Internet access
- ☎ Wi-fi access
- ☆ Swimming pool
- ▣ Bus
- ☆ Ferry
- ▣ Tram
- ▣ Train
- ▣ English-language menu
- ✈ Vegetarian selection
- ✦ Family-friendly

Find your best experiences with these Great For... icons.

- Art & Culture
- Beaches
- Budget
- Cafe/Coffee
- Cycling
- Detour
- Drinking
- Entertainment
- Events
- Family Travel
- Food & Drink
- History
- Local Life
- Nature & Wildlife
- Photo Op
- Scenery
- Shopping
- Short Trip
- Sport
- Walking
- Winter Travel

Sights

- Beach
- Bird Sanctuary
- Buddhist
- Castle/Palace
- Christian
- Confucian
- Hindu
- Islamic
- Jain
- Jewish
- Monument
- Museum/Gallery/ Historic Building
- Ruin
- Shinto
- Sikh
- Taoist
- Winery/Vineyard
- Zoo/Wildlife Sanctuary
- Other Sight

Points of Interest

- Bodysurfing
- Camping
- Cafe
- Canoeing/Kayaking
- Course/Tour
- Diving
- Drinking & Nightlife
- Eating
- Entertainment
- Sento Hot Baths/ Onsen
- Shopping
- Skiing
- Sleeping
- Snorkelling
- Surfing
- Swimming/Pool
- Walking
- Windsurfing
- Other Activity

Information

- Bank
- Embassy/Consulate
- Hospital/Medical
- Internet
- Police
- Post Office
- Telephone
- Toilet
- Tourist Information
- Other Information

Geographic

- Beach
- Gate
- Hut/Shelter
- Lighthouse
- Lookout
- Mountain/Volcano
- Oasis
- Park
- Pass
- Picnic Area
- Waterfall

Transport

- Airport
- BART station
- Border crossing
- Boston T station
- Bus
- Cable car/Funicular
- Cycling
- Ferry
- Metro/MRT station
- Monorail
- Parking
- Petrol station
- Subway/S-Bahn/ Skytrain station
- Taxi
- Train station/Railway
- Tram
- Tube Station
- Underground/ U-Bahn station
- Other Transport

Our Story

A beat-up old car, a few dollars in the pocket and a sense of adventure. In 1972 that's all Tony and Maureen Wheeler needed for the trip of a lifetime – across Europe and Asia overland to Australia. It took several months, and at the end – broke but inspired – they sat at their kitchen table writing and stapling together their first travel guide, *Across Asia on the Cheap*. Within a week they'd sold 1500 copies. Lonely Planet was born.

Today, Lonely Planet has offices in Franklin, London, Melbourne, Oakland, Dublin, Beijing, and Delhi, with more than 600 staff and writers. We share Tony's belief that 'a great guidebook should do three things: inform, educate and amuse'.

Our Writers

Andy Symington

Andy has written or worked on over a hundred books and other updates for Lonely Planet and other publishing companies, and has published articles on numerous subjects for a variety of newspapers, magazines, and websites. He part-owns and operates a rock bar, has written a novel, and is currently working on several fiction and non-fiction writing projects. Andy, from Australia, moved to Northern Spain many years ago. When he's not off with a backpack in some far-flung corner of the world, he can probably be found watching the tragically poor local football side or tasting local wines after a long walk in the nearby mountains.

Sally Davies

Sally landed in Seville in 1992 with a handful of pesetas and five words of Spanish, and, despite a complete inability to communicate, promptly snared a lucrative gig handing out leaflets at Expo '92. In 2001 she settled in Barcelona, where her daily grind involves nose-to-tail eating, getting lost in museums and finding ways to convey the beauty of this spectacular city.

Catherine Le Nevez

Catherine's wanderlust kicked in when she roadtripped across Europe from her Parisian base aged four, and she's been hitting the road at every opportunity since. Over the past dozen-plus years she's written scores of Lonely Planet guides and articles covering Paris, France, Europe and far beyond. Her work has also appeared in numerous online and print publications. Topping Catherine's list of travel tips is to travel without any expectations.

STAY IN TOUCH LONELYPLANET.COM/CONTACT

AUSTRALIA The Malt Store, Level 3, 551 Swanston St, Carlton, Victoria 3053
☏ 03 8379 8000,
fax 03 8379 8111

IRELAND Digital Depot, Roe Lane (off Thomas St), Digital Hub, Dublin 8, D08 TCV4

USA 124 Linden Street, Oakland, CA 94607
☏ 510 250 6400,
toll free 800 275 8555,
fax 510 893 8572

UK 240 Blackfriars Road, London SE1 8NW
☏ 020 3771 5100,
fax 020 3771 5101

twitter.com/lonelyplanet

facebook.com/lonelyplanet

instagram.com/lonelyplanet

youtube.com/lonelyplanet

lonelyplanet.com/newsletter